Peter Fischli Tuesday till Sunday

BY ART MATTERS 天目里美术馆
Verlag der Buchhandlung Walther und Franz König, Köln

彼得 · 费茨利 周二到周日

WU Tian

Gaze Upon the Mundane

Whether or not you've seen Peter Fischli's exhibition *Tuesday till Sunday* at BY ART MATTERS, you'll get something of the experience flipping through this book of the same name. This was my experience when, a few years ago in a Cologne bookstore, I stumbled upon a small book called *Will Happiness Find Me?*, co-authored by Peter Fischli and his then creative partner David Weiss. In it, scribbly, playful handwriting asks a series of questions that cut to readers' hearts. We all ask ourselves questions from time to time, and Fischli and Weiss are no exception.

Today, we are familiar with the uniform grid of photos in our mobile phones. But if this grid appeared on floor mats covering a large area, would it change the way you saw the cup of cappuccino in the photo? What about a photo of that enlarged grid laid next to the original array? By now, I imagine you've guessed that I'm describing the book you are holding. It's full of images of daily life, but it organizes them with unusual attention. The artist creates meaning by canceling meaning, filling the work with contradictions, nestings, and meta-narrative fun. The same was true of Fischli's exhibition, which contained both the familiar and many surprises.

Tuesday till Sunday was Peter Fischli's first solo exhibition outside of Europe. Thanks to a recommendation from our director Francesco Bonami, BY ART MATTERS is happy to present Fischli's solo work, expanding our understanding of his work beyond the well known collaborations with Weiss. In the works, we see him freely traveling through cities around the world, stopping, squinting, looking, and quickly pressing the shutter. Looking closer at the work presented, we can experience his attention to urban spaces and networks of underground energy: electricity, physics, and intelligence.

In the process of preparing for the exhibition, Fischli's humorous rigor, subtle observation, and clever adaptation of space impressed us. Fischli originally planned to lay the work *Vertigo Vinyl Floor Pattern I, II, III*

吴天

对日常的一次不平凡注目

当你翻阅手中这本《周二到周日》时，无论你是否已经看了艺术家彼得·费茨利在 BY ART MATTERS 天目里美术馆的同名展览，我相信你都能有所获得。一如前些年我在科隆的一家书店偶然发现彼得·费茨利和彼时的创作搭档大卫·威斯共同创作的小书《幸福会降临在我身上吗？》。真诚拙朴的手写字体让人在心里默默跟读书中的一连串问题——我们都会时不时对自己发问，费茨利和威斯也不例外。

时至今日，我们对手机相册里的方块阵列照片已再熟悉不过。但当看到这些照片被印成了地垫大面积铺开，你会不会对里面的一杯卡布奇诺另眼相看？如果对满铺照片的地面再拍一张，并将之并置在初始的阵列旁呢？我想你已经猜到了，我就在描述你手中的这本书。它充满日常，但又用一次次不寻常的注目把这些画面都组织了起来。艺术家用取消意义的方式来呈现意义，让作品充满矛盾、多重嵌套和元叙事的趣味。这也正如费茨利此次展览中的作品，既熟悉又充满惊喜。

“周二到周日”是彼得·费茨利在欧洲以外的首个个展。多亏馆长弗朗切斯科·博纳米的推荐，BY ART MATTERS 天目里美术馆有幸能为观众呈现彼得·费茨利在双人组合之外的个人创作。在作品中我们仿佛看到了他自由自在地穿梭于世界各个城市，在各处驻足、眯眼、观察，快速按下拍照按键的身影。而向内看我们更能在本次展览的作品中体会他对城市空间和地下能量网络——电能、物理、智力的关注。

在筹备展览的过程中，费茨利的幽默严谨以及对空间的细微观察和巧心适配让我们印象深刻。费茨利原本计划将作品《眩晕乙烯基地板图案 I, II, III》（也就是本书所演绎的原作）直接铺于美术馆的地面，但地送风系统给艺术家出了难题，遮盖在所难免。费茨利在跟美术馆团队的同事们沟通之后，决定局部切割地垫，露出通风口。这些切割口

directly on the museum's floor. But the floor vents posed a problem for the artist, as the work would certainly cover them. After communicating with colleagues in the museum team, Fischli decided to partially cut the floor mat to expose the vents. These cuts are interspersed between photos of cities, making the work more three-dimensional, suggesting a way into the city's underground system.

Because of his interest in urban landscapes, Fischli carefully produced a video work *Cinema* for this exhibition. The film focuses on the subway network, one of the artist's urban systems, incorporating daily scenes from the Hangzhou subway. The work expands out of the exhibition hall and into public space. He transforms *Work, Summer 2018*, a piece originally meant for display on a small screen, into a video that can be played on a 60-meter advertising screen in a subway corridor. The video shows a GoPro advertisement reshot by the artist, and the result is very similar to the original. Yes! Did you notice it too? This multiply-nesting, almost obsessive echoing of the past and present is a prime example of Peter Fischli's creation of contrasts from the ordinary.

We would like to thank Buchholz Gallery and Reena Spaulings Fine Art Gallery for their help, as well as the Embassy of Switzerland in China and the Consulate General of Switzerland in Shanghai for their support of this exhibition. We would also like to thank Walther König for his help in publishing this book. Peter Fischli Studio worked closely with us during this exhibition to ensure its success. Once again, we would like to express our sincerest gratitude to all who have given their time and support!

Deputy Director at BY ART MATTERS
WU Tian

穿插在艺术家拍摄的城市照片之间，反而让作品更立体了，彷佛能直通城市的地下系统，和他所关注的议题不谋而合。

因为对城市景观的关注，费茨利精心为这次展览特地制作了一件影像作品《影院》。这部作品着眼城市系统之一的地铁网络，并融入了杭州地铁的日常画面。而在展厅之外，费茨利也没轻易放过公共空间。他将《2018年夏天的工作》这一件原本只能在小型播放器上展示的作品改制为一段能在地铁通道长廊60米广告屏幕播放的影像。影像内容是一段由艺术家翻拍的GoPro广告画面，恰好酷似广告。是的！你也发现了吧？这种奇妙的多重嵌套和近似强迫症的前后呼应让人啧啧暗赞，这与彼得 · 费茨利带来的"平凡"相映成趣。

我想特别感谢布赫霍尔兹画廊和 Reena Spaulings Fine Art 画廊的协助，以及瑞士驻华大使馆和瑞士驻上海总领事馆对本次展览的支持。对于本书的出版，我们还要感谢 Walther König 给予的帮助。同时，彼得 · 费茨利工作室在展览期间与我们紧密合作，确保了展览的圆满效果。再次向所有给予我们支持和帮助的人表达最诚挚的感谢！

BY ART MATTERS 天目里美术馆 副馆长
吴天

Alongside his kinetic traffic light sculptures, Peter Fischli's recent photo-printed-floor installations reflect a moment where constant circulation overdetermines every physical structure. Considering that Fischli is the son of an architect, it's tempting to interpret his *Vertigo Vinyl Floor Pattern I, II, III* (2023–2024) as playful jabs at this paternal discipline, mocking its pretense of grounding an already floating reality. With Fischli's photo-floor, architecture literally surrenders its ground to the image: we are walking on JPEGs. These works also challenge the museum's traditional mission of sheltering and preserving art by separating it off from the mad, mad world of capital. What happens to the museum's institutional authority when art takes on the sprawling dimensions of outdoor advertising?

By flattening, expanding, and spreading his work beneath the feet of its viewers and across the gallery's entire floor plan, Fischli pushes art to the limits of its ability to be experienced as such. Printed onto 80 × 80 cm vinyl squares, these black-and-white photographs are arranged in a checkerboard pattern, covering the entire exhibition floor. His image carpets immediately recall the aggressive visual language of pop-up retail environments and wrap-around, immersive advertising campaigns. It's the sort of all-encompassing branding strategy one might encounter at a convention center or trade fair.

Now that digital imaging techniques have conquered the threshold of scale, no urban surface is beyond the reach of the inkjet printer. And wherever we look, the image absorbs architectural space into its own communicational dimension. The visual content of Fischli's *Vertigo Vinyl Floor Pattern I, II, III,* meanwhile, consists entirely of iPhone photos taken on walks in Zurich, New York, Paris, and other cities. So the photo-floor is a sort of city symphony, a mash-up of multiple walks in different Western capitals, taking the form of an ongoing grid pattern very much like the display on our mobile phone's camera app, where we access our pictures to remember our lives.

与他的动态雕塑作品交通信号灯一样，彼得·费茨利近期创作的一系列印有照片的地板装置体现了这样一个时刻：各种永不停息的流通都在多重地决定着每一个具有物理实体的结构。如果我们知道费茨利的父亲其实是一位建筑师的话，一定忍不住会想象《眩晕乙烯基地板图案I, II, III》（2023－2024）是对他父亲所从事的这门学科的恶搞，是在嘲笑建筑学还要自欺欺人地为业已悬浮的现实建构地基。在费茨利铺开的"照片地板"上，建筑在字面的意义上将其地基让位于图像：我们此刻正行走在JPEG图像上。这些作品也挑战了美术馆的传统使命。过去，美术馆总是将艺术与无序的资本世界分隔开来从而使之得到保护或保存。而当艺术本身采取了铺天盖地的户外广告那肆意扩张的维度特性时，美术馆作为艺术机构的权威又将受到怎样的影响？在将自己的作品展平，铺开于观众脚下，从展厅地面的一端延伸至另一端的过程中，费茨利将艺术推向了它所能被体验的可能性极限。一系列黑白图像印刷在 80×80 厘米的方形乙烯基地垫上，以国际象棋棋盘格般黑白间隔式排列平铺，覆盖住了整个展厅空间的地面。这些填满两端墙面之间空地的图像地垫会让人立刻想到快闪店或全方位沉浸式广告宣传活动那种极具侵略性的视觉语言。这种环绕整个空间的品牌宣传手法，是我们可能在会展中心或展览会上看到的。

如今，由于数字成像技术已经征服了尺度的阈限，喷墨打印机可以无远弗届地触及城市的每一寸表面。无论当下的我们望向何处，建筑空间都被图像吸收进了自己交流维度之中。《眩晕乙烯基地板图案I, II, III》的视觉内容全部由用 iPhone 捕捉到的照片组成，而这些照片都是费茨利在苏黎世、纽约、巴黎等城市中漫步时拍摄的。因此可以说，这个照片地板是某种在西方不同大都市中漫步的场景所混搭而成的一出"城市交响曲"，它以一种持续不绝的网格模式呈现在观众面

To experience one of Fischli's compositions, the viewer must physically traverse the work, surfing it with their pedestrian body. Here, scrolling becomes indistinguishable from strolling—both in our minds and in space and time. Are we inside or outside the phone? We find ourselves in the immersive dimension of an enlarged digital timeline, spread out and de-virtualized in the museum. And we are already physically within the artwork before we can comprehend its full layout: we encounter it as we go, square by square, much like scrolling through a social media feed on our phone: pretzel, black dog, cappuccino foam heart, Eiffel Tower at night, martini glass, another pretzel, white dog, another cappuccino, and so on.

Since the advent of the smartphone, architects have had to grapple with the challenge of designing physical environments for a society increasingly absorbed in virtual space—with citizens who are not fully here. How can we architecturally convince everyone that the new info-structure in which we've become immersed is still a tangible place? The iPhone poses a dilemma for architecture because the more we rely on its interface to navigate and understand the city, the more the city itself seems to vanish. More accurately, the city is reduced to just one layer among several in a digital stack, and architecture begins to lose its connection to reality.[1] Meanwhile, the phone appears to acknowledge that the physical, architectural city still exists (our pictures prove it!) as signals and screens proliferate across every solid surface. Since we last looked up, the entire cityscape has transformed into a giant interface.

---

1 Benjamin Bratton, *The Stack*, The MIT Press, 2016.

前，非常类似于我们为了提取自己的生活记忆而要访问自己的照片时，打开手机相册后会显示的那种网格视图。

要体验费茨利这一系列覆盖整个展厅地面的作品，观众必须亲身穿越其中，利用他们身体的行走，在这个图像网格上“冲浪”。当我们这样做时，我们究竟是在自己的思维中、在时间与空间中刷动屏幕，还是在其中漫步游走，这种界限已经即刻消失了。我们置身于一个放大版数字时间线的沉浸式维度之中，它在美术馆中铺展开来，并去虚拟化而获得了物理实体。而在我们领会作品的整体布局之前，我们其实就已然置身其中了：我们一边行走，一边观看，掠过一格接一格的图像，就好像我们在手机上刷社交媒体的动态更新：我们浏览到了椒盐卷饼、黑狗、卡布奇诺上的心形奶泡拉花、埃菲尔铁塔夜景、一杯马提尼、又一块椒盐卷饼、白狗、又一杯卡布奇诺，等等，等等。

当世界进入智能手机时代以来，建筑师们不得不去应对这样一个问题：如何为一个越来越消隐于虚拟空间的社会、为那些并未百分之百“在场”的市民来建造具备物理实体的环境。如何从建筑的角度说服每一个人，我们已经沉浸于其中的这个新的信息结构，依然是一个实际的地点呢？对建筑来说，iPhone 构成了一个问题，因为我们越是依赖手机界面来导航和理解城市，城市本身就越是消隐。或更确切地说，城市被限缩为只是一个数字“堆栈”所具有的多重层叠的其中之一而已……建筑则开始失去了它对现实的掌控。[1]

1　本杰明·布拉顿，《堆栈》，麻省理工学院出版社，2016

So, where are we when we're connected, and when we're not? Is the city inside or outside our phone? Fischli's photo-floors pose this question in an overly loud manner, akin to a villager lost in the capital. We all understand precisely what the artist means by the vertigo of looking up and down as we navigate our surroundings on a mobile device. With our attention now divided between screen and street, we inhabit our own dislocation.

Phone pictures of snacks and dogs, cocktails, and tourist views of everyday reality capture the strange banality of the contemporary urban commons—or what remains of it. Today, what is common is less a public place we cohabit than an image-space we all utilize, and the code that programs it. Indeed, what is striking about Fischli's photo-floor images is their apparent ordinariness and strange familiarity. There's nothing overtly personal in his photographs, nor anything political. He reduces his content to images that could easily be mistaken for similar pictures on anyone else's phone. The impression is that it's not quite art—or, if it is art, it's not quite Fischli's. There are no selfies, nothing too existential. The artist presents us with what everyone already sees: a cappuccino's foam heart (each tile bears its own title: *Foam*), a work glove dropped in the street (*The Empire*), a pretzel (*Time Travel*), a broken cellphone screen (*Sunshine*)—a sort of normcore Surrealism. The imagery is both childlike and slightly senile in its willful artlessness, reminiscent of an AI's best attempt at envisioning the human city. This is urban reality consumed at the level of the CAPTCHA image—stoplights and bicycles recognizable to an almost hallucinatory degree. Meanwhile, isn't there something vertiginous about our human attempts to prove to the algorithm that we're not a robot? An inescapable shiver of doubt lingers.

而与此同时，手机似乎不得不承认，随着信号与屏幕无处不在地在每一个坚固表面增殖扩散，那个物理的、建筑的城市仍然在一定程度上存在在那里（我们为它拍下的照片就能证明这一点！）。自我们最后一次抬头向上看周身的都市景观以来，它已经变成了一块巨大的界面。因此，当我们与网络成功连接时，我们身处何处？而未能连接时，又位于哪里？城市在我们的手机之中还是之外？费茨利的照片地板用一种过度夸大的方式提出了这一问题，就像一个迷失在大都会中的农民一样。而当我们在移动设备上导航周遭环境时，也能确切理解艺术家所说的那种需要同时向上仰视和向下俯瞰所带来的“眩晕”。在我们的注意力被同时分散给屏幕和街道的当前情况下，我们必须尽最大努力来安放自己的错位感。

手机记录下来的零食和狗，鸡尾酒和游客视角中的日常现实——这些照片捕捉了当代城市的共同领域（或其残存仅余的部分）所展现出的那种奇怪的庸常性。因为，如今的所谓共同领域，已经不再是我们所共同栖身的公共地点，而是我们每一个人都在使用的图像空间——以及编写它的代码。的确，这些图片的特别之处，恰恰在于它们看起来是如此地不特别，让人感到异常熟悉。他挑选的照片中没有过于个人化或者政治化的东西。他将展出内容简化成了那些可能很容易就会与每一个人手机里的类似图片相混淆的照片。这些照片让人感觉仿佛它们并不是艺术——或者说，如果它们是艺术，那也不是独属于费茨利的艺术。这里找不到自拍，也看不到太存在主义的元素。他向我们展示了每个人都已经看到的东西：卡布奇诺上心形奶泡（每一块照片地板都有各自的标题，这一块叫《泡沫》），一只掉落在街道上的劳动手套（《帝国》），椒盐脆饼（《时空旅行》），破碎的手机屏幕（《阳光》）……某种基本款超现实主义。这些图像在其故意展现出的无艺术性上，既显得有些天真，又有一些老成。或者说，它们就像人工智能在幻想人类城市时所能给出

As GPS reorients the global citizen towards abstraction, an interactive map replaces the city in our minds. The map on our phones not only deceives us into thinking we know where we are in Paris or New York, it also leads us to believe we know when we are there. It implies that time is now part of its map. Thus, as we navigate urban spaces on our phones, we find ourselves wandering through a digital timeline. To put it plainly, the society of control conceals a clock within its map, and as we move through this urban image-space, we become increasingly enmeshed in its peculiar mechanisms. Life, attention, memory… so much of human experience is now represented and tracked on the timeline's grid, fundamentally altering everything for the contemporary pedestrian. While out for a walk, we find ourselves wandering inside a map that monitors our movements and counts our steps.

For the flâneur or the dog walker who has become a gawking tourist in the abstraction of their own city, the primary activity is to extend the poodle-cappuccino matrix modeled in Fischli's floor patterns. We accomplish this with our phones, through the constant translation of reality into digital content and back again, perpetually scanning, decoding, and recoding the cityscape in real time, within the ever-refreshing now of the interface. We've come a long way from the Situationist *dérive*; the flâneur is now relegated to the role of operator of the urban apparatus.[2] Fischli's photo-floors create a vivid simulation of this new version of what we once considered simply taking a walk. We were surprised, circa 2012, to see Google's roving cameras scanning every inch of urban space, but now we perform this task ourselves, for free and without a second thought. "I am not a robot", these will likely be the last words of this new pedestrian.

---

2 Vilém Flusser, *Communicology: Mutations in Human Relations?*, Stanford University Press, 2022.

的最好尝试。这是在以类似处理验证码图像——诸如需要你选出红绿灯和自行车——的方式被感知和接受的城市现实，它所展现出的高度可识别性几乎达到了一种幻觉的程度。同时，在我们人类试图向算法证明我们自己“不是机器人”的过程中，难道不存在某种让你感到眩晕的东西……某种无法自已的惊疑颤栗吗?

而随着 GPS 再度引导全球公民走向抽象，在我们脑海中，城市就被手机里的这幅交互式地图所取代了。手机地图不仅使我们误以为知道自己在巴黎或纽约身处何地，它还让我们相信我们也知道自己是在“何时”身处此地。它让我们认为，“何时”现在也已经是地图的一部分了。因此，当我们用手机在城市空间中导航时，我们会突然意识到，我们其实是在时间……是在一个数字时间线中游走。更直白地说：控制社会将一个时钟隐藏在其地图中，而当我们在这个城市图像空间中穿行时，我们会变得日益啮合于它的诡异齿轮。生活、注意力、记忆……如此多的人类经验此刻都在时间线的图像网格上被表征和追踪着，这使当代行人的一切都发生了改变。当我们出门散步，我们其实是游走在一幅会记录我们移动并计算我们步数的地图中。那些游荡者或遛狗的人，他们在自己栖居的城市的抽象之中，却变成了目瞪口呆地四处张望的游客。对他们来说，头号重要的活动就是延伸我们在费茨利的地板图案中看到的贵宾犬－卡布奇诺矩阵。我们借助手机，利用它不断地将现实转化为数字内容，然后再转化回来，在手机界面不断刷新的“此刻”中，持续地“实时”扫描、解码和重新编码城市景观。相比于情境主义国际的“漂移”，我们已经走得更远：游荡者被重新安排了工作，成为城市装置的人类操作员。[2]

[2] 威廉·弗卢塞尔，《传播学：人类关系的变异？》，斯坦福大学出版社，2022年

Writing in the early 1980s, Michel de Certeau conceptualized pedestrian behavior as a spatial practice whereby clandestine territories are carved out within the panoptic discipline of the urban plan. In *The Practice of Everyday Life*, he described walking in the city as a creative act and a re-appropriation of urban space-time from its owners and architects.[3] Nothing has changed in the meantime, except for the crucial, game-changing difference that the pedestrian's freedom of movement is now instrumentalized in the production of the metaverse. This means the info-flâneur is immediately involved in the extension of the technical image that the city is swiftly and inexorably becoming.[4] It doesn't matter where we actually are or where we're going; what matters is that our mobile attention remains connected to the info-structure, allowing it to sense and signal to itself in real-time. By extending and personalizing the poodle-cappuccino matrix, we let the city know it's still there.

To complete a feedback loop, in other words, the city needs us to walk around and look at things with our phones. Fischli's imagery emphasizes this roving, phone's-eye view of the metropolis: easy, casually composed shots of the usual, immediate subjects that phones seem to favor, captured on the go—sometimes looking down (dogs, manholes, plates of food) and sometimes looking up (skyscrapers, escalators). The edge-to-edge alternation of these contrasting views within the photo-floor's ongoing grid performs a sort of spatial practice of the interface itself. We might say that Fischli composes an image of how the city sees itself through us.

3 Michel de Certeau, *The Practice of Everyday Life*, University of California Press, 1984.

4 Vilém Flusser, *Communicology: Mutations in Human Relations?*, Stanford University Press, 2022.

费茨利的照片地板生动地模拟了我们曾经认为只是单纯漫步的行为在当下的最新版本。2012 年左右，当我们看到 Google 的街景车在街头扫描每一寸城市空间时还会感到惊讶，但现在，我们毫不犹豫地自发执行起了这项任务。“我不是机器人”将成为这种新型行人被传扬下去的遗言。

1980 年代初，米歇尔 · 德 · 塞尔托以“空间实践”这一概念来构想行人在城市中步行的行为，经由这种实践，行人可以在城市规划所设下的全景敞视规训中，开掘出一些秘密的领地。在《日常生活实践》中，他将城市漫步描述成一种具有创造力的行为，是从所有者和建筑师那里重新夺取城市时空。[3]与此同时，一切又都没有发生改变，除了一项颠覆性的关键差异：行人的行动自由现在被用作工具来生产“元宇宙”。也就是说，就城市正迅速且无可阻挡地转变成为的这种“技术图像”而言，信息浪游者是直接参与到它的扩充和延展中来的。[4]我们实际在哪里或实际要去哪里并不重要，重要的是，我们的移动注意力始终保持与这个信息结构相连相通，从而能够实时地感知并向自身发送信号。正是通过扩展和个性化这个贵宾犬 - 卡布奇诺矩阵，我们才让城市知道，它依然存在在那里。换句话说，为了完成一个完整的反馈循环，城市需要我们四处走动，用手机来看周遭的东西。费茨利展示的图像突出彰显了这种在漫游的手机镜头视角中捕捉到的大都会景象：一些轻松随意捕捉到的日常即时场景，这些场景似乎很适合用手机来拍摄，并且是在漫步

---

3 米歇尔 · 德 · 塞尔托，《日常生活实践》，加利福尼亚大学出版社，1984年

4 威廉 · 弗卢塞尔，《传播学：人类关系的变异？》，斯坦福大学出版社，2022年

We recognize simple shapes, respond to signals and prompts, like, shop, and eat: we are in communication with the info-structure. Taking a walk is a constant translation of everyday experience into data, into shareable content. However, the content of our walks holds no inherent meaning, or at least none that is urgent; content is merely a means of extending and adding resolution to the technical image of the city. We extend this image by taking our phones for a walk, moving through the city like dogs or drones.

The iPhone pictures that provide the content for Fischli's floor patterns seem to recognize and capture something emoji-like in the new cityscape. These images could also be seen as a joke on post-war street photography, which was all about encountering reality through a camera lens and realizing the "decisive moment" (Henri Cartier-Bresson) in the exposure of film to light. Now, every moment is as decisive as any other in the digital timeline: where and when was this poodle or that pretzel, in a matrix where Zurich and New York relinquish their distinct place-ness? Haven't we all experienced by now the uncanny sensation that it is the phone that remembers for us, whether regarding what we did last summer or a best friend's birthday? The same applies to all the people, places, and cappuccinos captured by the phone: we can only be certain they happened to the extent that they appear on our timeline.

Fischli's iPhone pictures were taken during walks in cities such as Zurich, New York, Paris, and Chicago, but in the grid patterns of his vinyl floors, this content is all mixed together, as if all these places and times were one city, one image. The vertigo effect is also this: the experience of every city as one and the same walk, accompanied by the uncanny sensation of time traveling through a grid of memories that belong to no one in particular.

中拍到的，有时视角向下俯瞰（狗，窨井盖，一盘盘食物），有时向上仰视（摩天大楼，自动扶梯）。在覆盖整个展厅地面的绵延网格中，这些交替排列的对比视图执行了一种界面本身的空间实践。

可以说，费茨利构建了一幅城市通过我们来看待它自己的图像。我们可以识别简单的图形，我们会对信号和提示词作出反应，我们点赞，我们购物，我们进食：在做所有这些动作的时候，我们都是在与这个信息结构进行交流。出门漫步是将日常经验不断转化为数据，转化为可被分享的内容。但是，我们的漫步内容本身并没有意义，或者说，至少不具有紧迫的重要性：内容仅仅是扩展和增加这幅城市技术图像分辨率的一种手段。我们在漫步时带着手机，以此扩展这幅图像。我们就像狗或无人机那样穿行在城市中。

为费茨利的地板图案提供内容的 iPhone 照片似乎在这个新的城市景观中识别并捕捉到了某些类似表情符号的元素。这些图像也可能是对完全依靠使用相机镜头来邂逅现实，并在胶片曝光的那一时刻实现"决定性瞬间"（亨利·卡蒂埃-布列松语）的战后街头摄影开的一个玩笑。因为在数字时间线上，每一个时刻都和任何其他时刻一样是决定性的：在这个苏黎世和纽约都已经消退了它们独特地方性的矩阵中，这只贵宾犬或那个椒盐卷饼出现在哪个地点、哪一时刻？而且，这种诡异的不安感——手机在帮助我们记忆，无论是去年夏天我们做了什么，还是最好朋友的生日——我们难道不是都体验过吗？而对于手机捕捉到的所有人、所有地点和每一杯卡布奇诺来说，这种感觉同样存在：我们只能确信，那些事物确实发生过，因为它们出现在了我们的时间线上。费茨利的 iPhone 照片是在苏黎世、纽约、巴黎和芝加哥等城市漫步时拍下来的，但在他的乙烯基地板网格图案中，所有这些内容全都混杂在了一起，就好像所有这些地点和时刻都只是一个

Fischli's images are not quite our own in the same way that our iPhone memories both do and do not belong to us. Yet, when viewing his photo-floor, there's an odd feeling of déjà vu, as if we've taken this walk before. Whose walk is this? Whose streets? Isn't this a sensation we sometimes experience when scrolling through our timelines—that this wasn't one hundred percent my walk or my life, but it was absolutely the phone's or Google's? Fischli's floor patterns activate the robot within us as we scan his gridded content with our bodies and minds. We recognize this walk, which seems to occur within the no-when of the technical image and its built-in clock, in the real-time of its operation, involving us in ways we somehow consent to ("I agree") without fully comprehending our roles as operators. By mirroring our everyday walks within the human-facing metaverse, and by de-virtualizing this experience into a material floor in the gallery, these works bring our personal, inner robots physically into view.

Fischli's photo-floor models and mirrors the technical image by materially feeding back the content of his walks as vinyl tiles within the gallery or museum. Some images are repeated frequently, while others appear hardly at all. Within his installations, the artist plays on a push-pull dynamic between order and chaos, creating the impression of a repeating pattern, only to scramble this expectation by introducing randomness into the grid. The grid, meanwhile, remains the only constant here: the disciplinary matrix of an urban plan, a chessboard, and the layout of thumbnail images on an iPhone's screen. To engage with the work, viewers must physically enter, traverse, and scan Fischli's composition tile by tile with their bodies, looking downward. In doing so, we see our own feet and legs merging with the floor's photographic content. Here we find ourselves in the pretzel-cappuccino matrix, operating the photo-floor. It's an artwork that continually displaces its viewer: there is no other way to perceive it. Vertigo, meanwhile, may be the most human dimension of this matrix, as it is an experience we probably do not share with robots.

城市、一幅图像而已。它所具有的眩晕效应还在于此：对每个不同城市的体验都如同是一次相同的漫步。以及，在不属于任何特定人的记忆网格中进行时间旅行所带来的诡异不安感。

费茨利的图像并不完全属于我们，就好像我们的iPhone记忆既属于我们，又不属于我们一样。然而，当我们在观看他的照片地板时，心中会滋生一种奇怪的既视感，仿佛我们从前也曾经进行过这趟漫步。这是谁的漫步？这是谁的街道？当我们滑动浏览自己的时间线时，不是时而也会产生这种感觉吗：这并不百分之一百是我自己的漫步、我自己的生活……但它们绝对属于手机或谷歌？当我们开始借由自己的肉身和思维来扫描费茨利图像网格里的内容时，这些地板图案就激活了我们内心中的机器人。我们认识到，这种漫步似乎发生在技术图像的"无时刻"和它所内置的时钟之中，发生在它的实时操作之中，我们以某种表达出同意（点击协议末尾的"我同意"按钮）的方式参与其中，而我们其实并未完全理解自己作为操作员的角色。这些作品在面向人类的元宇宙中映射着我们的漫步，并在此刻将这种体验去虚拟化地呈现在展厅空间中形成实体的地面，由此将我们个人化的内在机器人以物理的方式呈现了出来。

通过将他的漫步内容以乙烯基方块的形式赋予物质实体，并呈现在画廊或美术馆中，费茨利的照片地板实现了对这幅技术图像的模仿和映射。某些照片重复出现过很多次，而某些照片则几乎是孤立存在的。在这一系列装置中，艺术家营造出了一种重复模式的印象，但又通过在网格中引入若干随机排列的照片来动摇观众的这种期待，从而精心安排了一种在秩序和混乱之间拉锯的张力。与此同时，装置中唯一不变的模式是网格：这种网格，是城市规划或国际象棋棋盘或iPhone屏幕上显示的照片缩略图布局所设下的规训矩阵。要观看作品，观众必

We operate while simultaneously drifting. In our minds and in time, with our phones and our bodies, we extend the communicating labyrinth of the virtual city, which increasingly resembles the city we remember. We drift in the constantly refreshed no-when of a non-place, and there's perhaps something cool and cowboy-like about how our mobilized attention participates in the abstraction of everything. With each step, we extend the same matrix that counts our movements, whether in Zurich, Hangzhou, or wherever we happen to go.

De Certeau insisted on an untrackable, delinquent dimension of the walk, which he referred to as our style. Even if the surrounding info-structure knows exactly where we are right now and precisely where we were this time last year, it will never understand how we got there or how we managed to escape. In a chapter titled 'Spatial Stories', he explains the difference between place and space: a place is where we appear on the map; it has a proper name and does not belong to us. Space, on the other hand, is defined by how we move or the creative dimension of our improvised trajectory: "Space is a practiced place." But what happens when the creativity of our freewheeling spatial practice—our style—is co-opted by the info-structure and its feedback loops? We could argue that space now creates its own operators. The desert begins to hallucinate its own cowboy. As the info-flâneur becomes enmeshed within these urban operations, he may start to feel a predictable longing for solid architecture and the oppressive old magic of places with names—the terrible village square, church bells, gates… Yes, but nostalgia too is a hallucination, combining with vertigo in the virtual hobo's experiential drift. Now, there's a ringtone that sounds a lot like church bells. Fischli's photo-floor, meanwhile, puts the space of the poodle-cappuccino matrix into practice by making it return as a simplistic physical model we can walk back into and onto. It is a work that mirrors the rampant dimensionality of the technical image, a walk the artist refreshes and extends with each installation, adding new images as he goes.

须亲身踏足进入作品之中，经由他们的肉身，在作品上穿行，并低头向下望去，一块一块地扫描费茨利构造的图像网格。而当我们俯瞰时，我们望见了自己的脚和腿，与地板上的摄影混为一体。在此，我们身处这个椒盐卷饼－卡布奇诺矩阵之中，操作着脚下的照片地板。这是一件使观众不断离开所在位置的艺术品：因为没有其他任何方式能够观看它。同时，这一矩阵所带来的眩晕，也许是它最具人性化的维度，因为这可能是我们并不与机器人共享的一种体验。

我们同时既在操作，又在漂移。在我们的思想中，在时间中，我们通过自己的手机和身体，扩充和延展了这座虚拟城市的交流迷宫，而这座虚拟城市看起来也越来越接近我们记忆中的城市了。我们漂移在不断刷新的一个无时刻的非地点，我们处于移动中的注意力正在参与一切事物的抽象化，这可能有点酷，有点牛仔般的感觉。每踏出一步，我们都在扩展那相同的一个计算着我们步数的矩阵。无论我们身处苏黎世还是身处杭州，或在偶然中去到的任何地方。

德·塞尔托坚持认为，步行具有某种不可追踪、不循约束的维度，而他指的，是我们的“风格”。即便周遭的这一信息结构准确知晓我们此刻的位置和去年今日的位置，它永远也无法理解，我们是怎样到达这里、我们又是如何离开的。在题为“空间故事”的章节中，德·塞尔托解释了地点与空间之间的区别。地点，是我们在地图上出现的地方；它有一个专门的名称，它并不属于我们。而空间，则是我们行动的方式，是我们即兴开辟的轨迹所具有的创造性维度：“空间是一个被实践的地点。”但是，当我们随心所欲的空间实践所彰显的创造性——我们的风格——被这个信息结构及其反馈循环吸纳和利用时，会产生什么样的后果呢？我们也许可以说，空间此刻正在创造它自己的操作员。沙漠开始幻想它自己的牛仔。而随着信息游荡者越来越深陷于这些城

市操作之中，他也许会开始感受到一种可以想见的渴望，渴望着具有固态实体的坚实建筑，以及那些带有名字的地点，在往日所曾散发的压抑魔力，渴望着难看的村庄广场、教堂钟声、大门……没错，但怀旧同样也是一种幻觉，它在虚拟流浪者的体验漂移中与眩晕结合在了一起。现在，有一种手机铃声听起来就十分类似教堂钟声。而费茨利的照片地板，通过将这个贵宾犬－卡布奇诺矩阵复现为一块简单的物理模型，让我们可以漫步回去，踏足其上，由此实践着这个矩阵的空间。这是一件映照出技术图像肆意扩张维度的作品，也是一场每次呈现都会被更新和扩展的漫步，随着艺术家的行走不断添加新的图像。

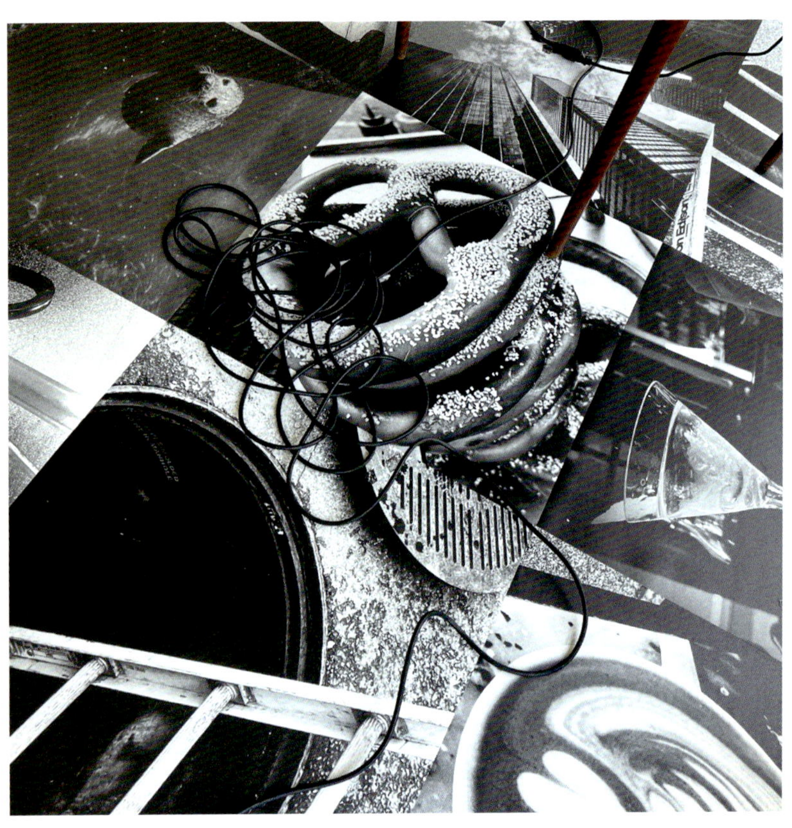

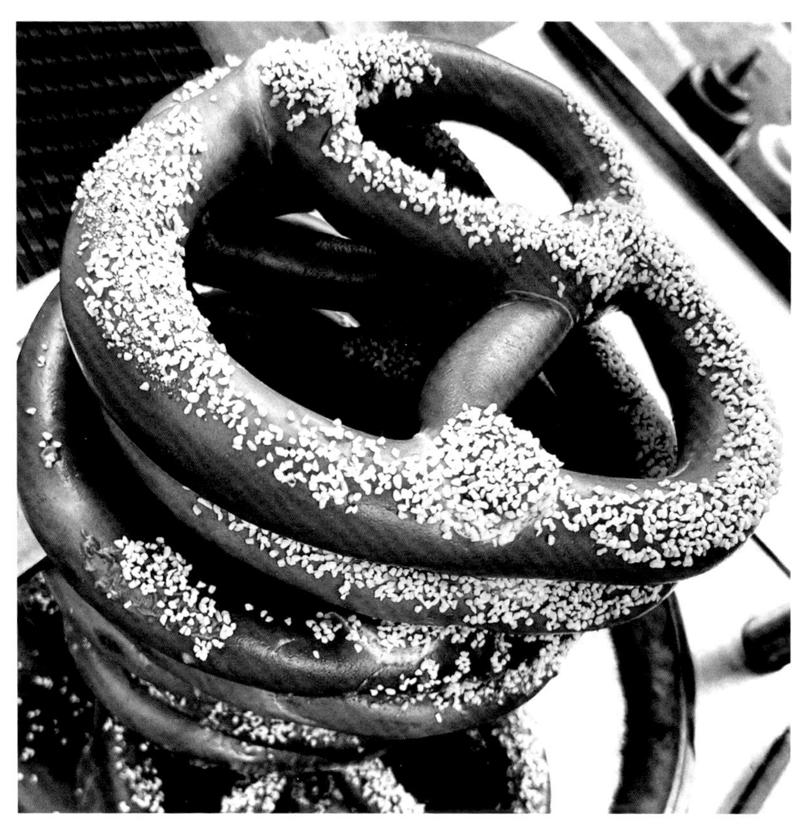

Time Travel

时空旅行

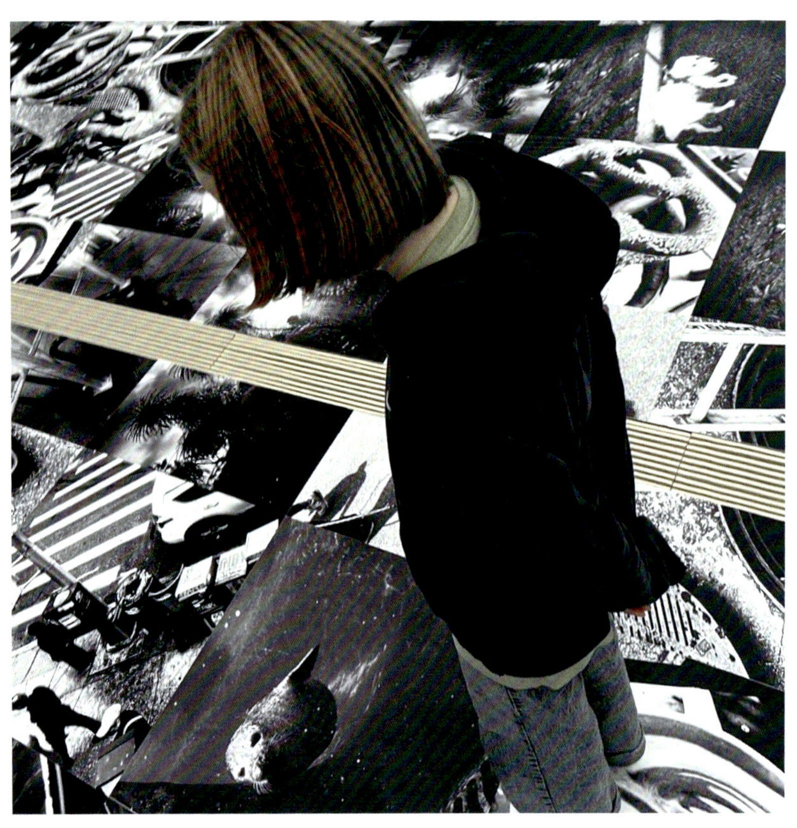

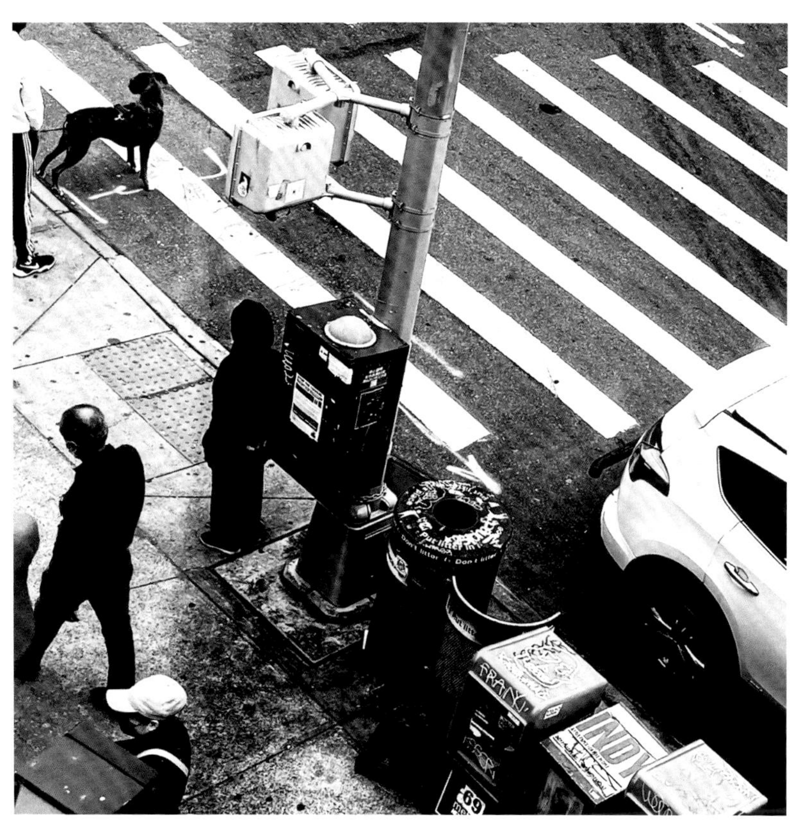

Composition with Stripes

条纹构图

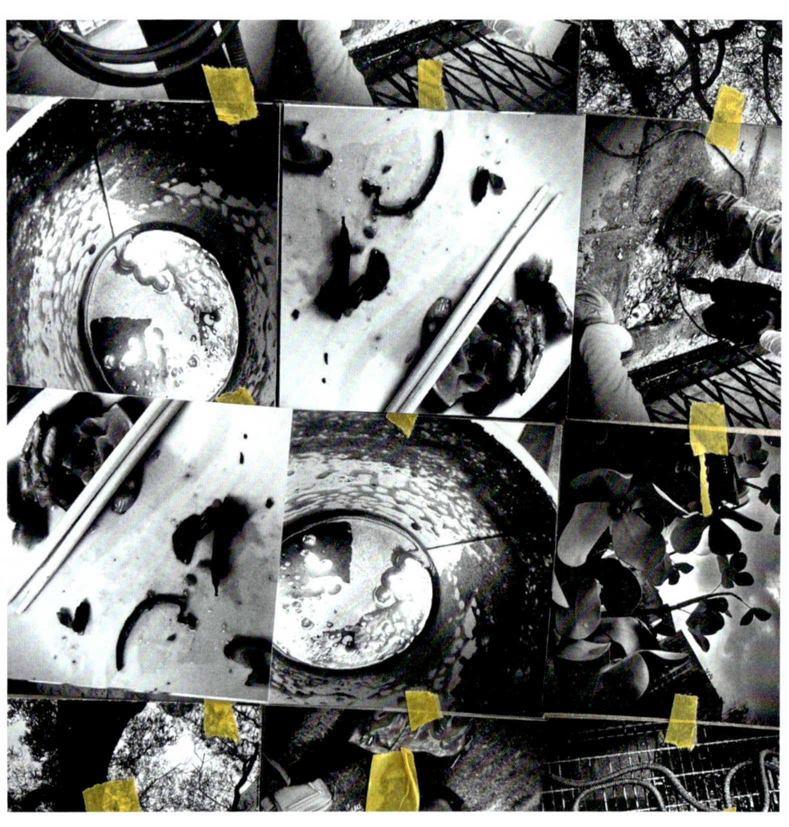

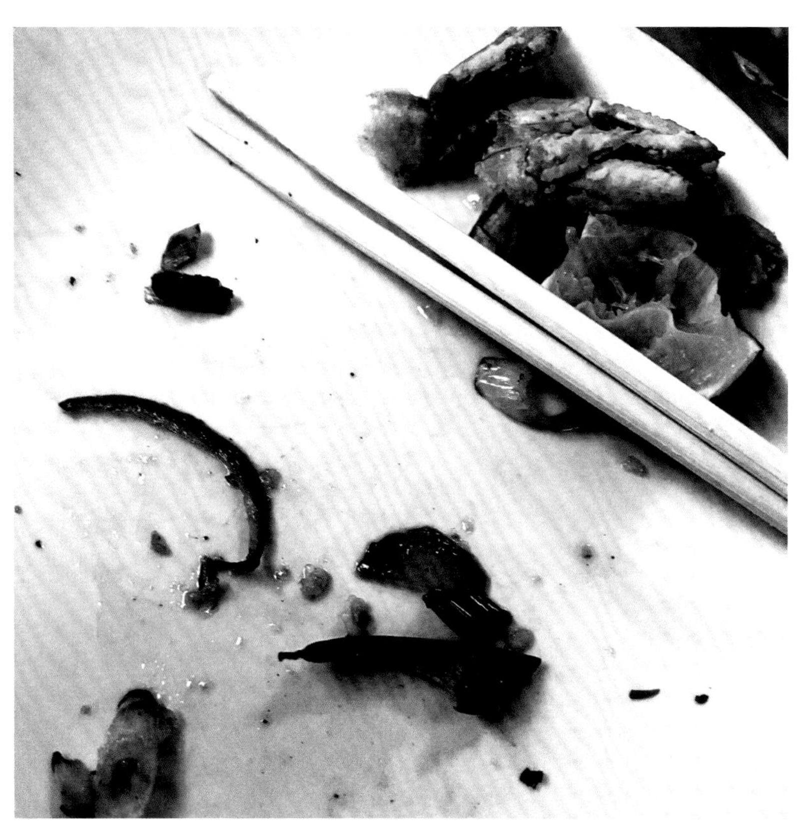

Enjoy Life More

狠享受生活

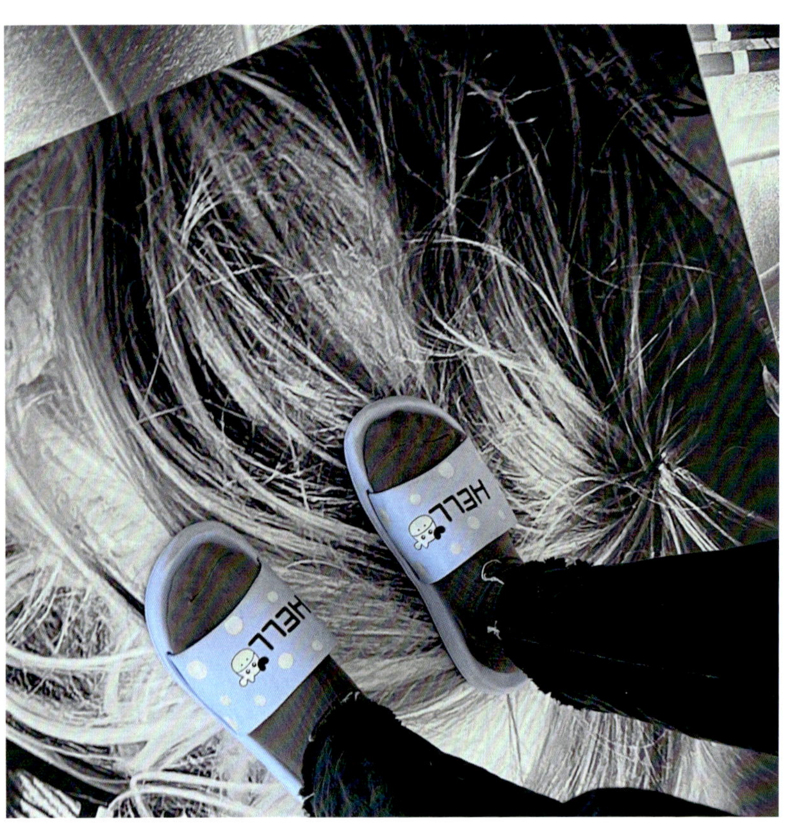
HELL
HELL

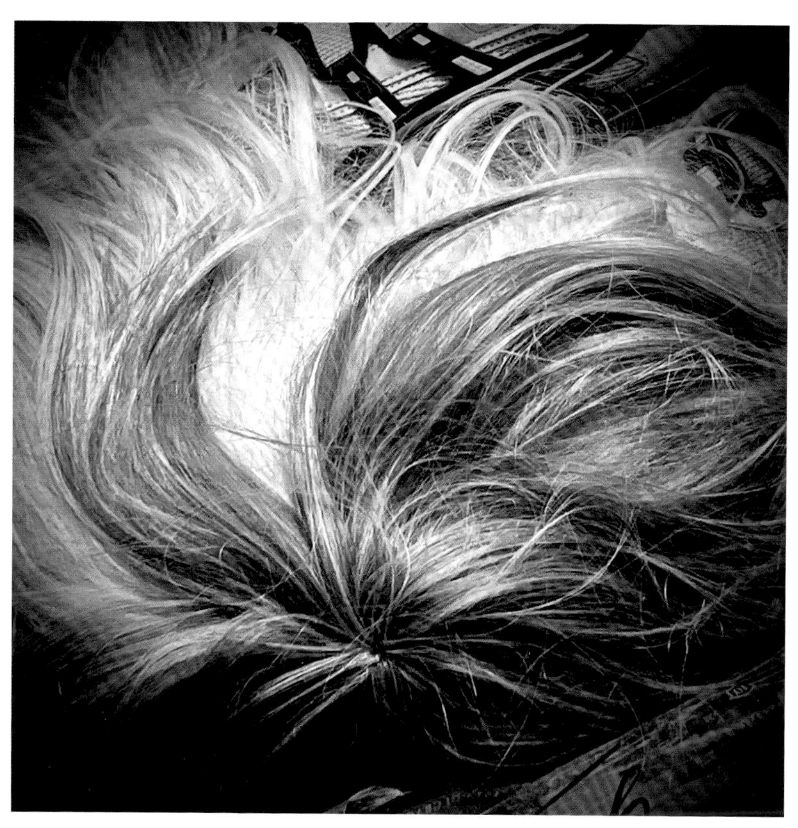

Hologram

全息图

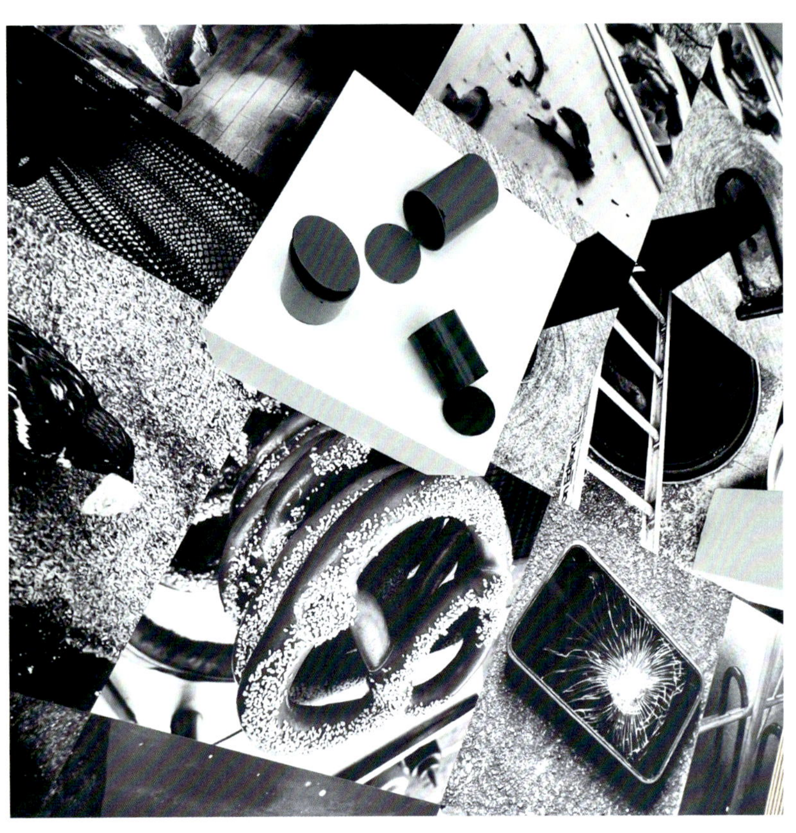

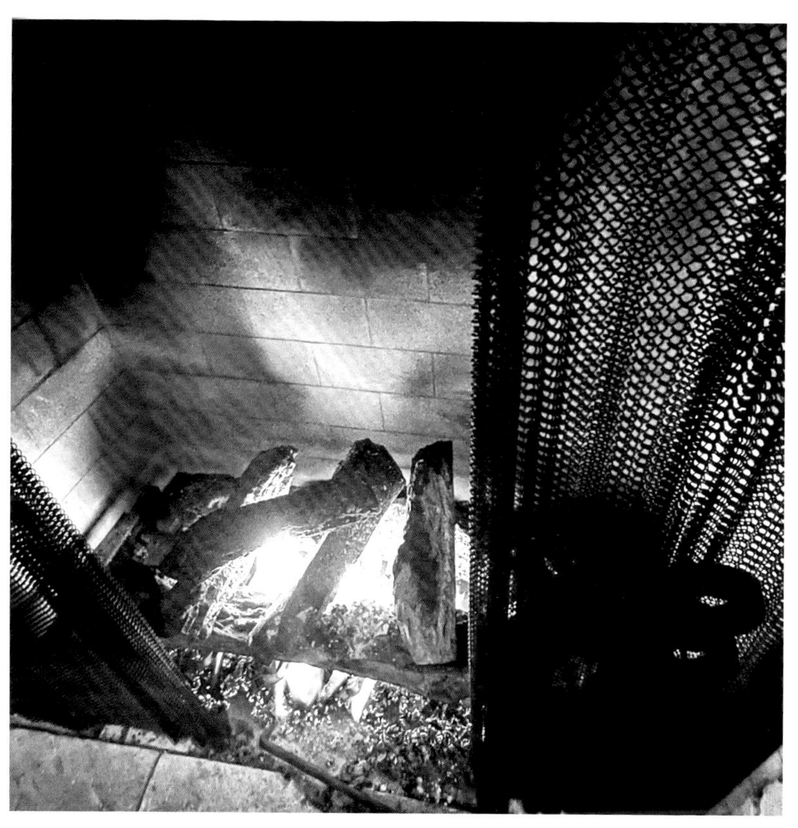

Dragon

龙

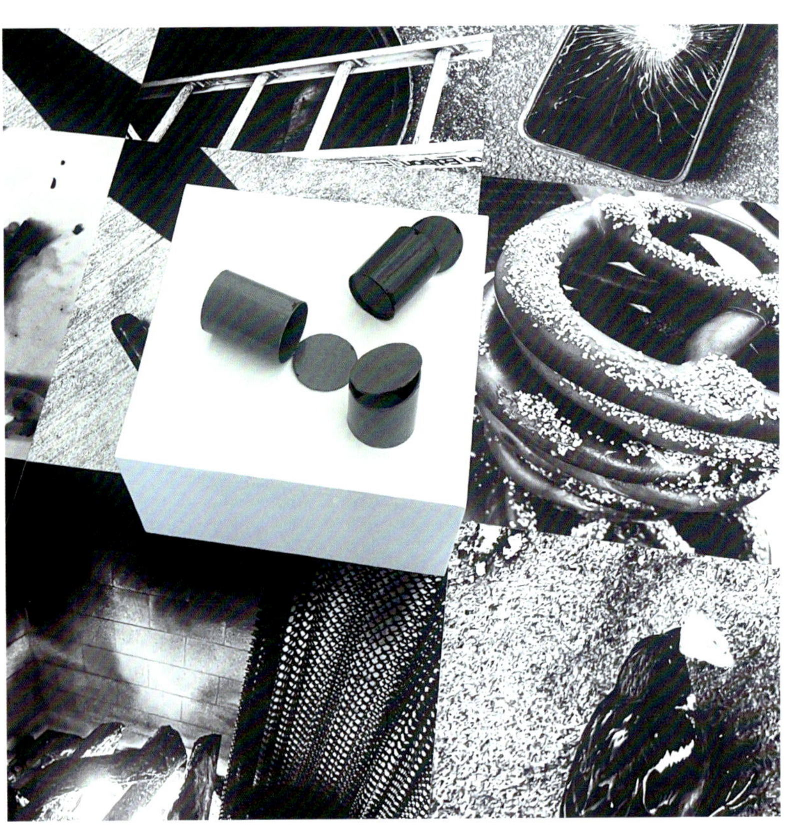

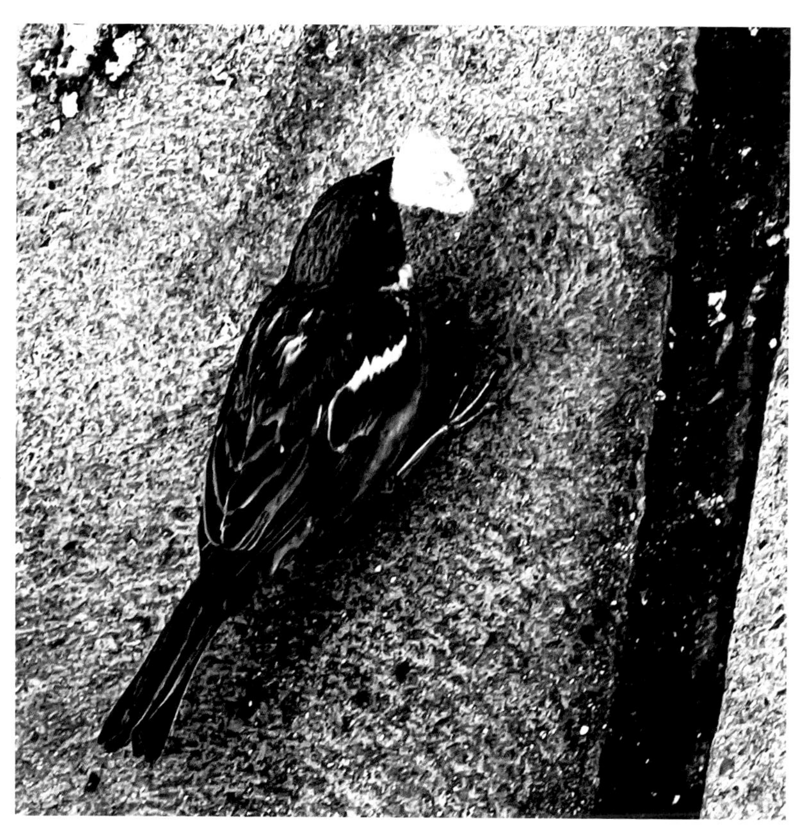

The Opportunist

机会主义者

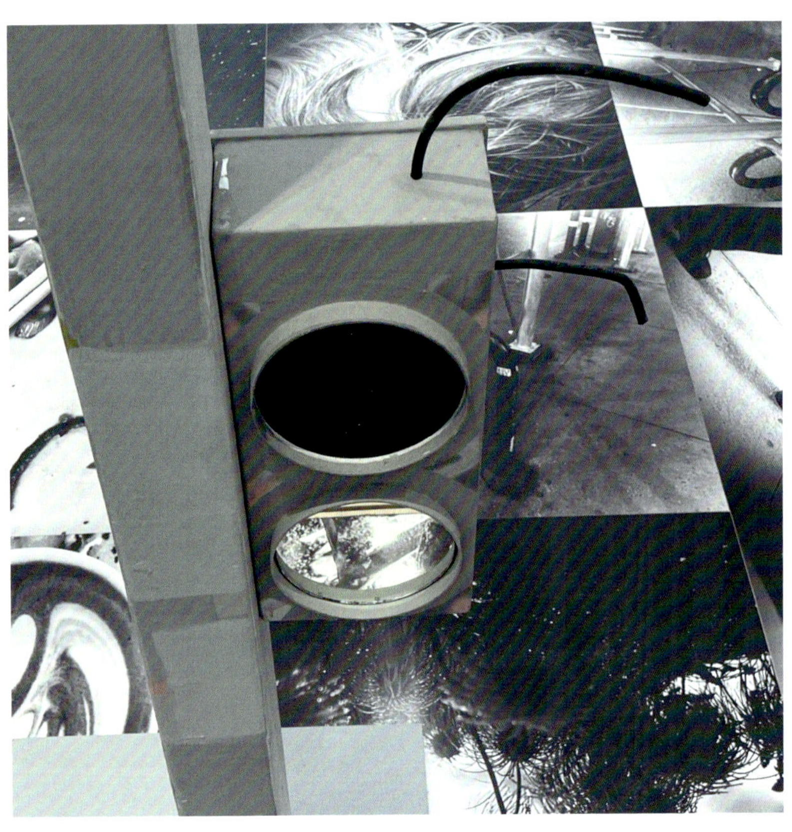

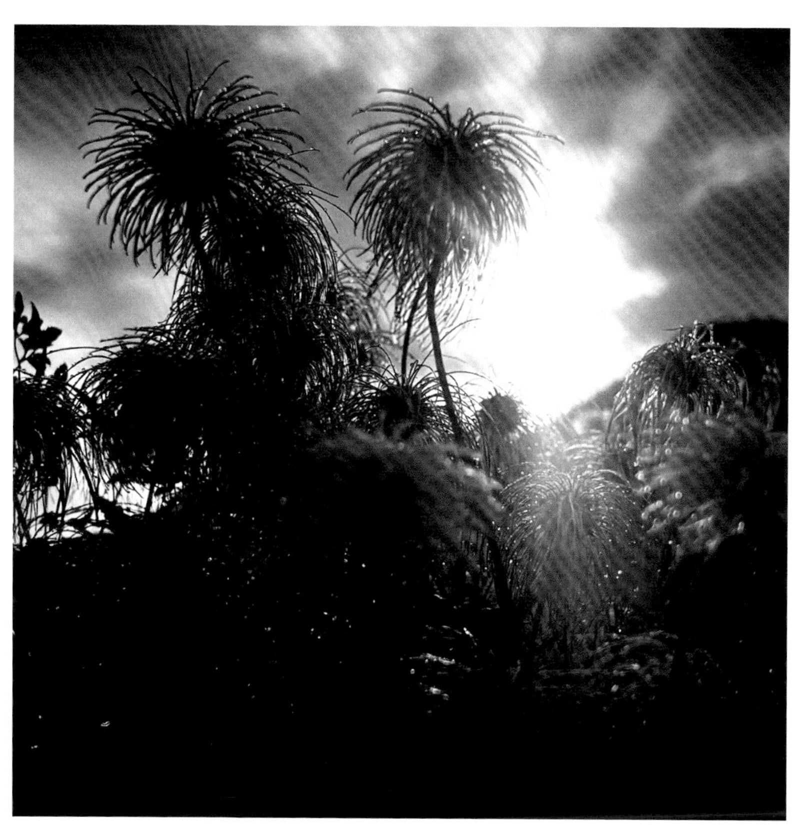

Wishful Thinking

一厢情愿

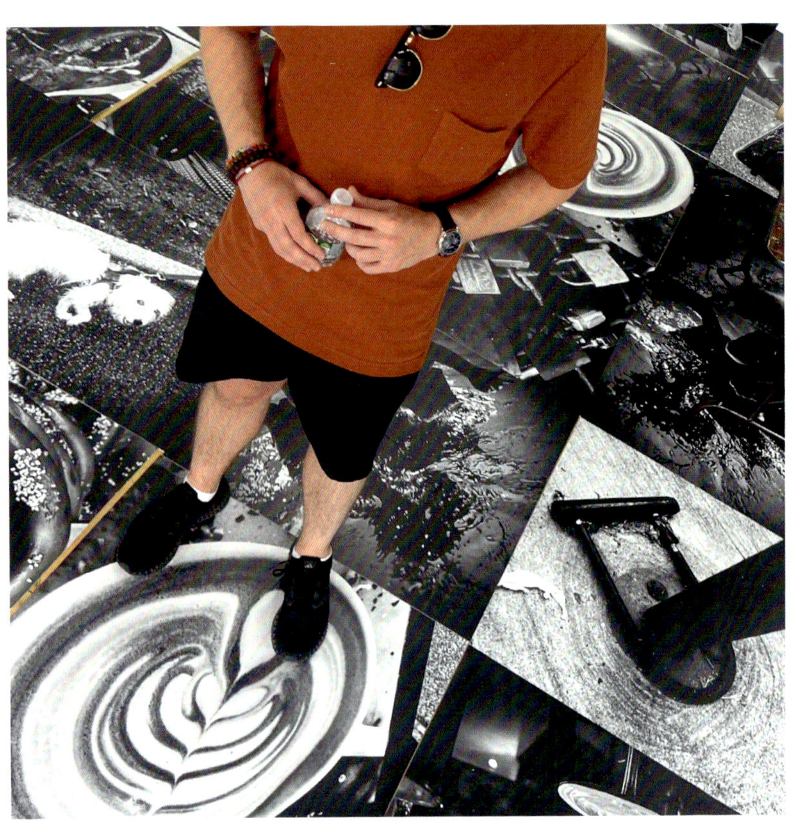

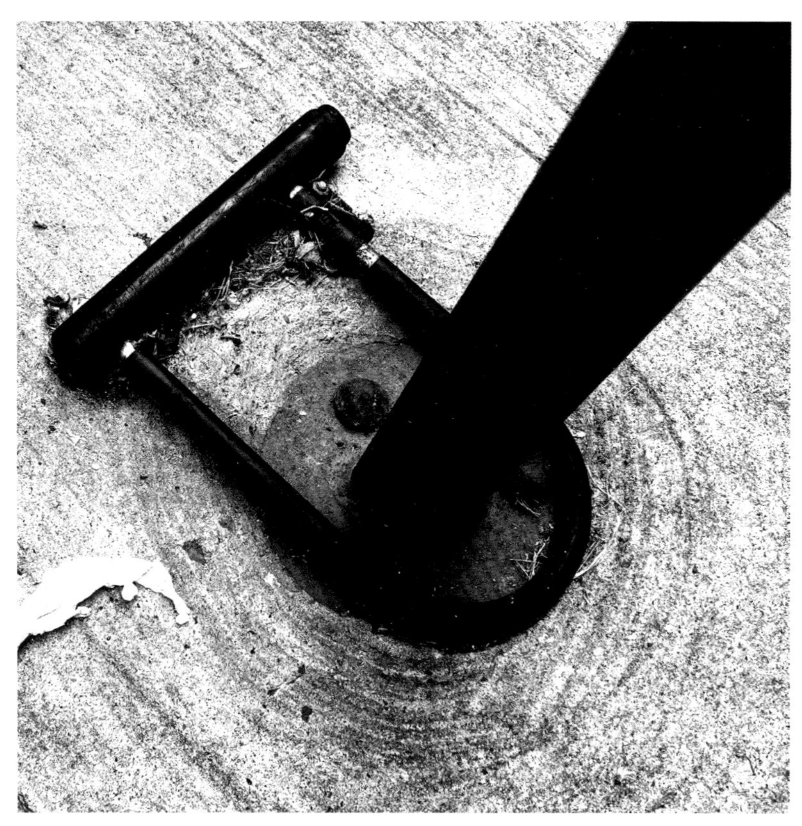

Superego

超我

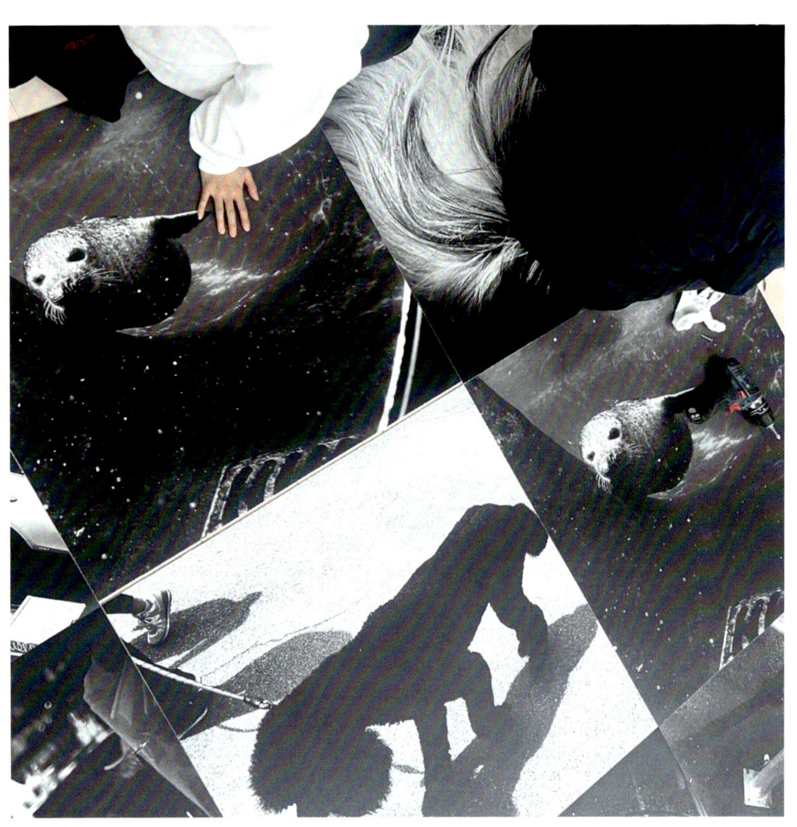

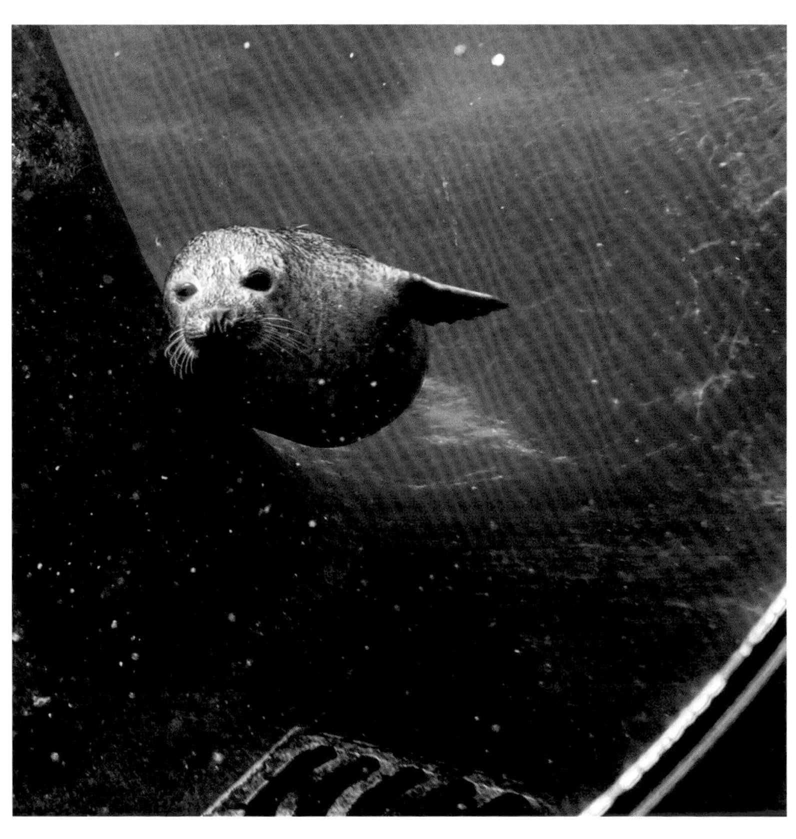

In the Basement

在地下室

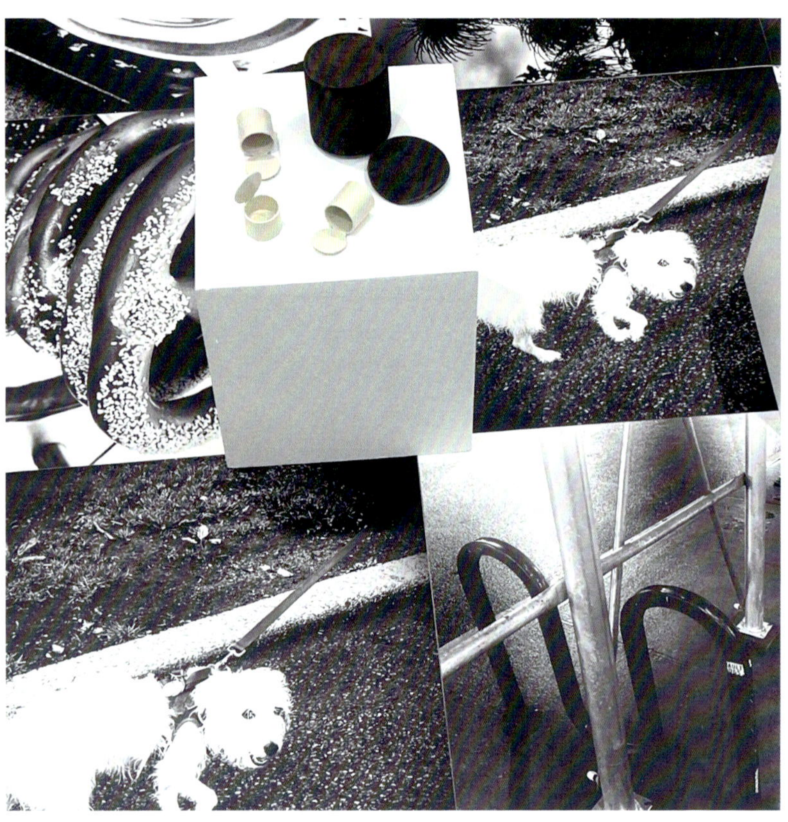

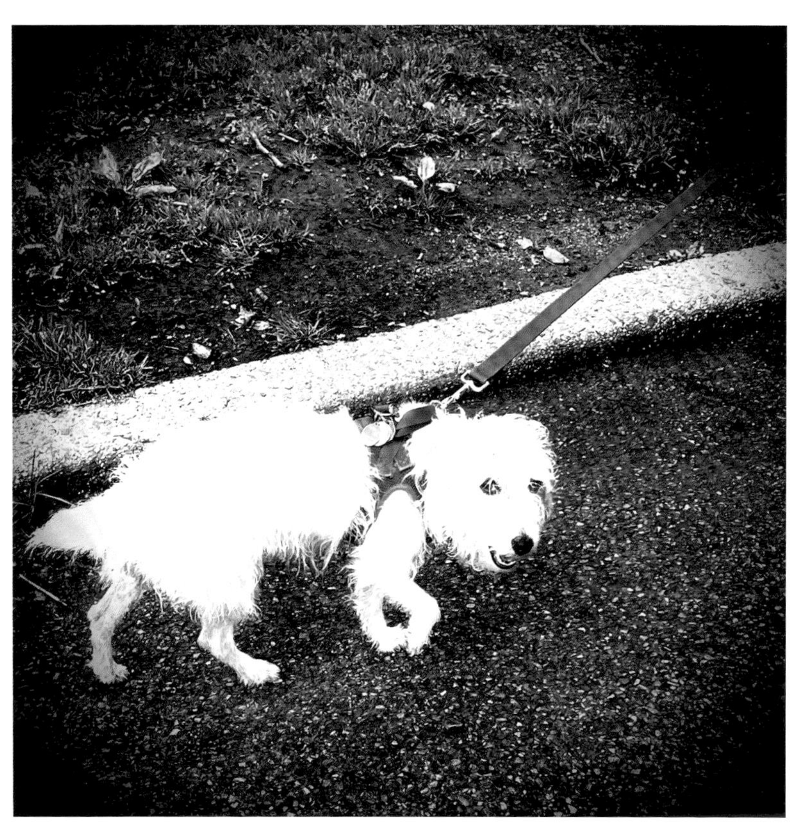

Emotional Support

情感支持

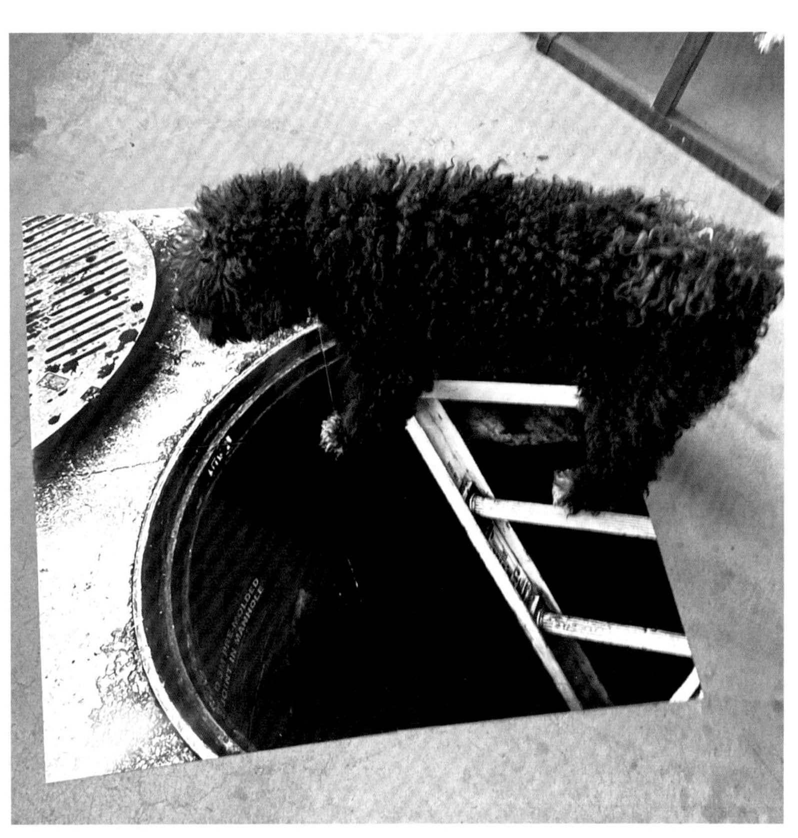
MOLDED
IN MANHOLE

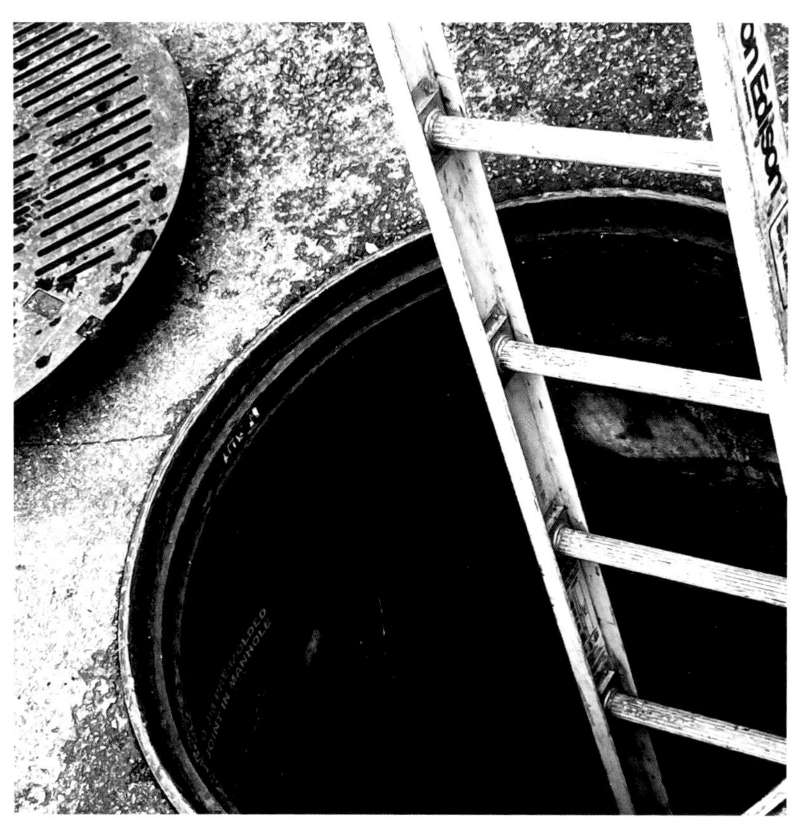

Index

量度

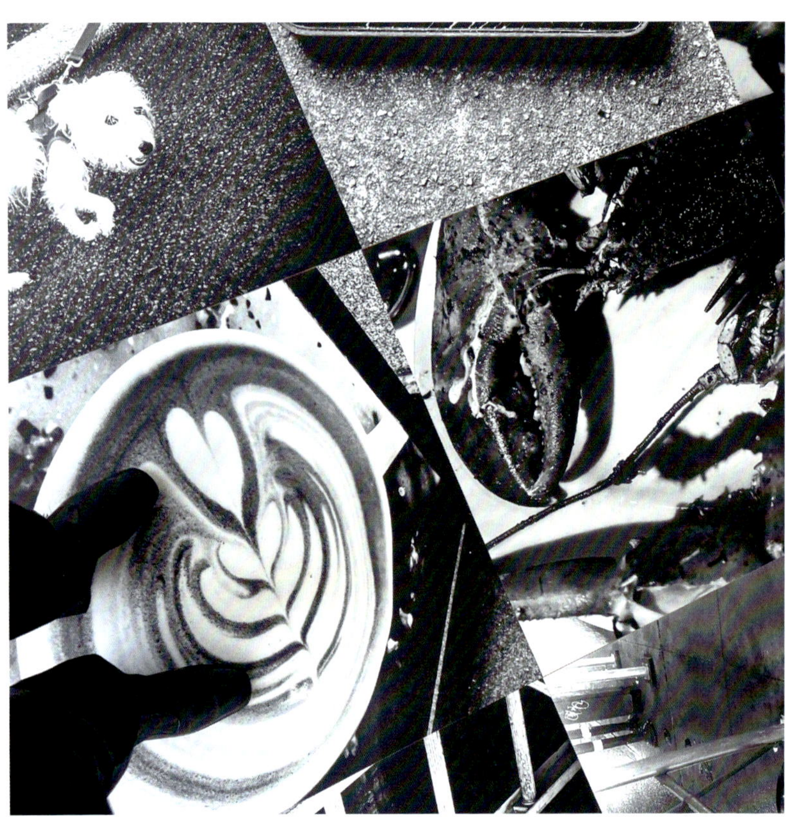

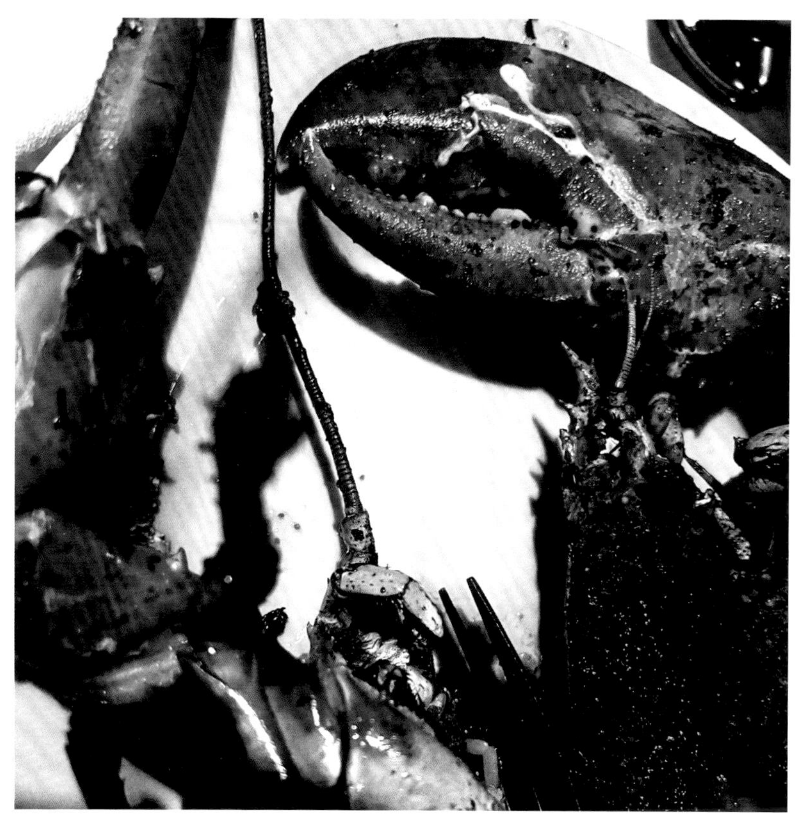

Caretaker

看守者

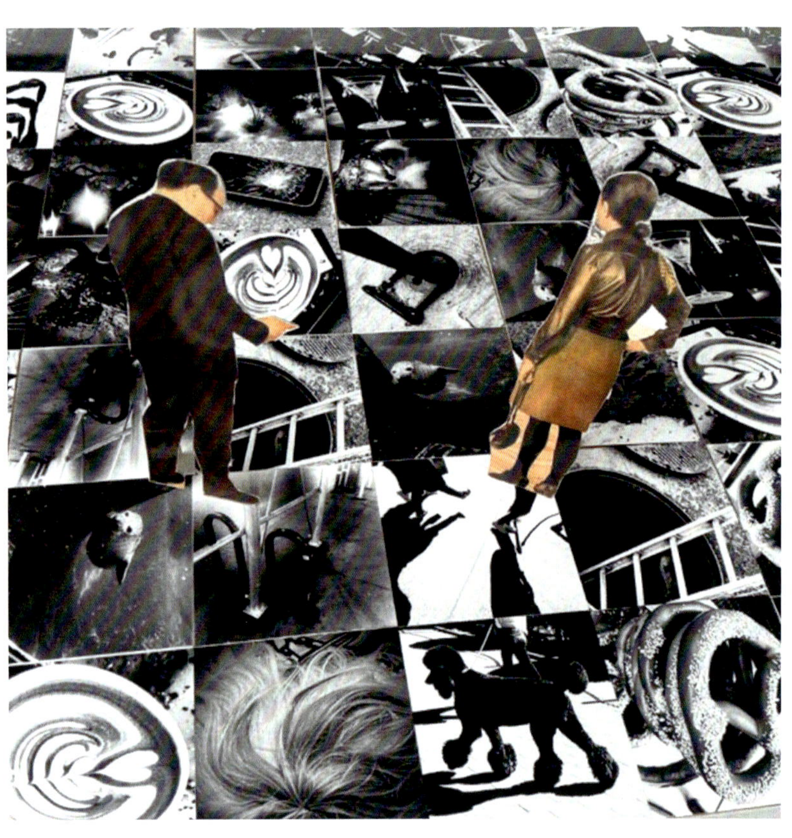

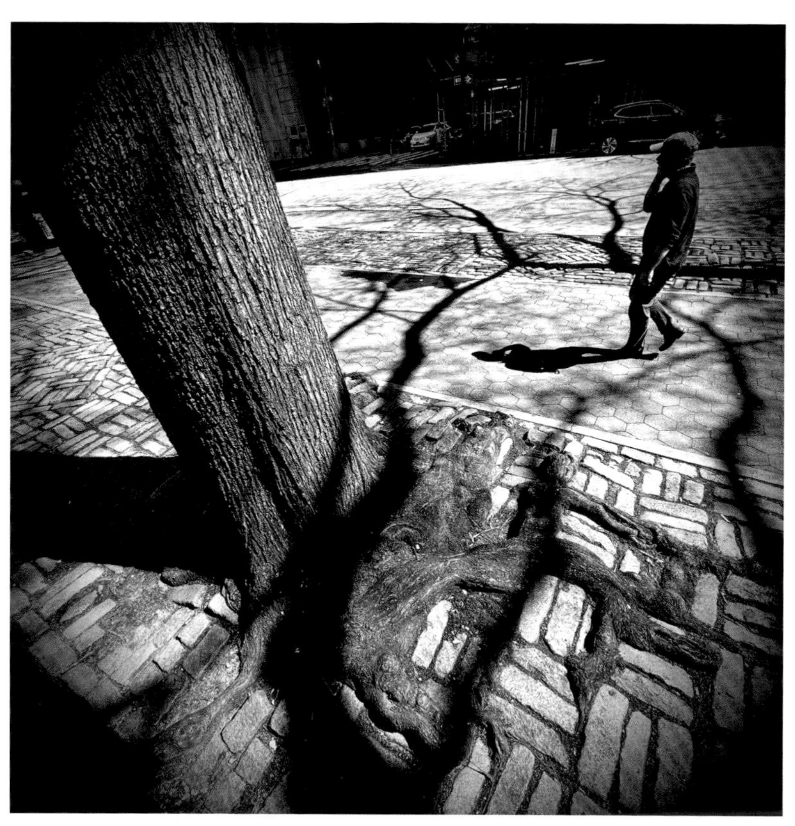

Palindrome

回文

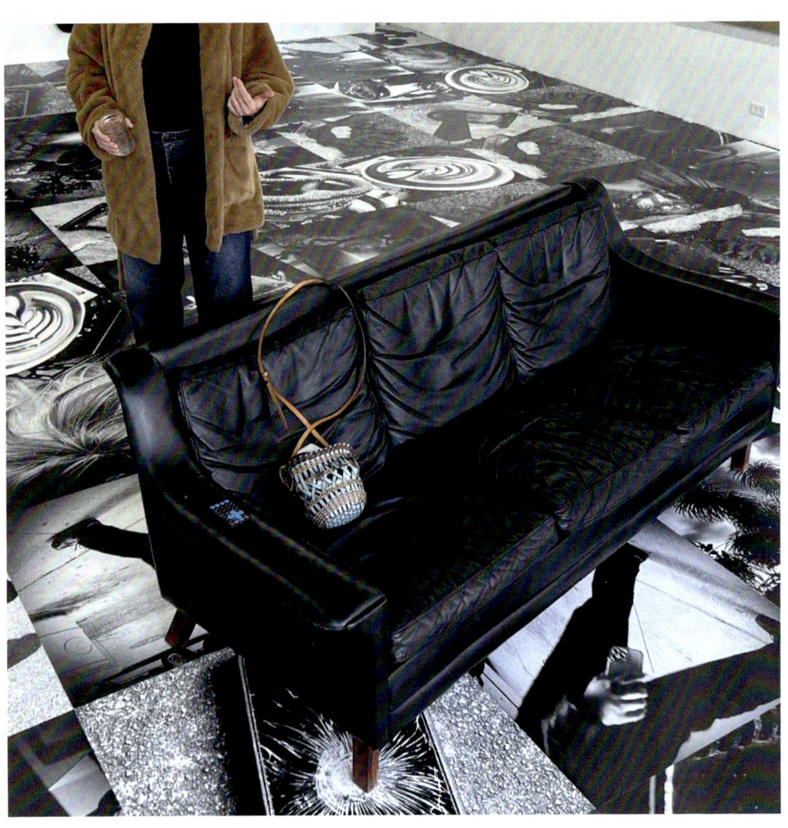

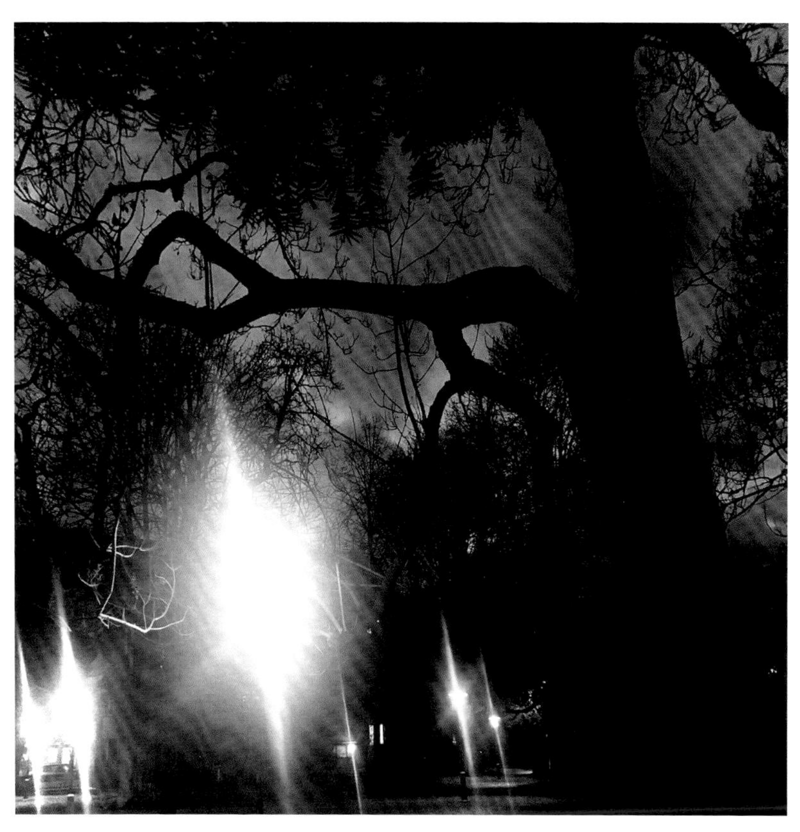

Investing in the Apocalypse

发末日财

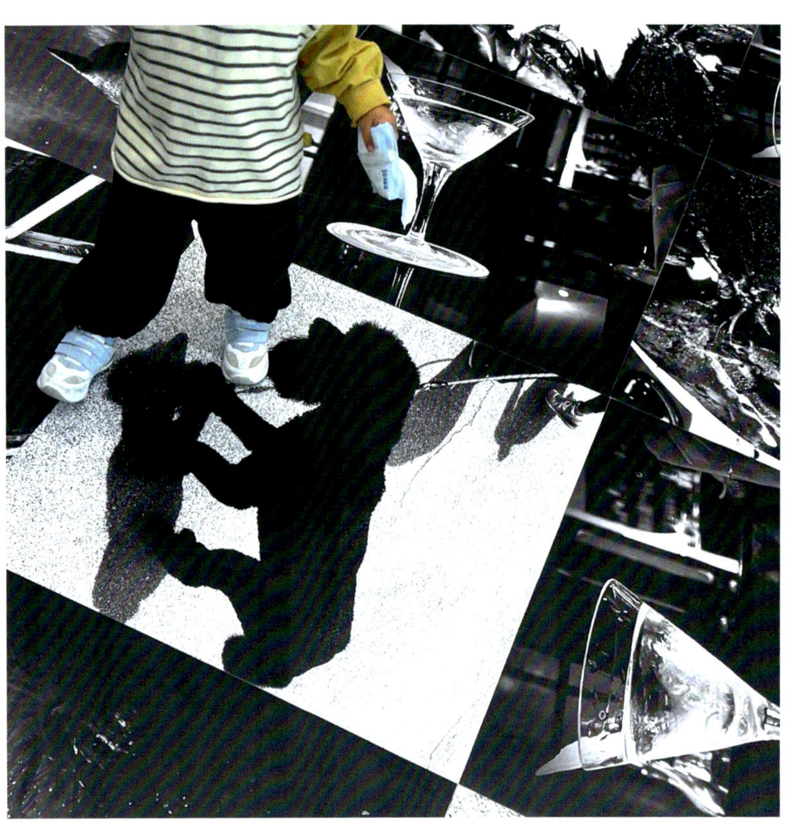

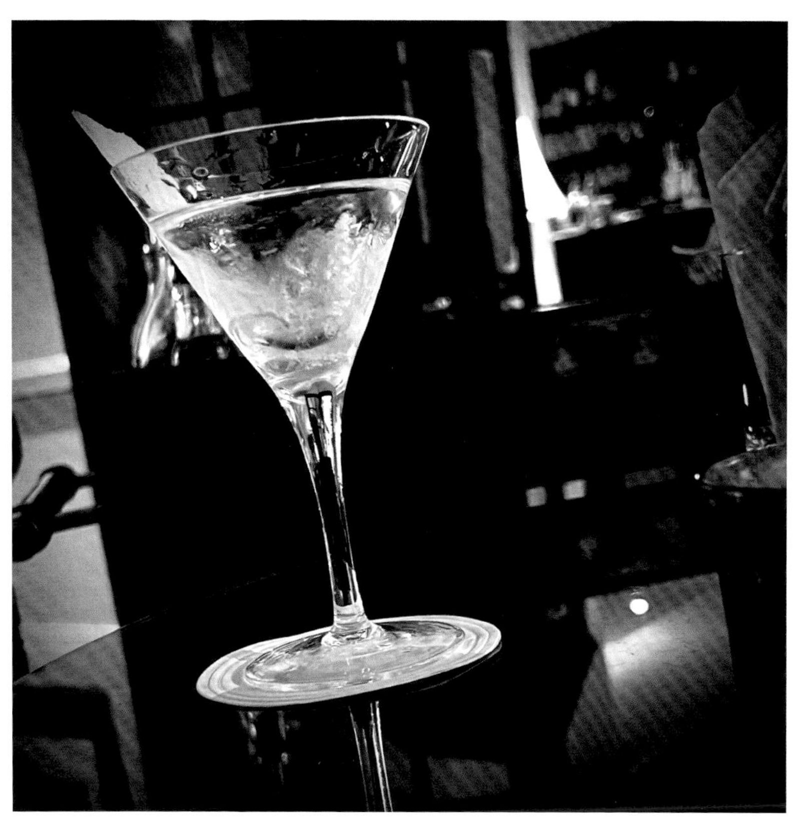

An Element for a Pattern

模式中的一环

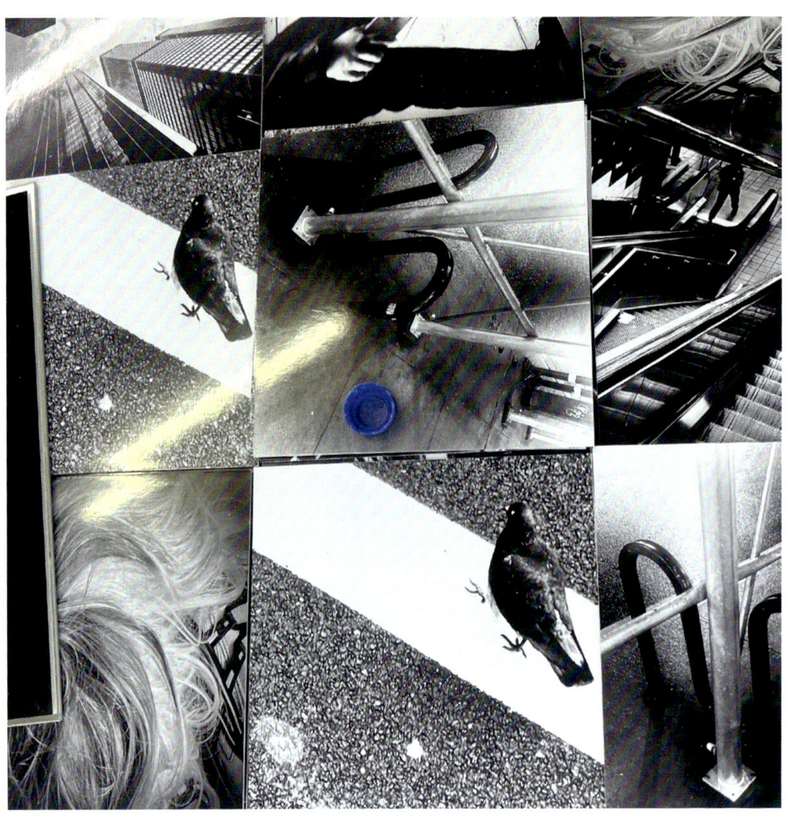

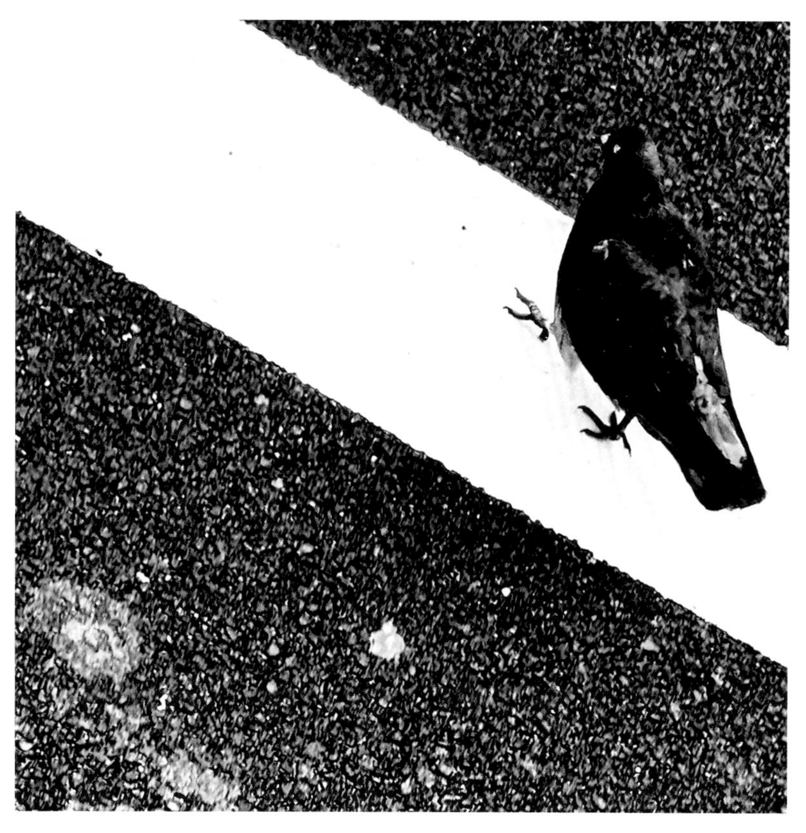

Bird Is Free

鸟儿自由了

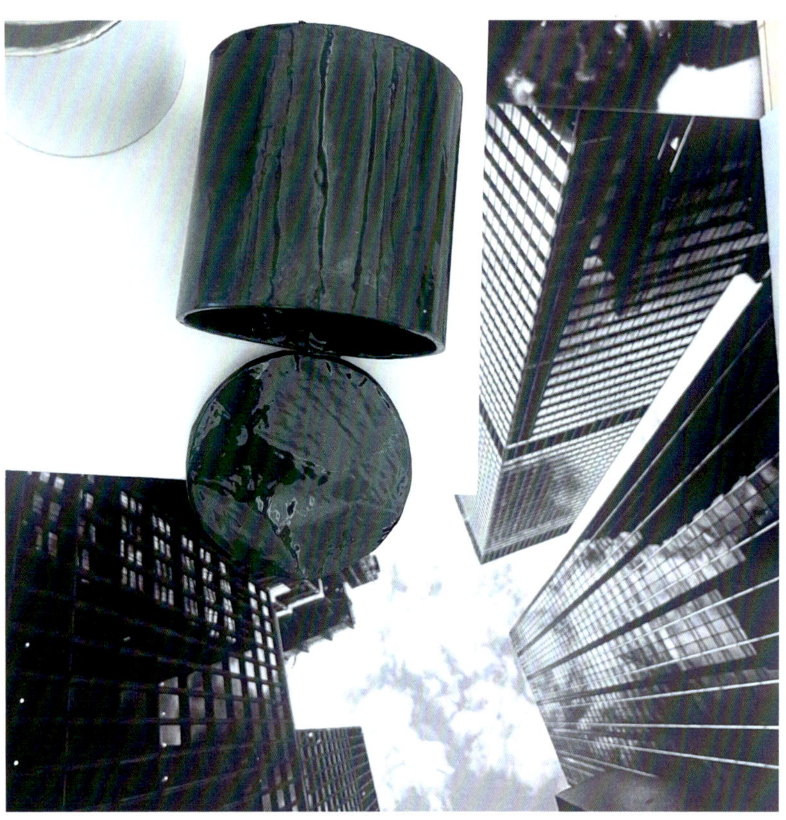

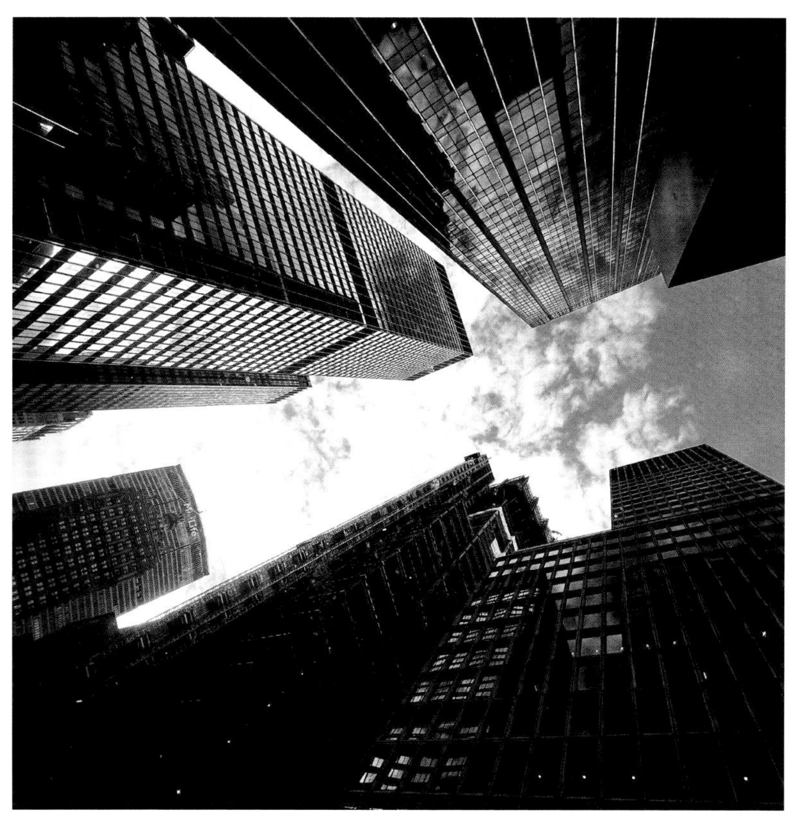

Economics of Emotion

情感经济学

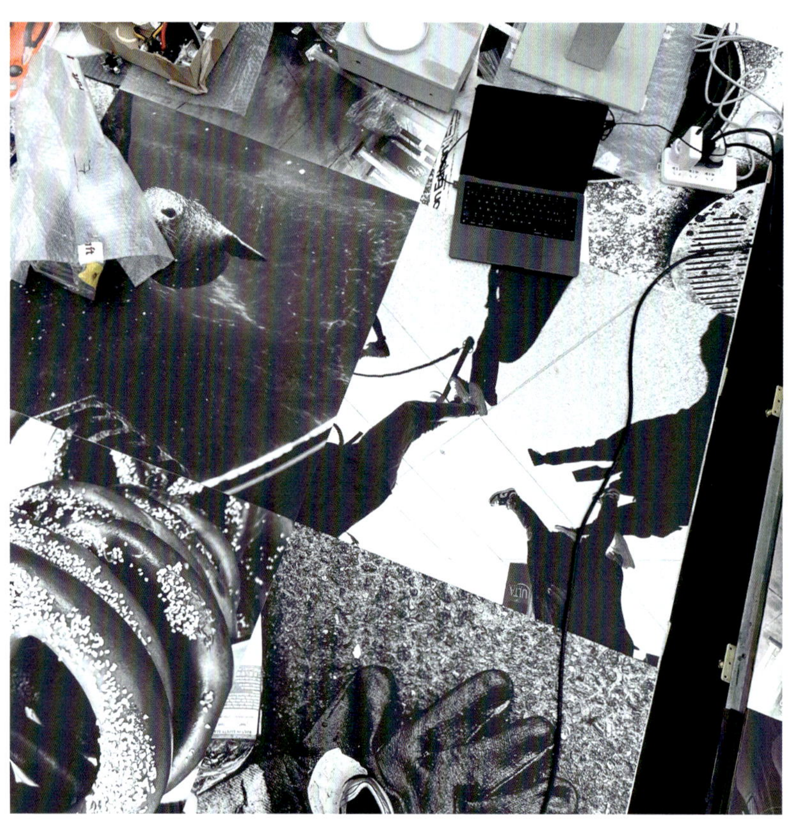

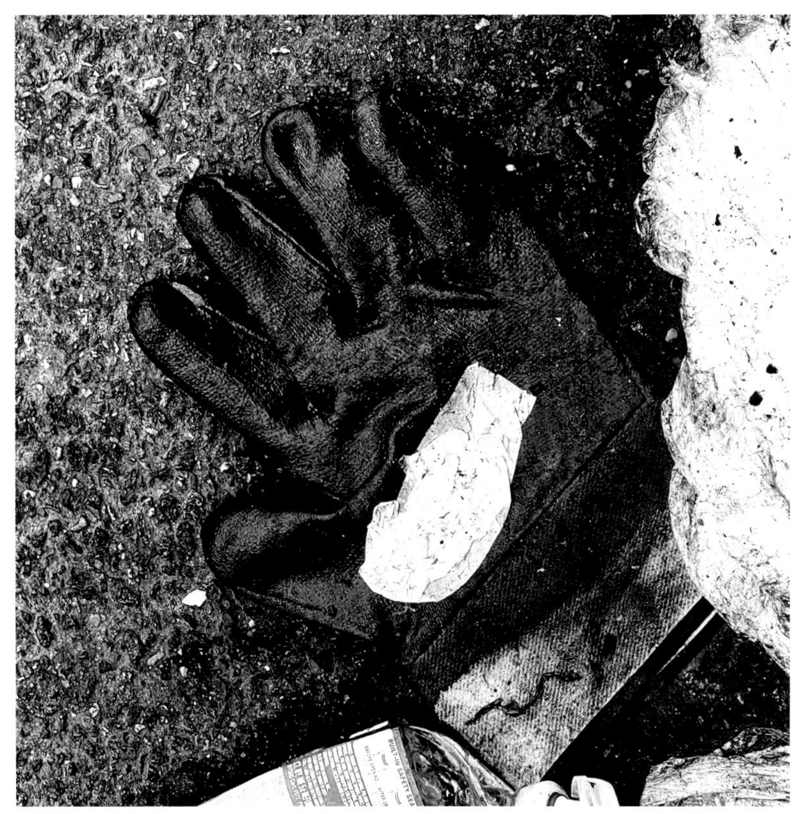

Empire

帝国

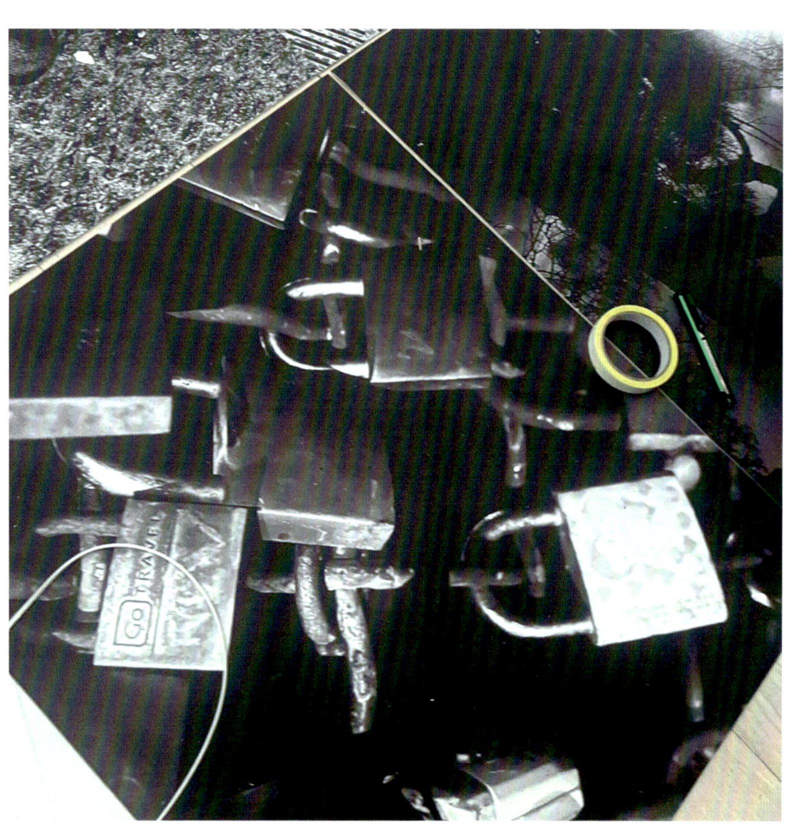
Go TRAVEL

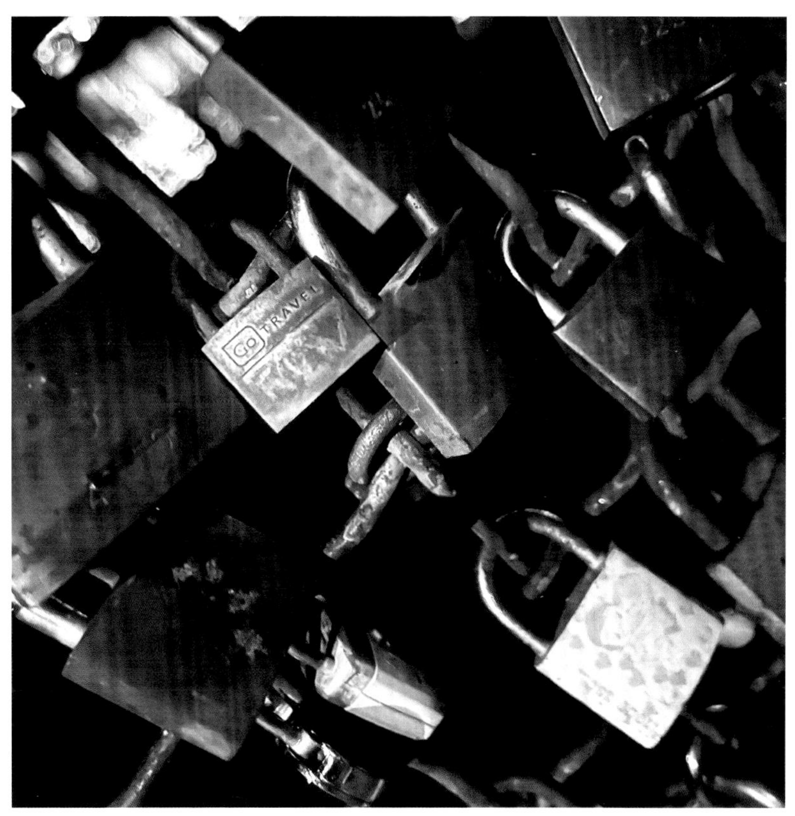

The Seven Rules

七条规则

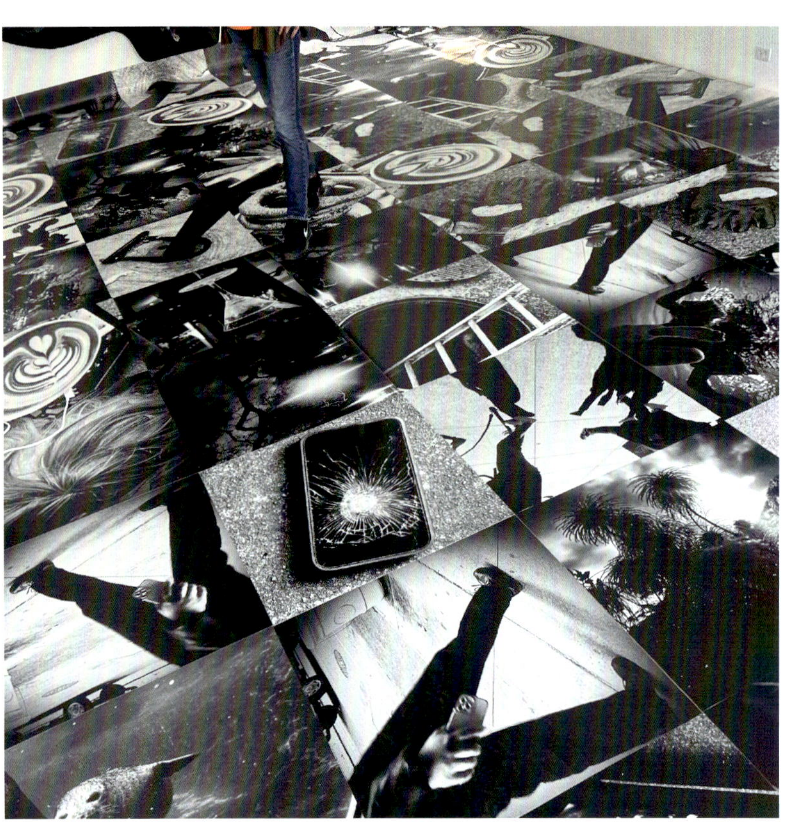

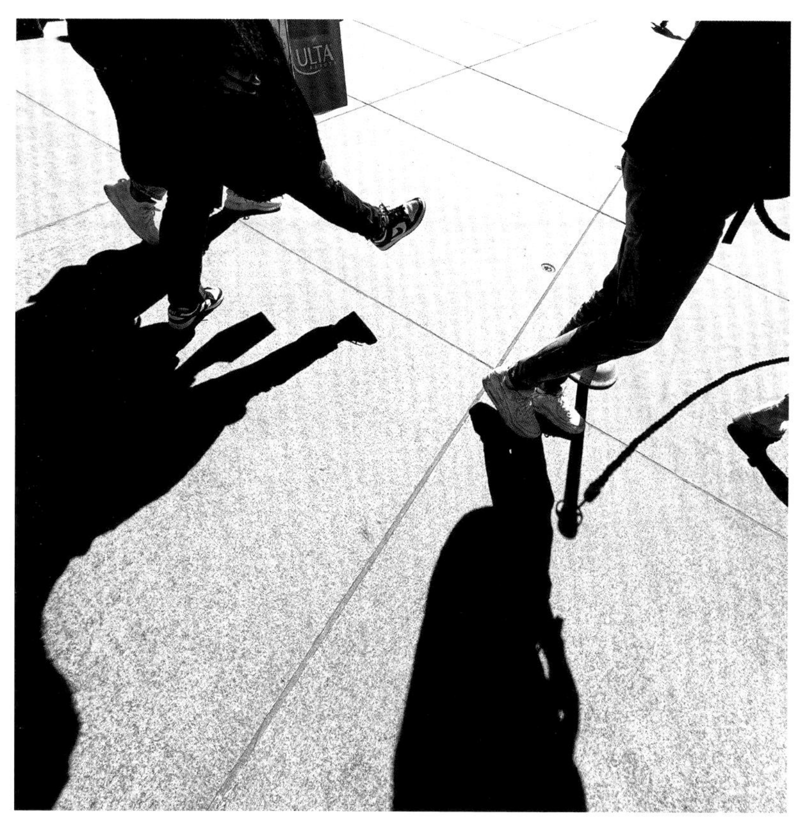

Carousel

旋转木马

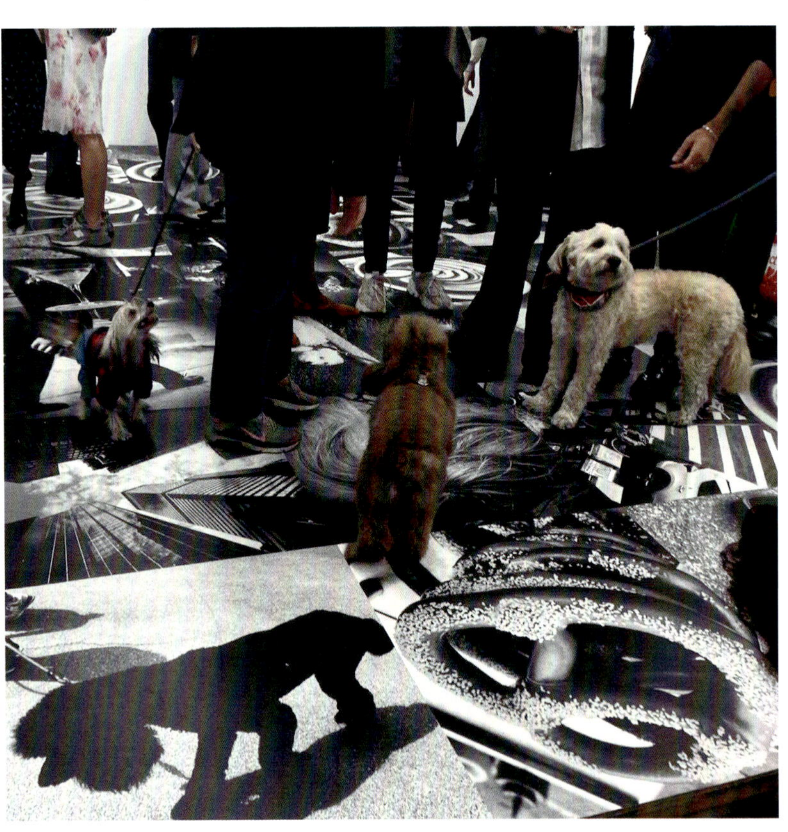

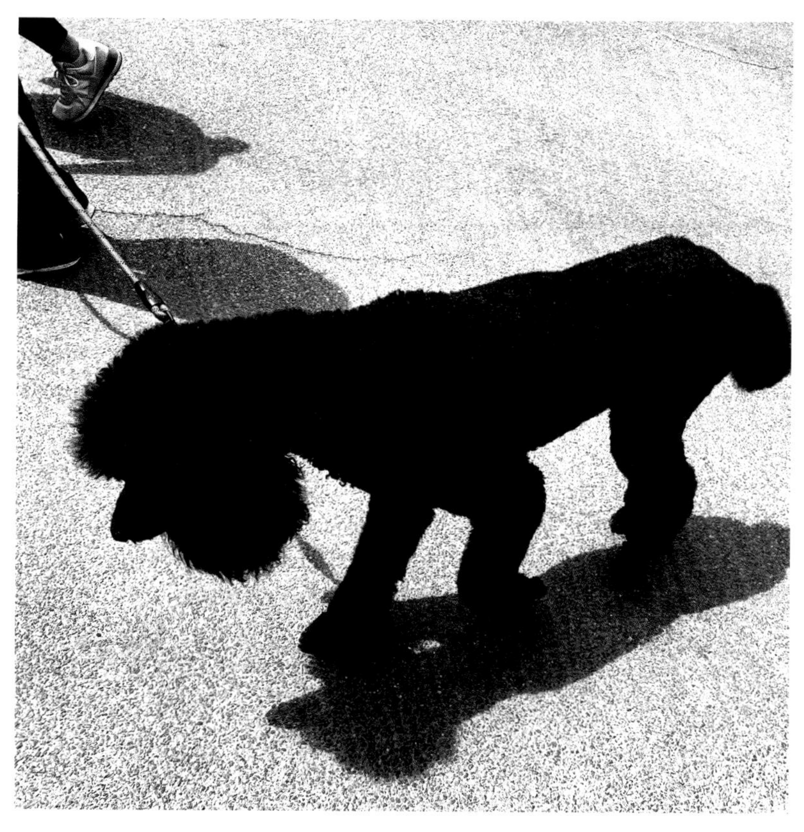

One of Us

我们中的一员

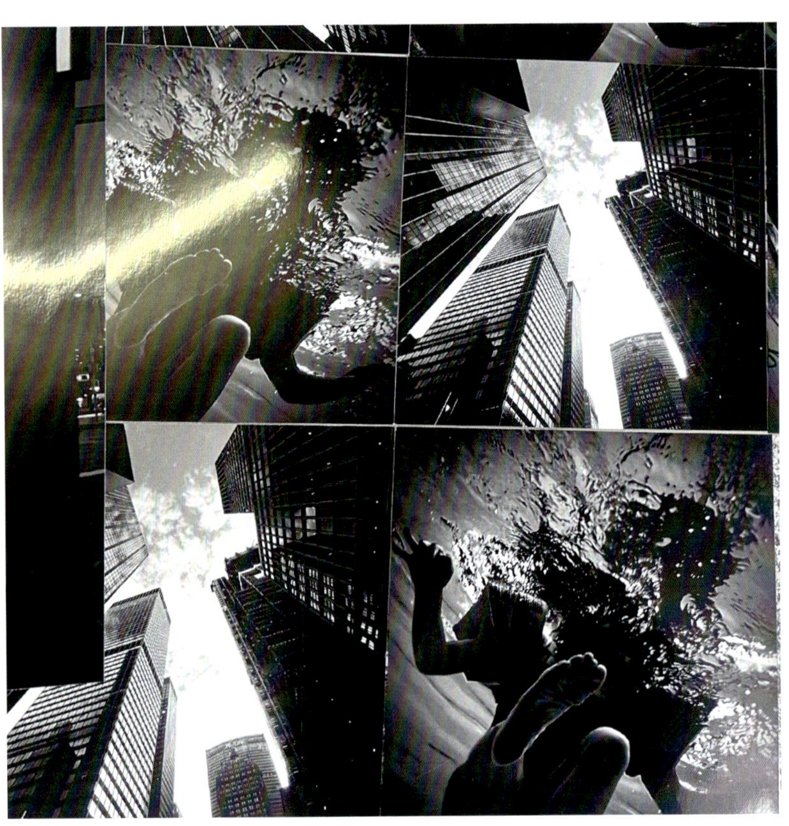

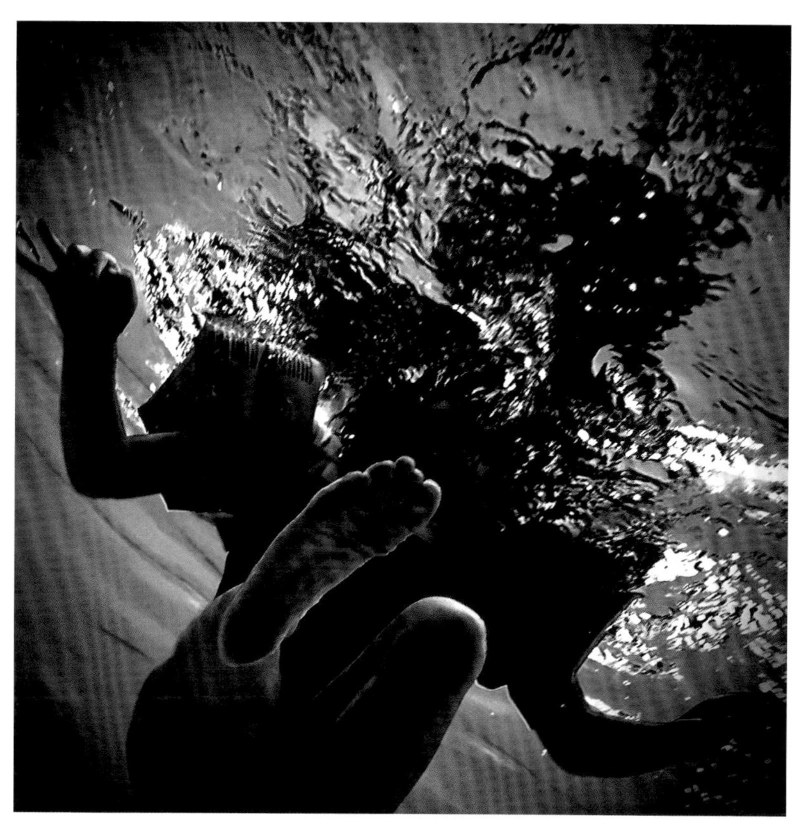

Escape into Space

逃入太空

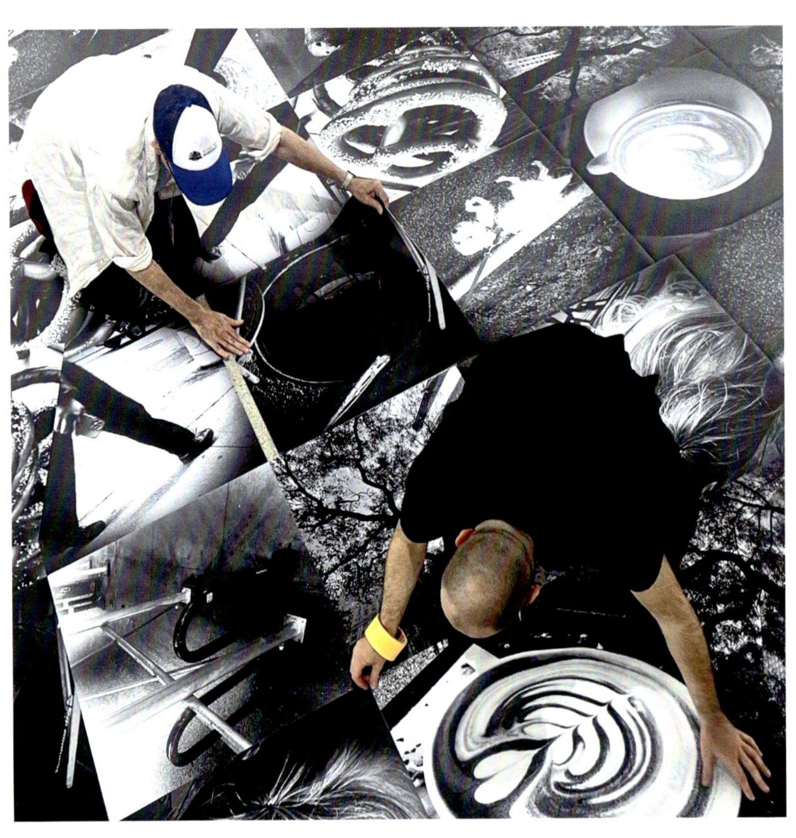

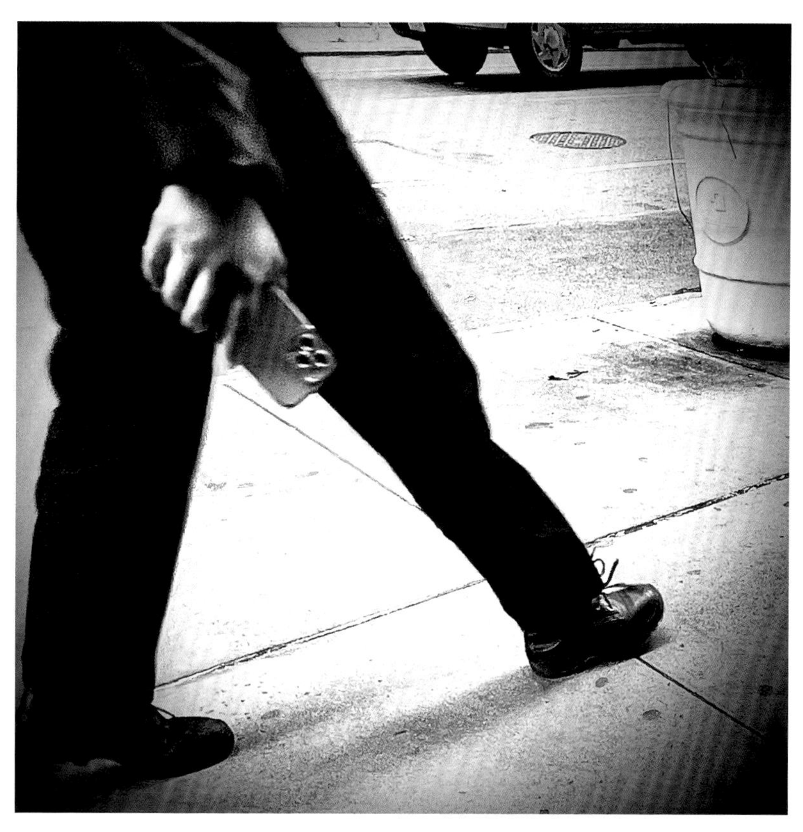

The Competitor

竞争者

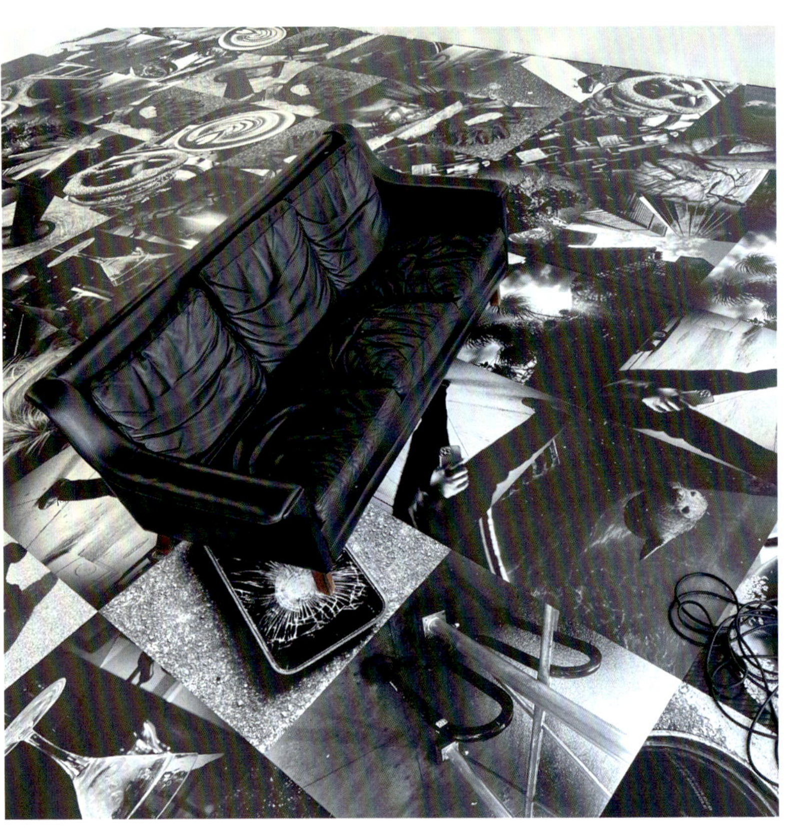

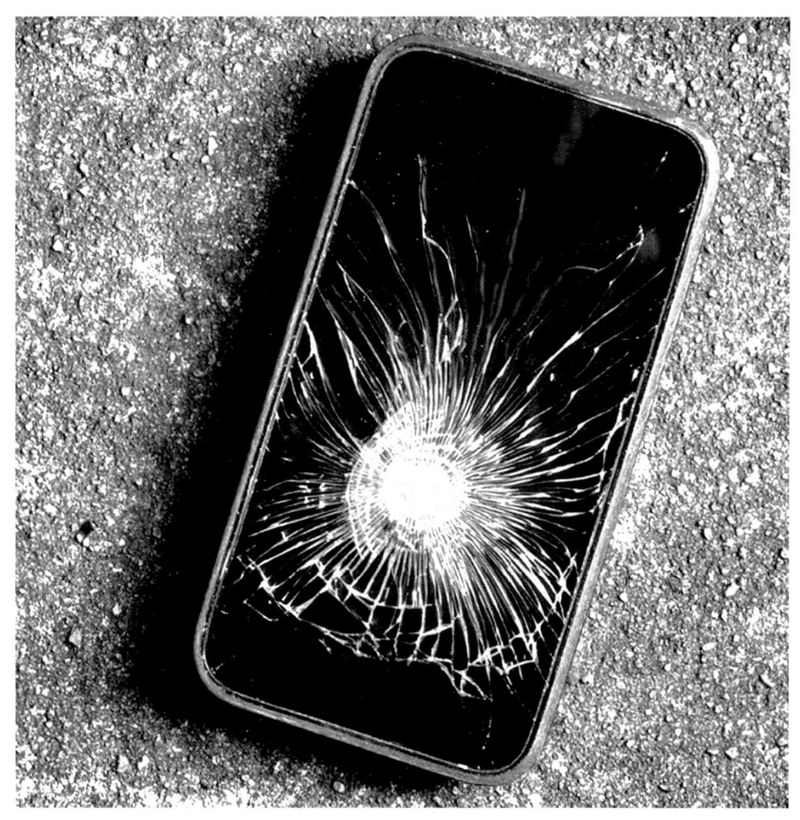

Sunshine

阳光

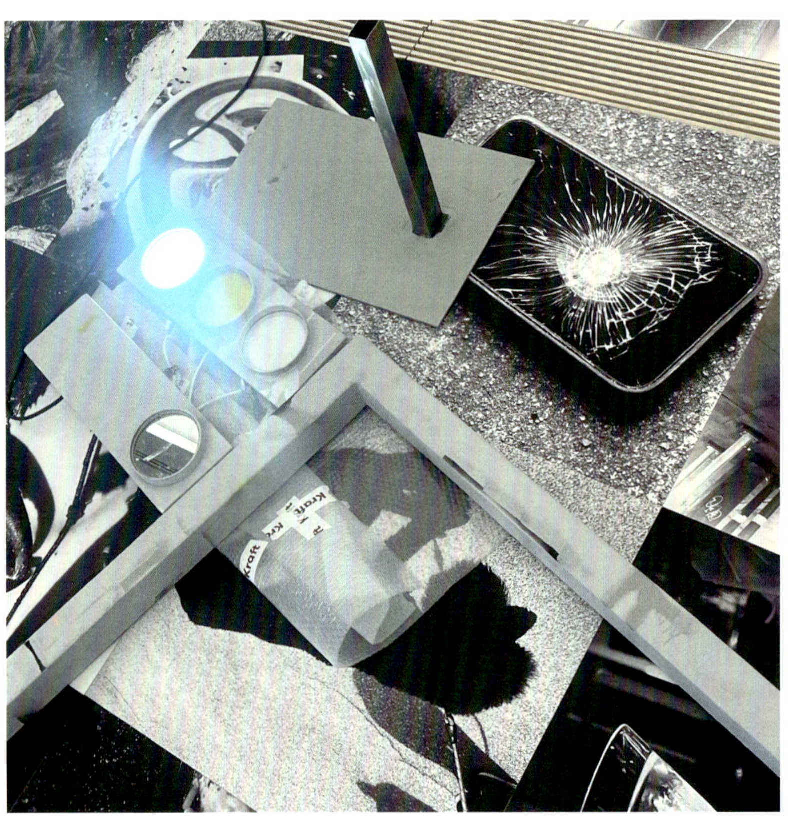
Kraft

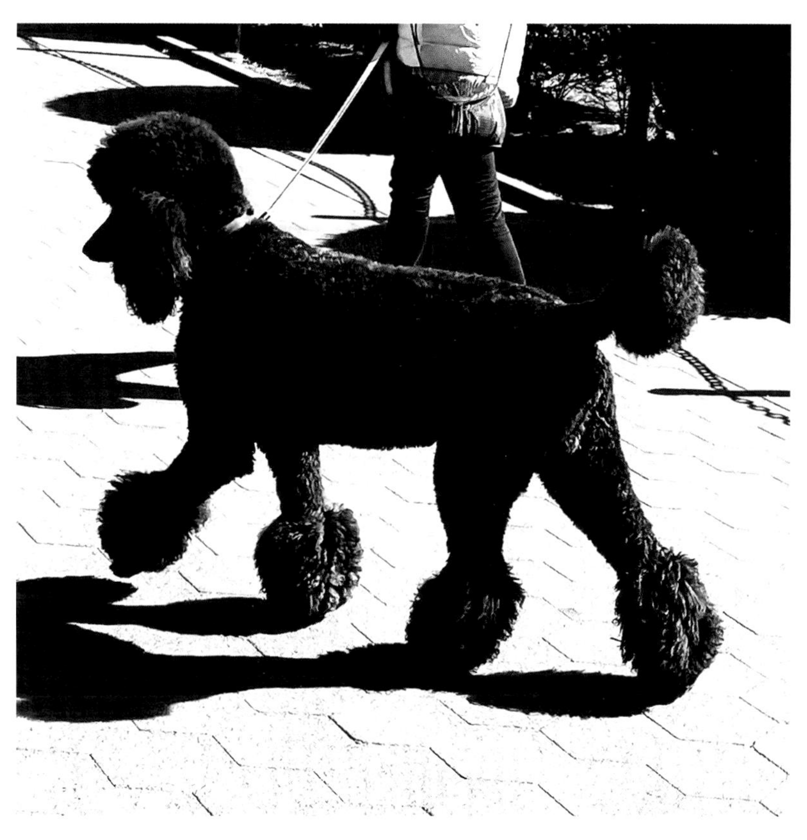

Perfect CV

完美简历

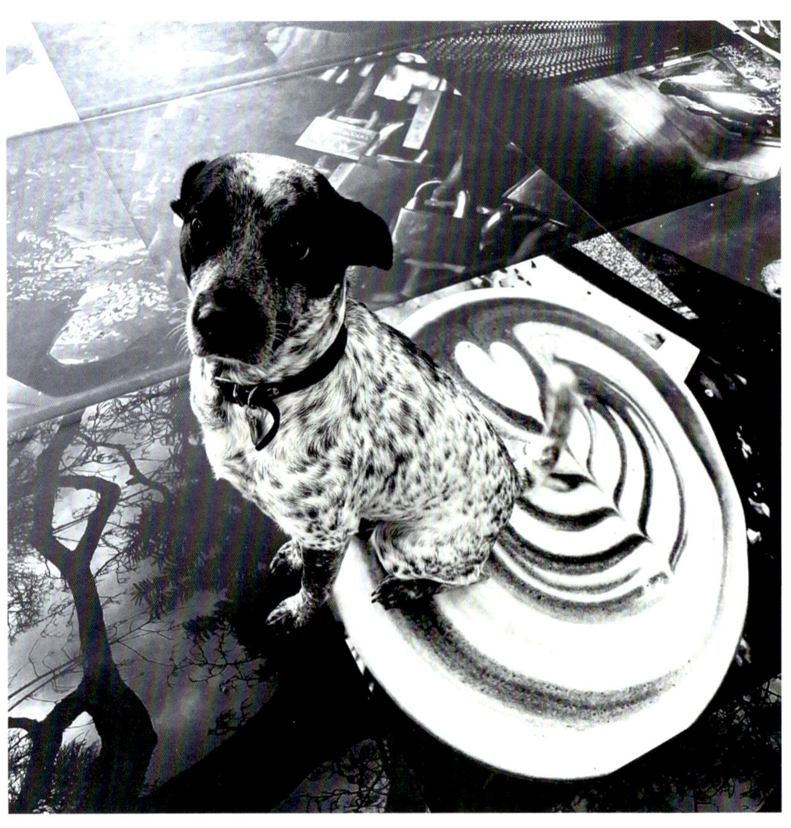

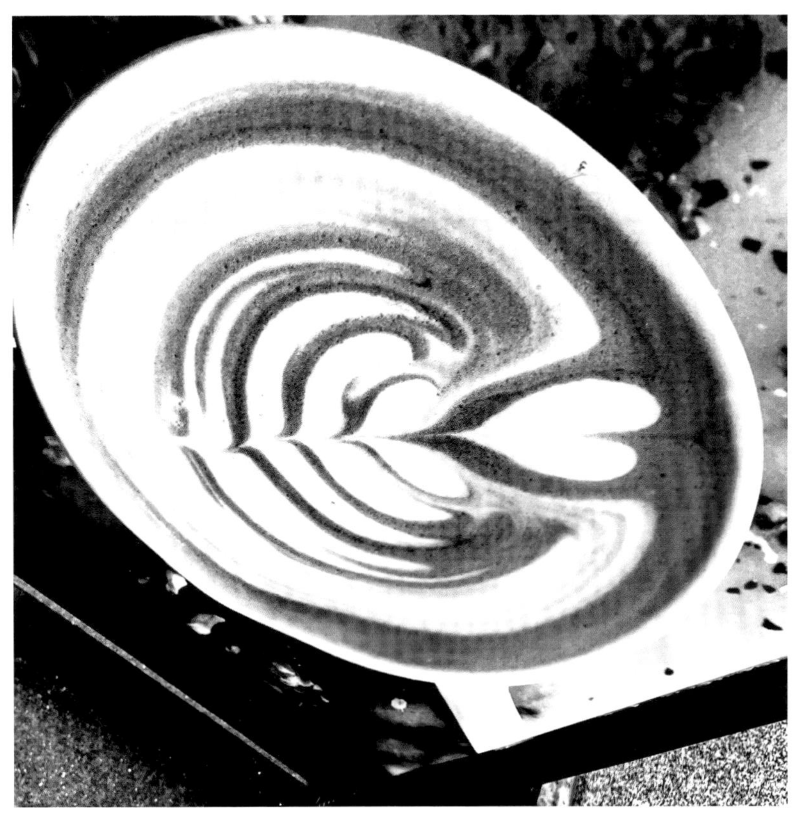

Foam

泡沫

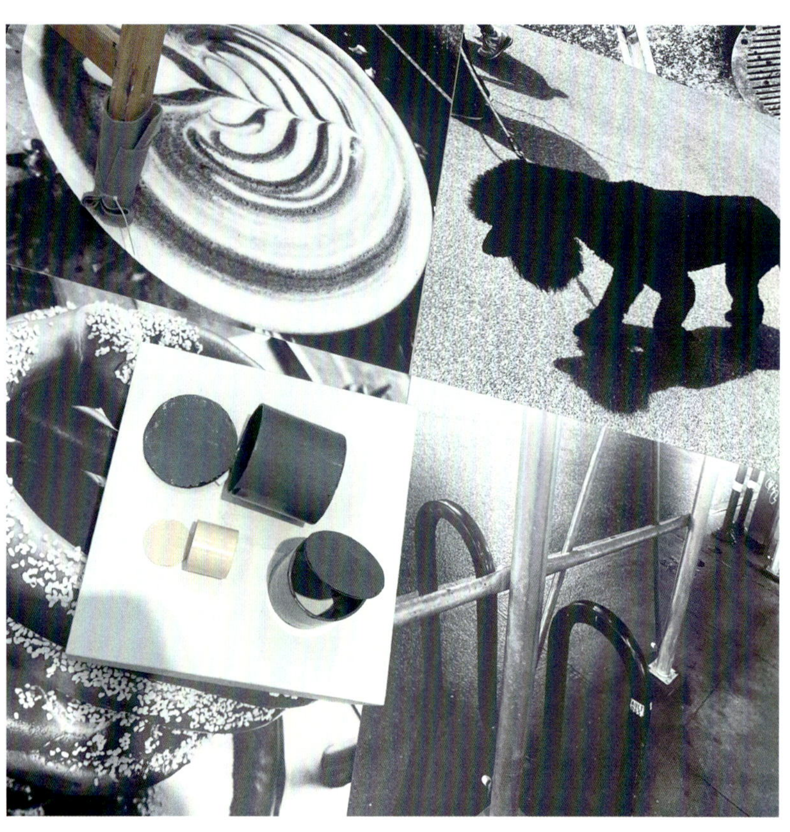

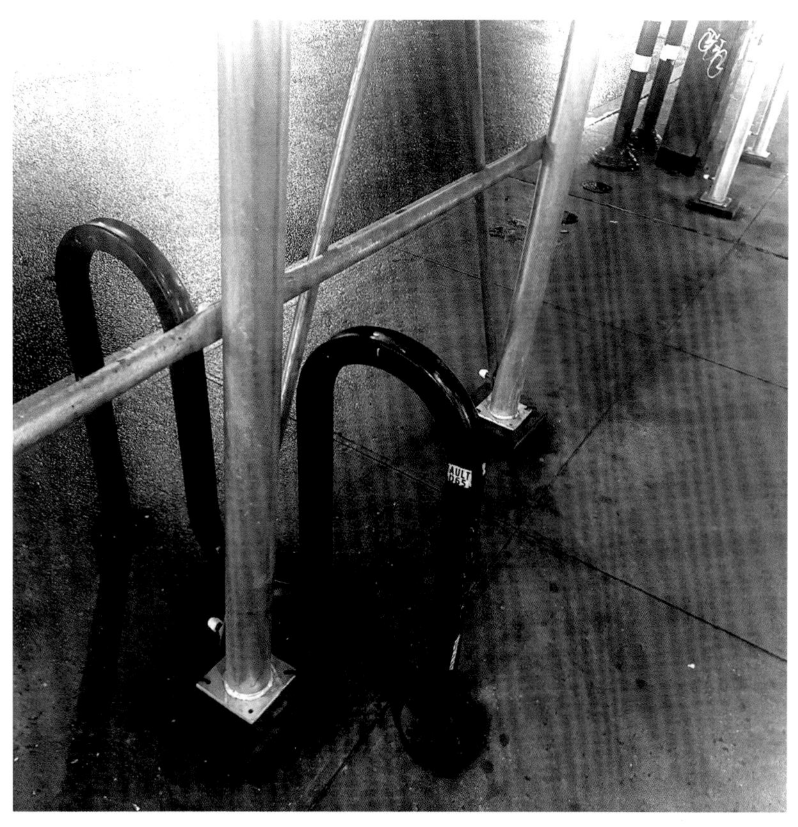

Emotional Intelligence

情商

Excerpt from *Folding Beijing*, a science fiction novel by Hao Jingfang.

(1)

At 4:50 a.m., Lao Dao walked through the bustling pedestrian street, heading to find Pengli.

After finishing his shift at the waste station, Lao Dao went home, took a shower, and changed his clothes. A white shirt and brown pants—his only decent set of clothes. The cuffs of the shirt were frayed, so he rolled the sleeves up to his elbows. Lao Dao was forty-eight years old, unmarried, and had long passed the age of caring about appearance. With no one to look after him, he had kept this outfit for years, wearing it for just a day at a time and then folding it away neatly after returning home. There was no need to dress up for his work at the waste station. He only brought out this outfit for the occasional wedding. This time, though, he didn't want to meet a stranger looking dirty. He had worked five straight hours at the waste station and worried about the smell lingering on him.

The pedestrian street was packed with people just off their shifts. Crowds of men and women gathered around stalls, loudly bargaining over local specialties. Diners hunched over plastic tables, devouring steaming bowls of sour and spicy noodles with the hunger of wild animals. The white steam masked their faces. The smell of fried food filled the air. Sour dates and walnuts were piled high on the stalls, and slabs of cured meat swung above. This was the liveliest time of day, as most had finished work, and the street was filled with people rushing to grab a hearty meal. The air buzzed with voices.

Lao Dao struggled to push through the crowd. A waiter, balancing trays, yelled for people to move aside, clearing a path. Lao Dao followed behind.

郝景芳 北京折叠

节选自郝景芳创作的科幻小说《北京折叠》。

(1)

清晨 4:50，老刀穿过熙熙攘攘的步行街，去找彭蠡。

从垃圾站下班之后，老刀回家洗了个澡，换了衣服。白色衬衫和褐色裤子，这是他唯一一套体面衣服，衬衫袖口磨了边，他把袖子卷到胳膊肘。老刀四十八岁，没结婚，已经过了注意外表的年龄，又没人照顾起居，这一套衣服留着穿了很多年，每次穿一天，回家就脱了叠上。他在垃圾站上班，没必要穿得体面，偶尔参加谁家小孩的婚礼，才拿出来穿在身上。这一次他不想脏兮兮地见陌生人。他在垃圾站连续工作了五小时，很担心身上会有味道。

步行街上挤满了刚刚下班的人。拥挤的男人女人围着小摊子挑土特产，大声讨价还价。食客围着塑料桌子，埋头在酸辣粉的热气腾腾中，饿虎扑食一般，白色蒸汽遮住了脸。油炸的香味弥漫。货摊上的酸枣和核桃堆成山，腊肉在头顶摇摆。这个点是全天最热闹的时间，基本都收工了，忙碌了几个小时的人们都赶过来吃一顿饱饭，人声鼎沸。

老刀艰难地穿过人群。端盘子的伙计一边喊着让让一边推开挡道的人，开出一条路来，老刀跟在后面。

彭蠡家在小街深处。老刀上楼，彭蠡不在家。问邻居，邻居说他每天快到关门才回来，具体几点不清楚。

Pengli's home was deep in a narrow street. Lao Dao climbed the stairs, but Pengli wasn't home. He asked a neighbor, who said Pengli usually returned right before closing time, but no one knew exactly when.

Lao Dao felt uneasy. He glanced at his watch. It was 5 a.m.

He returned to the entrance of the building to wait. Around him, hungry teenagers wolfed down their food. He recognized two of them—he'd seen them at Pengli's home once or twice. Each boy had a plate of fried noodles or fried rice noodles in front of them, sharing two dishes among the group. The plates were a mess, chopsticks prodding aimlessly through piles of chili peppers, searching for tiny scraps of meat. Lao Dao instinctively sniffed his forearm again, wondering if the stench of garbage still lingered on him. Everything around him was noisy and mundane, just like any other morning.

"Hey, do you know how much a plate of twice-cooked pork costs over there?" asked the boy named Xiao Li.

"Damn, there's sand in the food," said another boy, Xiao Ding, who was overweight. He suddenly covered his mouth, his fingernails still caked with black dirt. "What a rip-off! We should ask the boss for a refund."

"A plate of twice-cooked pork there costs three hundred and forty," Xiao Li continued. "Three hundred and forty! And a plate of spicy beef is four hundred and twenty."

老刀有点担忧，看了看手表，清晨5点。

他回到楼门口等着。两旁狼吞虎咽的饥饿少年围绕着他。他认识其中两个，原来在彭蠡家见过一两次。少年每人面前摆着一盘炒面或炒粉，几个人分吃两个菜，盘子里一片狼藉，筷子扔在无望而锲而不舍地拨动，寻找辣椒丛中的肉星。老刀又下意识闻了闻小臂，不知道身上还有没有垃圾的腥味。周围的一切嘈杂而庸常，和每个清晨一样。

“哎，你们知道那儿一盘回锅肉多少钱吗？”那个叫小李的少年说。

“靠，菜里有沙子。”另外一个叫小丁的胖少年突然捂住嘴说，他的指甲里还带着黑泥，“坑人啊。得找老板退钱！”

“人家那儿一盘回锅肉，就三百四。”小李说，“三百四！一盘水煮牛肉四百二呢。”

“什么玩意？这么贵。”小丁捂着腮帮子咕哝道。

另外两个少年对谈话没兴趣，还在埋头吃面，小李低头看着他们，眼睛似乎穿过他们，看到了某个看不见的地方，目光里有热切。

老刀的肚子也感觉到饥饿。他迅速转开眼睛，可是来不及了，那种感觉迅速席卷了他，胃的空虚像是一个深渊，让他身体微微发颤。他有一个月不吃清晨这顿饭了。一顿饭差不多一百块，一个月三千块，攒上一年就够糖糖两个月的幼儿园开销了。

他向远处看，城市清理队的车辆已经缓缓开过来了。

“What the hell? That expensive?” Xiao Ding mumbled, still holding his cheek.

The other two boys had no interest in the conversation, still engrossed in their noodles. Xiao Li stared down at them, his eyes seemingly looking through them, as if seeing something far beyond. There was a certain eagerness in his gaze.

Lao Dao’s stomach growled with hunger. He quickly looked away. But it was too late. The sensation overwhelmed him, an emptiness in his stomach that felt like a deep abyss, making his body tremble slightly. He hadn’t eaten breakfast in a month. One meal cost about a hundred yuan—three thousand for the month. If he saved for a year, that would cover two months of Tangtang’s kindergarten fees.

He looked into the distance. The city cleanup crew’s vehicles were slowly approaching.

He began to prepare himself. If Pengli didn’t return soon, he’d have to take action on his own. It would be difficult, but time wasn’t on his side—he had to move. The woman selling dates nearby kept shouting her sales pitch, her loud voice piercing through his thoughts and giving him a headache. At one end of the pedestrian street, the stalls were starting to pack up. The crowd scattered like fish in a stirred pond, darting away in all directions. No one wanted to mess with the cleanup crew at this hour. The stalls were slow to clear out, but the crew’s vehicles moved patiently. The pedestrian street was only a pedestrian street, except when it came to the cleanup crew. Anyone who lagged behind would be forcibly swept up.

他开始做准备，若彭蠡一时再不回来，他就要考虑自己行动了。虽然会带来不少困难，但时间不等人，总得走才行。身边卖大枣的女人高声叫卖，不时打断他的思绪，声音的洪亮刺得他头疼。步行街一端的小摊子开始收拾，人群像用棍子搅动的池塘里的鱼，倏一下散去。没人会在这时候和清理队较劲。小摊子收拾得比较慢，清理队的车耐心地移动。步行街通常只是步行街，但对清理队的车除外。谁若走得慢了，就被强行收拢起来。

这时彭蠡出现了。他剔着牙，敞着衬衫的扣子，不紧不慢地踱回来，不时打饱嗝。彭蠡六十多了，变得懒散不修边幅，两颊像沙皮狗一样耷拉着，让嘴角显得总是不满意地撇着。如果只看这幅模样，不知道他年轻时的样子，会以为他只是个胸无大志只知道吃喝的怂包。但从老刀很小的时 候，他就听父亲讲过彭蠡的事。

老刀迎上前去。彭蠡看到他要打招呼，老刀却打断他："我没时间和你解释。我需要去第一空间，你告诉我怎么走。"

彭蠡愣住了，已经有十年没人跟他提过第一空间的事，他的牙签捏在手里，不知不觉掰断了。他有片刻没回答，见老刀实在有点急了，才拽着他向楼里走。"回我家说，"彭蠡说，"要走也从那儿走。"

在他们身后，清理队已经缓缓开了过来，像秋风扫落叶一样将人们扫回家。"回家啦，回家啦。转换马上开始了。"车上有人吆喝着。
彭蠡带老刀上楼，进屋。他的单人小房子和一般公租屋无异，六平米房间，一个厕所，一个能做菜的角落，一张桌子一把椅子，胶囊床铺，胶囊下是抽拉式箱柜，可以放衣服物品。墙面上有水渍和鞋印，没做任何修饰，只是歪斜着贴了几个挂钩，挂着夹克和裤子。进屋

Just then, Pengli appeared. He was picking his teeth, his shirt unbuttoned, strolling back without a care, occasionally belching. Pengli was in his sixties now, lazy and unkempt, with sagging cheeks that made his mouth look permanently displeased. If you only saw him like this, you'd think he was just a small-minded man with no ambition beyond eating and drinking. But Lao Dao had heard stories about Pengli from his father ever since he was a child.

Lao Dao stepped forward. Pengli saw him and was about to greet him, but Lao Dao cut him off. "I don't have time to explain. I need to go to First Space. Tell me how to get there."

Pengli was taken aback. No one had mentioned First Space to him in ten years. The toothpick in his hand snapped in two. He hesitated for a moment, seeing that Lao Dao was in a hurry, then grabbed him and pulled him toward the building. "Come back to my place," Pengli said. "If you're going, that's where we'll start."

Behind them, the cleanup crew's vehicles were slowly rolling in, sweeping people off the streets like autumn leaves. "Go home, go home. The switch is about to begin," someone shouted from the vehicle.

Pengli led Lao Dao upstairs and into his apartment. His small, single-unit housing was no different from any other public rental. A six-square-meter room with a toilet, a small corner for cooking, a table, a chair, and a capsule bed. Underneath the bed was a pull-out drawer for clothes and belongings. The walls were stained with watermarks and shoe prints, with no decoration except for a few crooked hooks where jackets and pants hung. As soon as they entered, Pengli took down the clothes and towels from the wall and stuffed them into the furthest drawer. During the switch, nothing could be left hanging out. Lao Dao had lived in a similar single-unit public rental before.

后，彭蠡把墙上的衣服毛巾都取下来，塞到最靠边的抽屉里。转换的时候，什么都不能挂出来。老刀以前也住这样的单人公租房。一进屋，他就感到一股旧日的气息。

彭蠡直截了当地瞪着老刀："你不告诉我为什么，我就不告诉你怎么走。"

已经5点半了，还有半个小时。

老刀简单讲了事情的始末。从他捡到纸条瓶子，到他偷偷躲入垃圾道，到他在第二空间接到的委托，再到他的行动。他没有时间描述太多，最好马上就走。

"你昨天躲在垃圾道里？去第二空间？"彭蠡皱着眉，"那你得等24小时啊。"

"二十万块。"老刀说，"等一礼拜也值啊。"

"你就这么缺钱花？"

老刀沉默了一下。"糖糖还有一年多该去幼儿园了。"他说，"我来不及了。"

The moment he stepped inside, he was hit by a wave of old memories.

Pengli stared at Lao Dao bluntly. “If you don’t tell me why, I won’t tell you how to get there.”

It was already 5:30. Half an hour left.

Lao Dao briefly explained the situation. From the note in the bottle he found, to hiding in the waste chute, to receiving the commission in Second Space, and the actions he had taken since. He didn’t have time for too many details—they needed to leave as soon as possible.

“You hid in the waste chute yesterday? Went to Second Space?” Pengli frowned. “Then you’ve got to wait 24 hours.”

“Two hundred thousand yuan,” Lao Dao said. “I’d wait a week if I had to.”

“You’re that short on money?”

Lao Dao hesitated for a moment. “Tangtang’s got a little over a year before she starts kindergarten,” he said. “I’m running out of time.”

Lao Dao had been shocked when he first inquired about kindergarten. For even a halfway decent one, parents were camping out two days before registration. Taking turns—one would eat, drink, and relieve themselves while the other held their place at the door. They’d wait for over forty hours and still might not get in. The spots at the front had already been bought out, leaving only a few for those who braved the line. That was for a decent kindergarten. The better ones didn’t even allow queues—everything was paid for from the start. Lao Dao hadn’t had high hopes, but ever since Tangtang turned one and a half, she’d developed a special love for music.

老刀去幼儿园咨询的时候，着实被吓到了。稍微好一点的幼儿园招生前两天，就有家长带着铺盖卷在幼儿园门口排队，两个家长轮着，一个吃喝拉撒，另一个坐在幼儿园门口等。就这么等上四十多个小时，还不一定能排进去。前面的名额早用钱买断了，只有最后剩下的寥寥几个名额分给苦熬排队的爹妈。这只是一般不错的幼儿园，更好一点的连排队都不行，从一开始就是钱买机会。老刀本来没什么奢望，可是自从糖糖一岁半之后，就特别喜欢音乐，每次在外面听见音乐，她就小脸放光，跟着扭动身子手舞足蹈。那个时候她特别好看。老刀对此毫无抵抗力，他就像被舞台上的灯光层层围绕着，只看到一片耀眼。无论付出什么代价，他都想送糖糖去一个能教音乐和跳舞的幼儿园。

彭蠡脱下外衣，一边洗脸，一边和老刀说话。说是洗脸，不过只是用水随便抹一抹。水马上就要停了，水流已经变得很小。彭蠡从墙上拽下一条脏兮兮的毛巾，随意蹭了蹭，又将毛巾塞进抽屉。他湿漉漉的头发显出油腻的光泽。

“你真是作死，”彭蠡说，“她又不是你闺女，犯得着吗。”

“别说这些了。快告我怎么走。”老刀说。

彭蠡叹了口气：“你可得知道，万一被抓着，可不只是罚款，得关上好几个月。”

“你不是去过好多次吗？”
“只有四次。第五次就被抓了。”

Every time she heard music, her little face lit up and she'd start moving, dancing to the rhythm. In those moments, she was especially beautiful. Lao Dao had no resistance to it. It was like being surrounded by stage lights, seeing nothing but a blinding glow. Whatever the cost, he wanted to send Tangtang to a kindergarten where she could learn music and dance.

Pengli took off his jacket and started washing his face while talking to Lao Dao. It wasn't much of a wash—he just splashed some water around. The water supply was about to be cut off; the flow had already slowed to a trickle. Pengli yanked a dirty towel from the wall and gave his face a quick wipe before stuffing it into the drawer. His damp hair glistened with a greasy sheen.

"You're really asking for trouble," Pengli said. "She's not even your daughter. Is it worth it?"

"Enough. Just tell me how to get there," Lao Dao said.

Pengli sighed. "You do realize that if you get caught, it's not just a fine. You'll be locked up for months."

"Haven't you gone there plenty of times?"

"Only four times. Got caught on the fifth."

"That's more than enough. If I can go four times, getting caught once doesn't matter."

Lao Dao had to deliver something to First Space. Delivering it would earn him 100,000 yuan. Bringing back a response would earn him 200,000. It was a big risk, but if he used the right path and method, the chances of

“那也够了。我要是能去四次，抓一次也无所谓。”

老刀要去第一空间送一样东西，送到了挣十万块，带来回信挣二十万。这不过是冒违规的大不韪，只要路径和方法对，被抓住的几率并不大，挣的却是实实在在的钞票。他不知道有什么理由拒绝。他知道彭蠡年轻的时候为了几笔风险钱，曾经偷偷进入第一空间好几次，贩卖私酒和烟。他知道这条路能走。

5:45。他必须马上走了。

彭蠡又叹口气，知道劝也没用。他已经上了年纪，对事懒散倦怠了，但他明白，自己在五十岁前也会和老刀一样。那时他不在乎坐牢之类的事。不过是熬几个月出来，挨两顿打，但挣的钱是实实在在的。只要抵死不说钱的下落，最后总能过去。秩序局的条子也不过就是例行公事。他把老刀带到窗口，向下指向一条被阴影覆盖的小路。

“从我房子底下爬下去，顺着排水管，毡布底下有我原来安上去的脚蹬，身子贴得足够紧了就能避开摄像头。从那儿过去，沿着阴影爬到边上。你能摸着也能看见那道缝。沿着缝往北走。一定得往北。千万别错了。”

彭蠡接着解释了爬过土地的诀窍。要借着升起的势头，从升高的一侧沿截面爬过五十米，到另一侧地面，爬上去，然后向东，那里会有一丛灌木，在土地合拢的时候可以抓住并隐藏自己。老刀没有听完，就已经将身子探出窗口，准备向下爬了。

getting caught were slim, and the money was very real. He couldn't think of a reason to refuse. He knew Pengli had done the same thing in his younger years—sneaking into First Space several times to smuggle alcohol and cigarettes for quick cash. Lao Dao knew it was possible to pull this off.

5:45. He had to leave immediately.

Pengli sighed again, knowing it was useless to try and talk him out of it. He was getting old and had grown indifferent to everything, but he understood—before turning fifty, he would have been just like Lao Dao. Back then, he didn't care about things like prison. A few months inside, a couple of beatings, but the money was real. As long as you kept quiet about where it was hidden, eventually, you'd make it through. The officers from the Bureau of Order were just doing their jobs. He led Lao Dao to the window and pointed down to a narrow path hidden in the shadows.

"Climb down from under my place, follow the drainpipe. There are footrests I put in under the felt. If you press your body close enough, you'll avoid the cameras. From there, crawl along the shadows to the edge. You'll feel and see the crack. Follow it north. You have to go north. Don't mess that up."

Pengli then explained the trick to crossing the terrain. He told Lao Dao to use the rising momentum, crawl fifty meters along the ridge to the other side, and then climb up. From there, head east, where there would be a clump of bushes—he could grab onto them and hide when the ground closed in. Lao Dao didn't listen to the whole explanation, already leaning out the window, preparing to climb down.

Pengli helped Lao Dao out of the window, guiding him to the foothold just below the ledge. Suddenly, Pengli paused. "I'll be blunt," he said. "You

彭蠡帮老刀爬出窗子，扶着他踩稳了窗下的踏脚。彭蠡突然停下来。“说句不好听的，”他说，“我还是劝你最好别去。那边可不是什么好地儿，去了之后没别的，只能感觉自己的日子有多操蛋。没劲。”

老刀的脚正在向下试探，身子还扒着窗台。“没事。”他说得有点费劲，“我不去也知道自己的日子有多操蛋。”

“好自为之吧。”彭蠡最后说。

老刀顺着彭蠡指出的路径快速向下爬。脚蹬的位置非常舒服。他看到彭蠡在窗口的身影，点了根烟，非常大口地快速抽了几口，又掐了。彭蠡一度从窗口探出身子，似乎想说什么，但最终还是缩了回去。窗子关上了，发着幽幽的光。老刀知道，彭蠡会在转换前最后一分钟钻进胶囊，和整个城市数千万人一样，受胶囊定时释放出的气体催眠，陷入深深睡眠，身子随着世界颠倒来去，头脑却一无所知，一睡就是整整40个小时，到次日晚上再睁开眼睛。彭蠡已经老了，他终于和这个世界其他五千万人一样了。

老刀用自己最快的速度向下，一蹦一跳，在离地足够近的时候纵身一跃，匍匐在地上。彭蠡的房子在四层，离地不远。爬起身，沿高楼在湖边投下的阴影奔跑。他能看到草地上的裂隙，那是翻转的地方。还没跑到，就听到身后在压抑中轰鸣的隆隆和偶尔清脆的嘎啦声。老刀转过头，高楼拦腰截断，上半截正从天上倒下，缓慢却不容置疑地压迫过来。

really shouldn't go. That place isn't what you think. All you'll feel when you're there is just how much your life sucks. It's not worth it."

Lao Dao's feet were already testing the descent, his hands still gripping the windowsill. "Doesn't matter," he said, struggling a bit. "I already know how much my life sucks."

"Take care of yourself," Pengli said at last.

Lao Dao quickly descended along the path Pengli had pointed out. The footholds were perfectly placed. He glanced up and saw Pengli's silhouette in the window, lighting a cigarette. He took a few deep, fast drags, then stubbed it out. At one point, Pengli leaned out as if to say something, but in the end, he pulled back. The window closed, casting a faint glow. Lao Dao knew that in the final minutes before the switch, Pengli would crawl into his capsule like the millions of others in the city, succumbing to the gas released by the timed mechanism, slipping into a deep sleep. His body would move with the world as it turned, but his mind would remain unaware, unconscious for the full 40 hours until he opened his eyes the next evening. Pengli was old now—he had finally become just like the rest of the 50 million people here.

Lao Dao moved as quickly as he could, jumping down and dropping to the ground when he was close enough. Pengli's home was on the fourth floor, not far from the ground. Lao Dao got to his feet and ran, staying in the shadow cast by the high-rises along the edge of the lake. He could see the cracks in the ground ahead—those were the places where the world would flip. He hadn't yet reached them when he heard the low, restrained rumble behind him, punctuated by occasional sharp cracking sounds. Lao Dao turned and saw the high-rises sliced in half, the top sections slowly but inexorably descending from the sky.

老刀被震住了，怔怔看了好一会儿。他跑到缝隙，伏在地上。

转换开始了。这是24小时周期的分隔时刻。整个世界开始翻转。钢筋砖块合拢的声音连成一片，像出了故障的流水线。高楼收拢合并，折叠成立方体。霓虹灯、店铺招牌、阳台和附加结构都被吸收入墙体，贴成楼的肌肤。结构见缝插针，每一寸空间都被占满。

大地在升起。老刀观察着地面的走势，来到缝的边缘，又随着缝隙的升起不断向上爬。他手脚并用，从大理石铺就的地面边缘起始，沿着泥土的截面，抓住土里埋藏的金属断茬，最初是向下，用脚试探着退行，很快，随着整快土地的翻转，他被带到空中。

老刀想到前一天晚上城市的样子。

当时他从垃圾堆中抬起眼睛，警觉地听着门外的声音。周围发酵腐烂的垃圾散发出刺鼻的气息，带一股发腥的甜腻味。他倚在门前。铁门外的世界在苏醒。

当铁门掀开的缝隙透入第一道街灯的黄色光芒，他俯下身去，从缓缓扩大的缝隙中钻出。街上空无一人，高楼灯光逐层亮起，附加结构从楼两侧探出，向两旁一节一节伸展，门廊从楼体内延 伸，房檐延轴旋转，缓缓落下，楼梯降落延伸到马迷途上。步行街的两侧，一个又一个黑色立方体从中间断裂，向两侧打开，露出其中货架的结构。立方体顶端伸出招牌，连成商铺的走廊，两侧的塑料棚向头顶延伸闭合。街道空旷得如同梦境。

He was stunned, staring at the scene for a long moment. Then he bolted for the crack, diving to the ground.

The switch had begun. It was the moment of separation in the 24-hour cycle. The entire world was starting to turn. The sound of steel and concrete folding together was a constant roar, like a malfunctioning assembly line. The high-rises compressed, folding into cubes. Neon lights, shop signs, balconies, and annexes were all sucked into the walls, melding into the surface of the buildings. Every inch of space was filled as the structures merged seamlessly.

The ground was rising. Lao Dao watched the movement, climbing up the crack as it lifted. He scrambled up with hands and feet, starting from the marble edge of the ground, gripping onto the jagged metal buried in the dirt. At first, he was moving downward, carefully stepping back. But soon, as the entire section of land flipped, he was lifted into the air.

Lao Dao thought back to the night before and how the city had looked.

He had lifted his eyes from the pile of garbage, listening carefully to the sounds outside the door. The stench of rotting, fermenting trash filled the air, a sickly sweet odor with a trace of something foul. He leaned against the iron door. Beyond it, the world was waking up.

When the first sliver of yellow streetlight slipped through the crack in the door, he bent down and squeezed through as the gap slowly widened. The street was empty, and the lights of the high-rises flickered on, floor by floor. The auxiliary structures began extending from the sides of the buildings, unfolding segment by segment. Porches stretched out from the building façades, eaves rotated down from their axles, slowly descending, and stairways extended down toward the maze of streets. On either side of the

霓虹灯亮了，商铺顶端闪烁的小灯打出新疆大枣、东北拉皮、上海烤麸和湖南腊肉。

整整一天，老刀头脑中都忘不了这一幕。他在这里生活了四十八年，还从来没有见过这一切。他的日子总是从胶囊起，至胶囊终，在脏兮兮的餐桌和被争吵萦绕的货摊之间穿行。这是他第一次看到世界纯粹的模样。

每个清晨，如果有人从远处观望——就像大货车司机在高速北京入口处等待时那样——他会看到整座城市的伸展与折叠。

清晨六点，司机们总会走下车，站在高速边上，揉着经过一夜潦草睡眠而昏沉的眼睛，打着哈欠，相互指点着望向远处的城市中央。高速截断在七环之外，所有的翻转都在六环内发生。不远不近的距离，就像遥望西山或是海上的一座孤岛。

晨光熹微中，一座城市折叠自身，向地面收拢。高楼像最卑微的仆人，弯下腰，让自己低声下气切断身体，头碰着脚，紧紧贴在一起，然后再次断裂弯腰，将头顶手臂扭曲弯折，插入空隙。高楼弯折之后重新组合，蜷缩成致密的巨大魔方，密密匝匝地聚合到一起，陷入沉睡。然后地面翻转，小块小块土地围绕其轴，一百八十度翻转到另一面，将另一面的建筑楼宇露出地表。楼宇由折叠中站立起身，在灰蓝色的天空中像苏醒的兽类。城市孤岛在橘黄色晨光中落位，展开，站定，腾起弥漫的灰色苍云。

司机们就在困倦与饥饿中欣赏这一幕无穷循环的城市戏剧。

pedestrian street, black cubes split open, revealing the shelves within. Signs popped up from the tops of the cubes, forming a corridor of store-fronts, and plastic awnings stretched out overhead, sealing the street.

The neon lights flickered on. Above the shops, small flashing signs advertised Xinjiang red dates, Northeast *la pi*, Shanghai *kaofu*, and Hunan cured meats.

The image had stayed in Lao Dao's mind all day. He had lived here for forty-eight years and had never seen anything like it. His life had always begun and ended inside his capsule, moving through the grime-covered tables and the bickering-filled market stalls. This was the first time he had seen the world in its pure form.

Every morning, if someone were watching from afar—just like the truck drivers waiting at the Beijing highway entrance—they would see the entire city stretch and fold.

At 6 a.m., the drivers would always step out of their trucks, standing by the side of the highway, rubbing their bleary eyes after a rough night's sleep, yawning and pointing toward the distant city center. The highway ended outside the Seventh Ring Road; all the flipping and folding happened within the Sixth Ring. The distance wasn't too far, nor too close—like gazing at the Western Hills or a lone island on the sea.

In the dim morning light, the city folded in on itself, curling down to the ground. The high-rises, like the most humble servants, bowed low, breaking their bodies in two, bending until their heads touched their feet, tightly pressed together. Then, they bent again, twisting their tops and arms into the gaps. After folding, the buildings recombined, shrinking into dense, giant cubes, packed tightly together, falling into a deep slumber. Then the ground flipped. Small patches of land rotated 180 degrees on their axes,

revealing the buildings hidden on the other side. These new structures rose from the fold, standing up like waking beasts against the gray-blue sky. The island of a city took its place in the orange morning light, unfolding, standing firm, while a haze of gray clouds billowed around it.

The drivers, caught between drowsiness and hunger, watched this endless cycle of the city's drama.

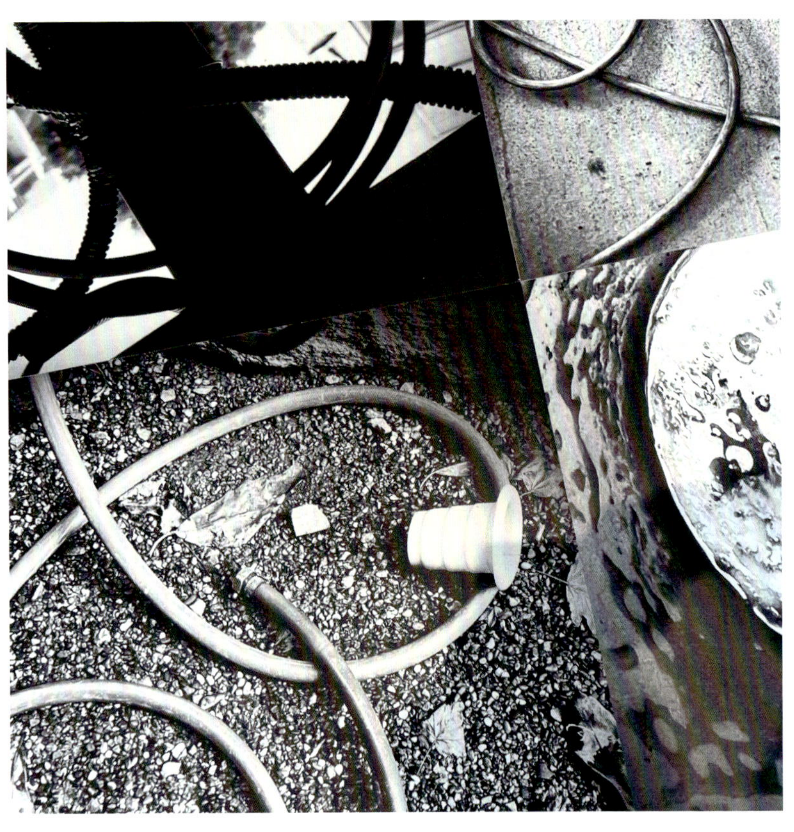

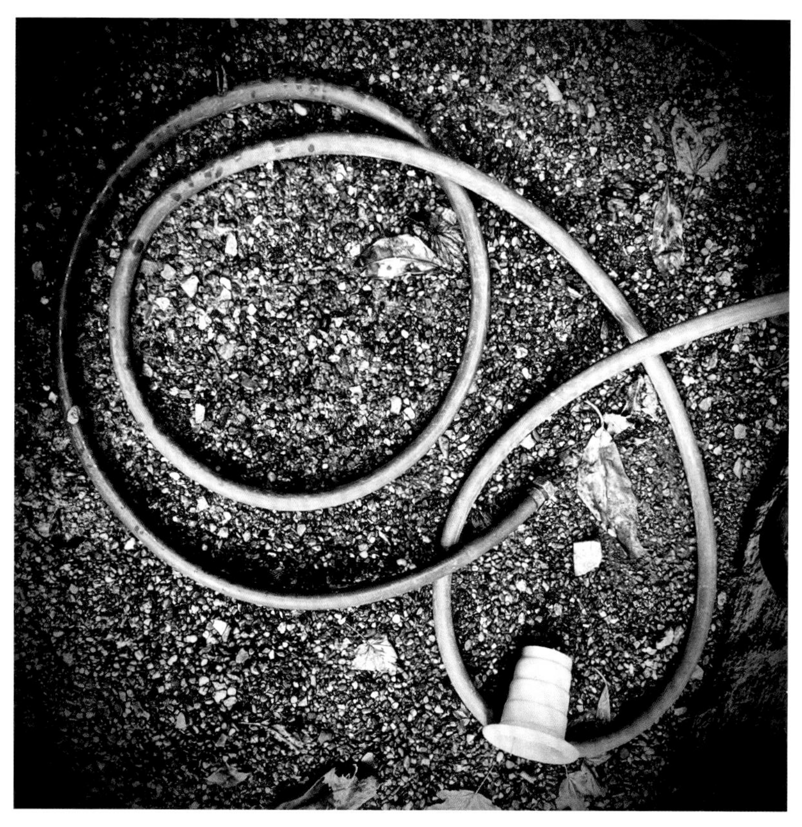

Figurative

具象

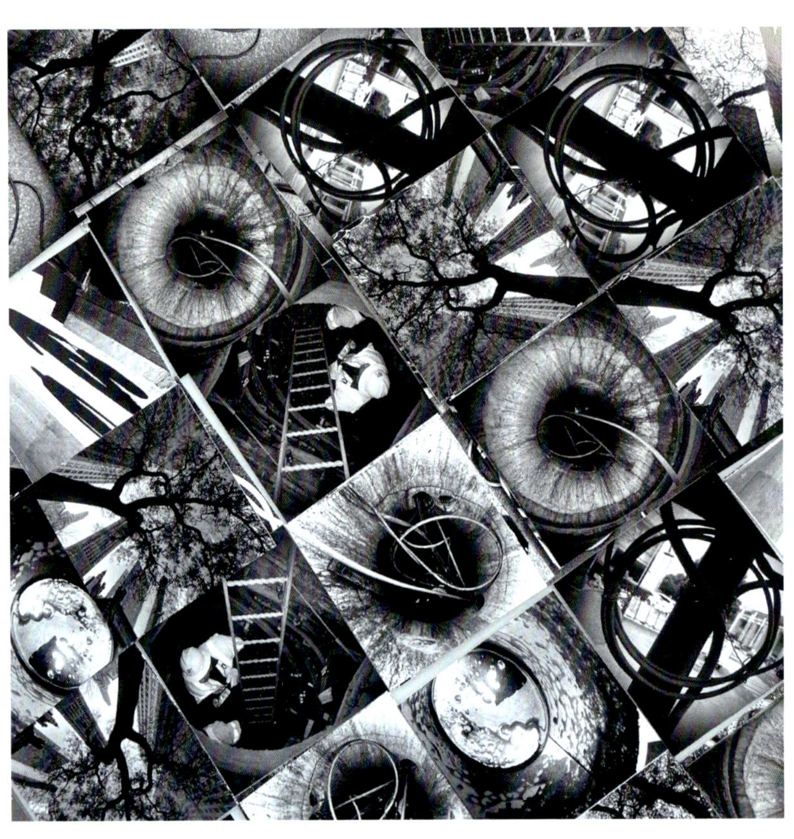

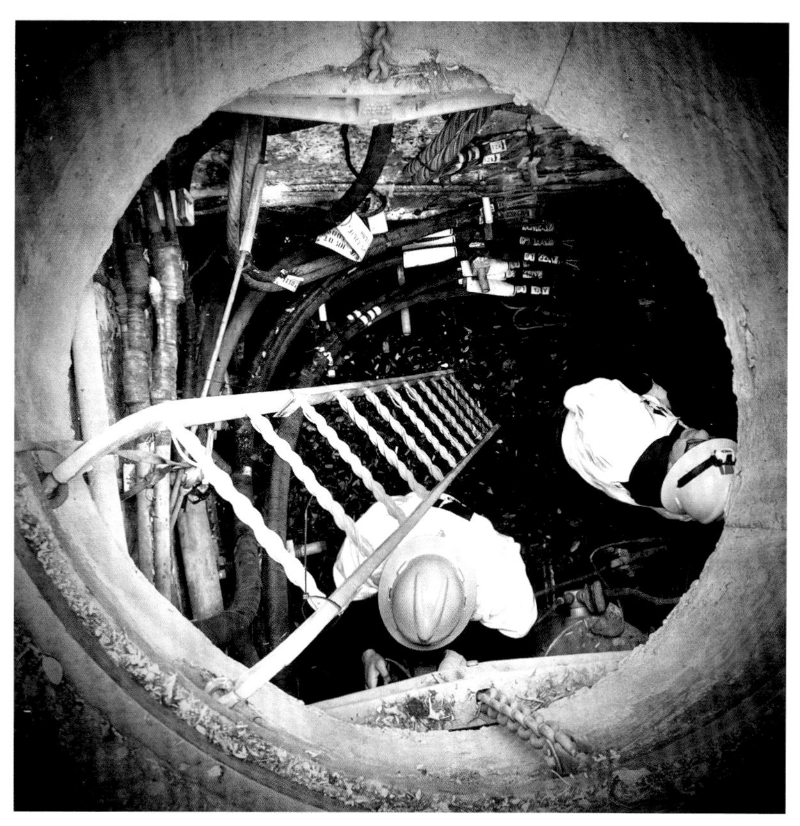

Introduction

介绍

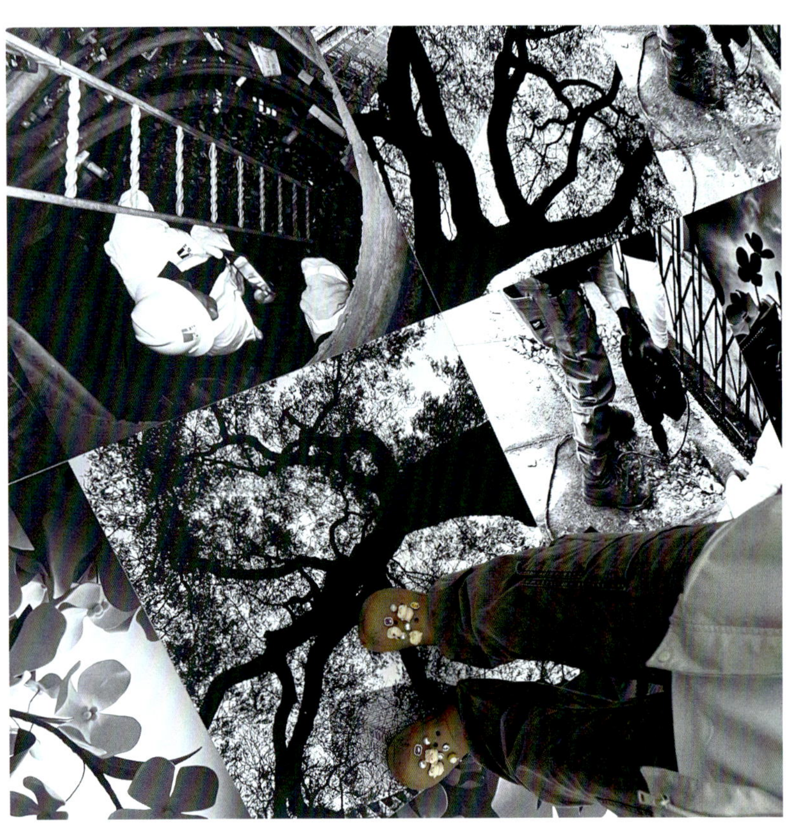

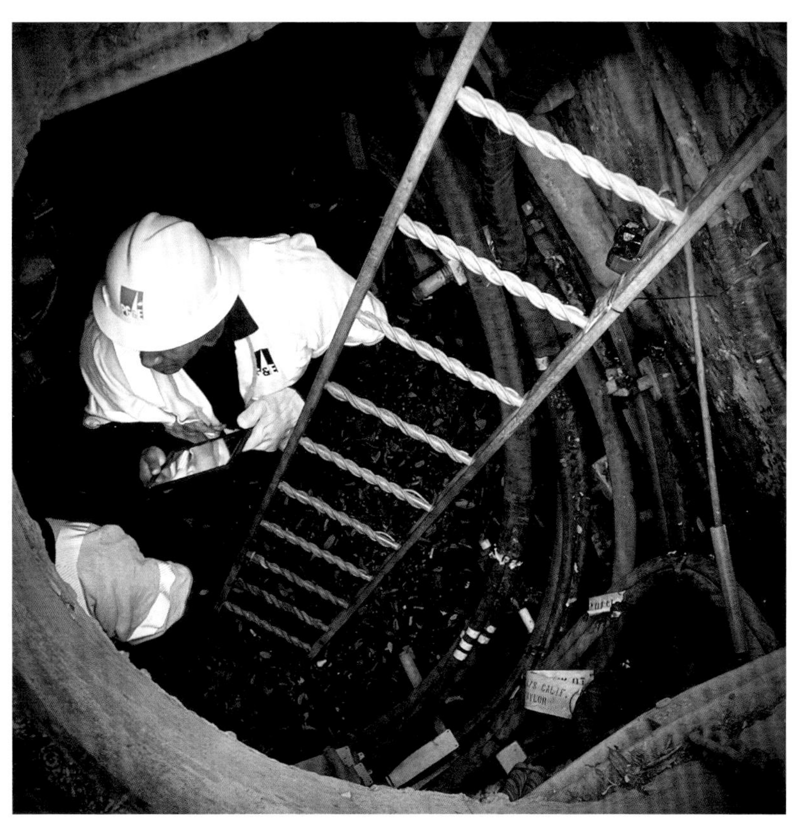

Why We Sleep

我们为何睡觉

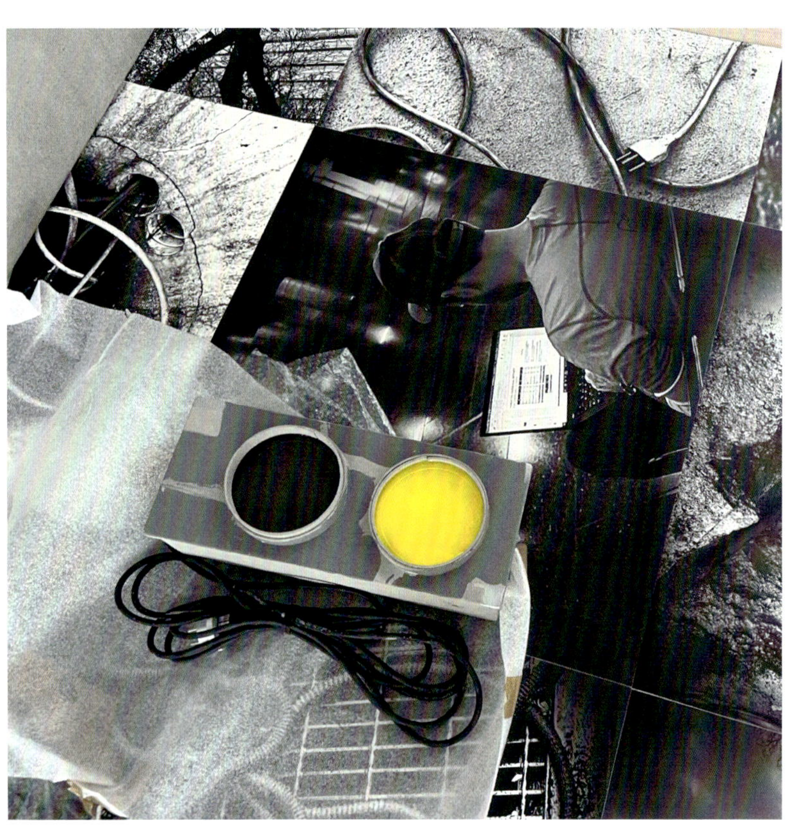

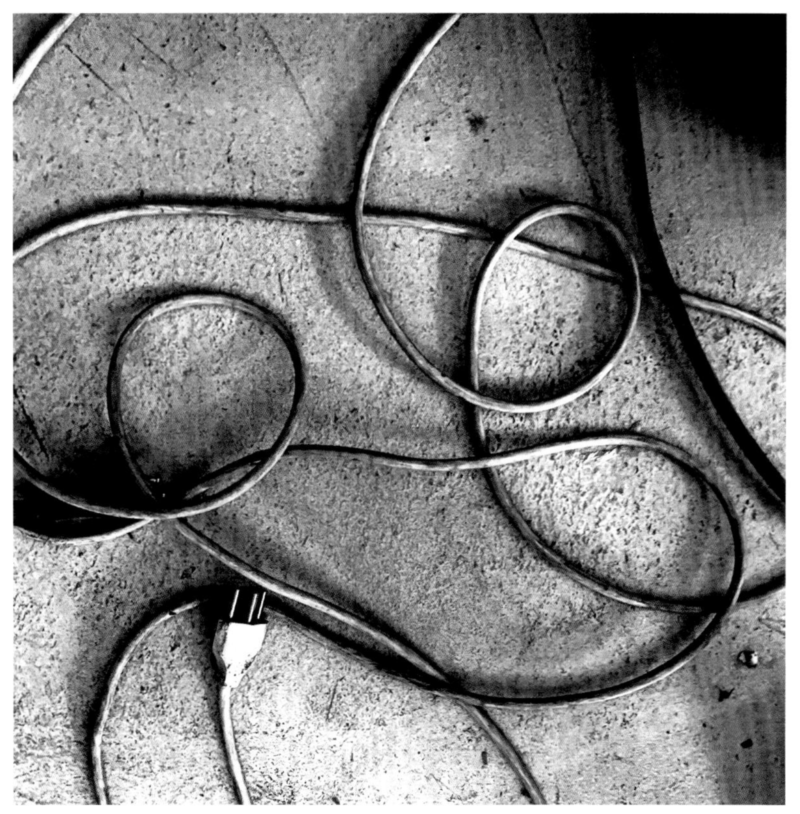

Painting

绘画

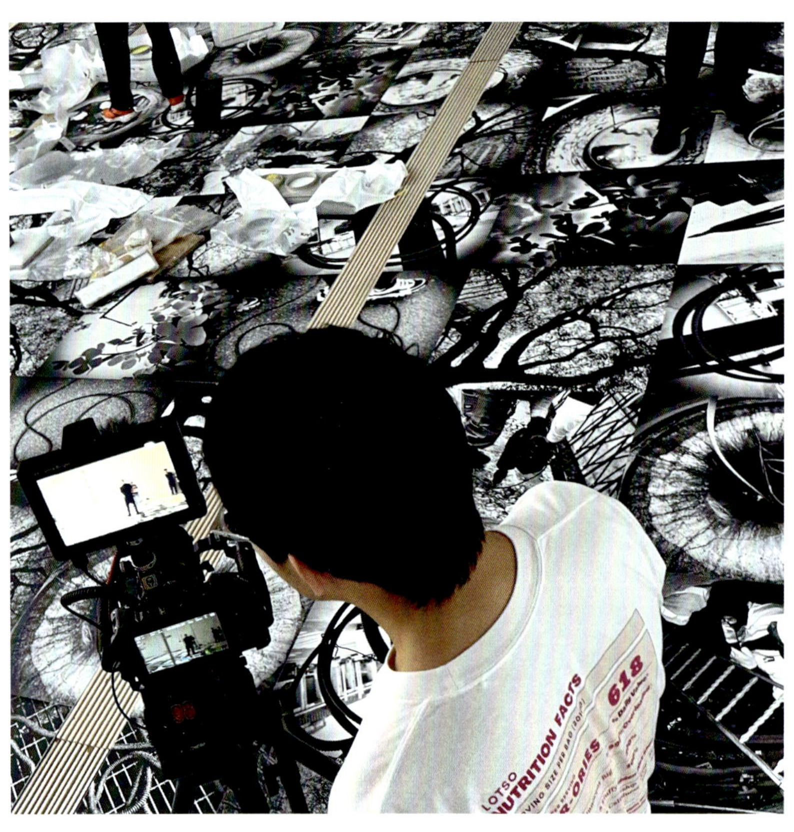
LOTSO
NUTRITION FACTS
618

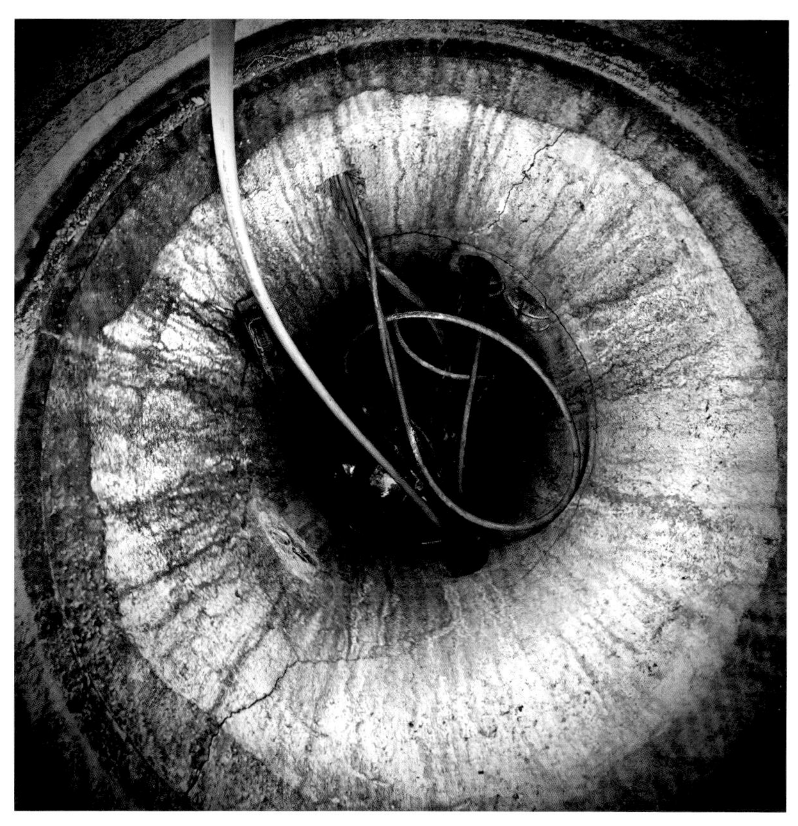

Predictability

可预测性

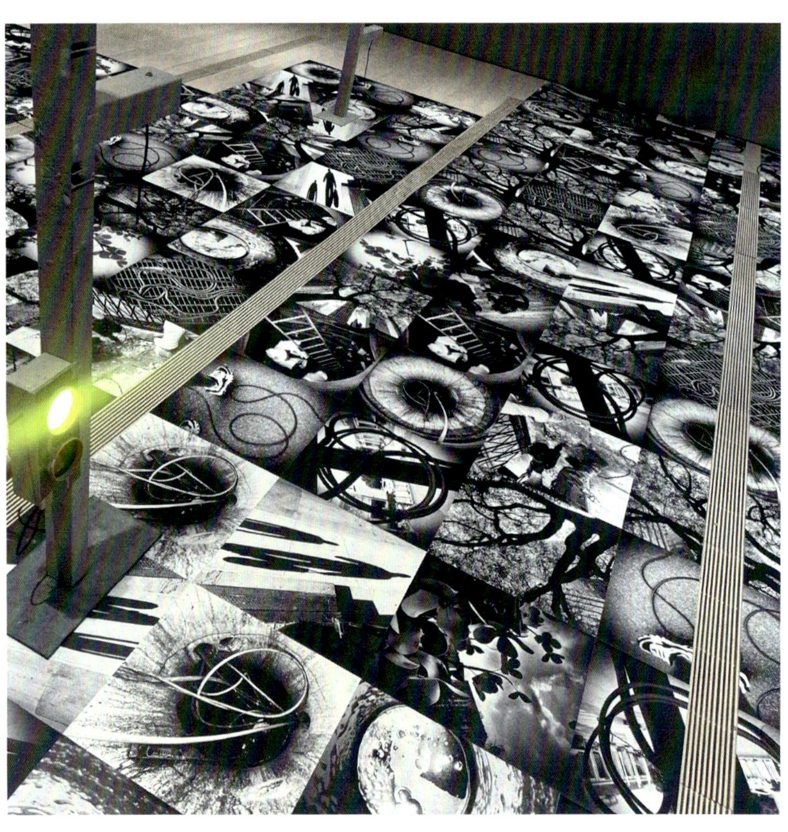

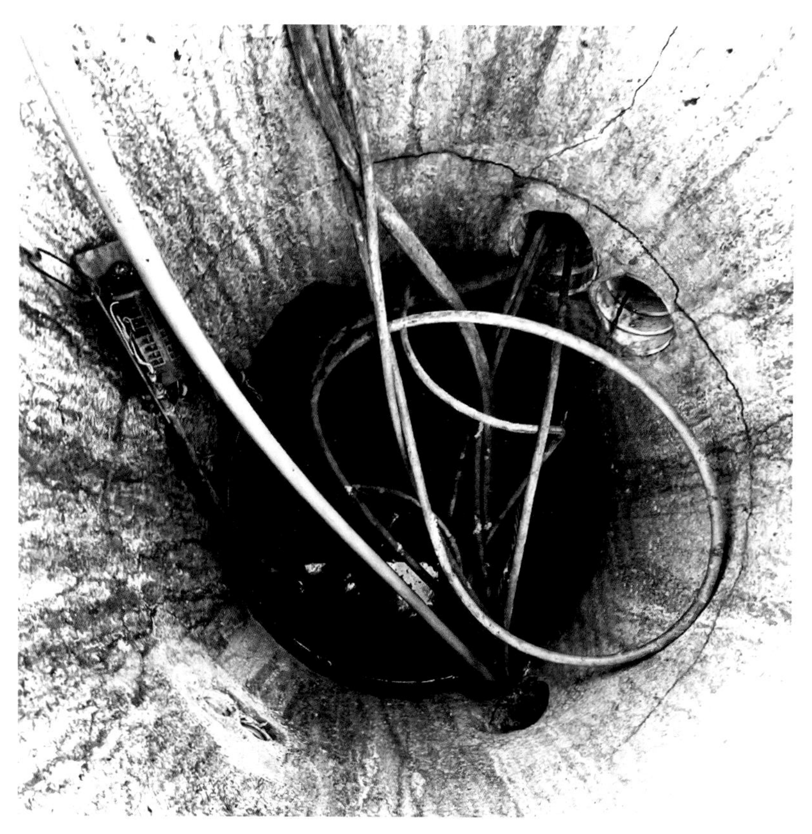

The 3rd Eye

第三只眼

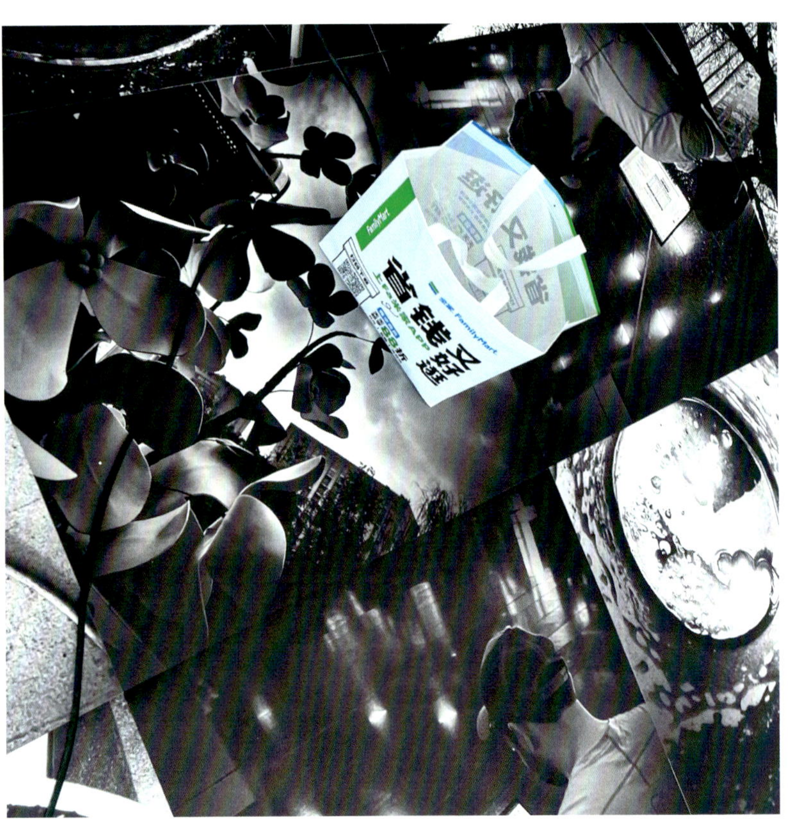
FamilyMart
省錢又好逛
FamilyMart

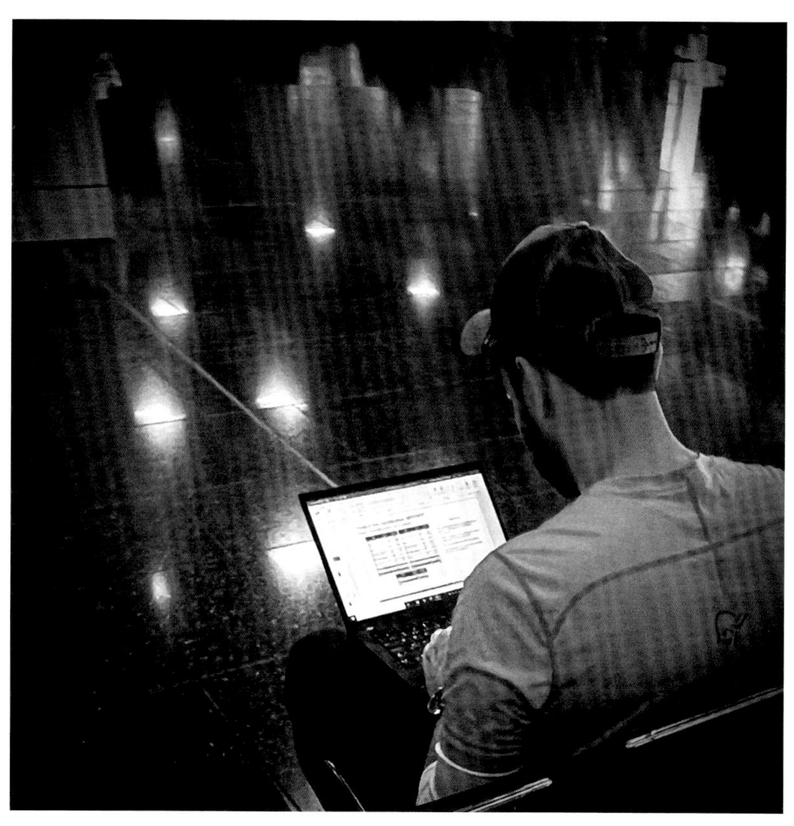

Seven Suns

七个太阳

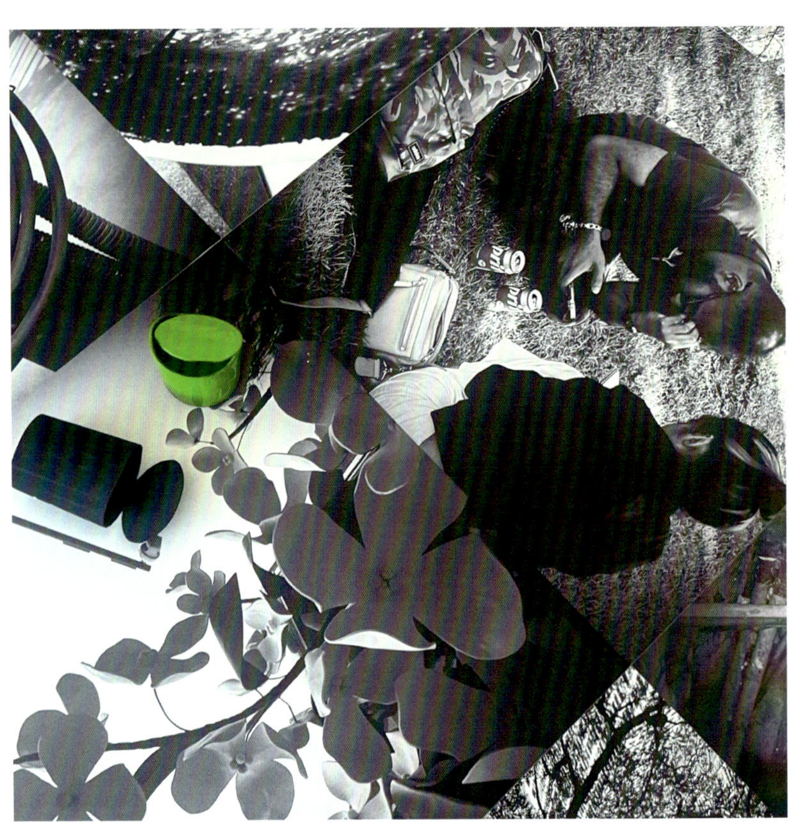

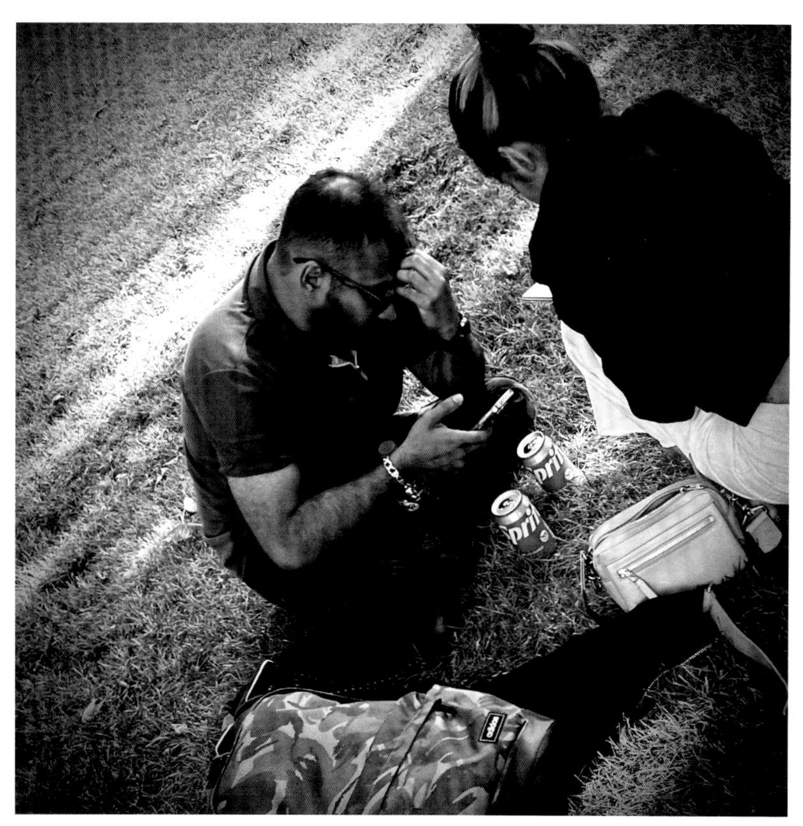

Overcast

郁闷

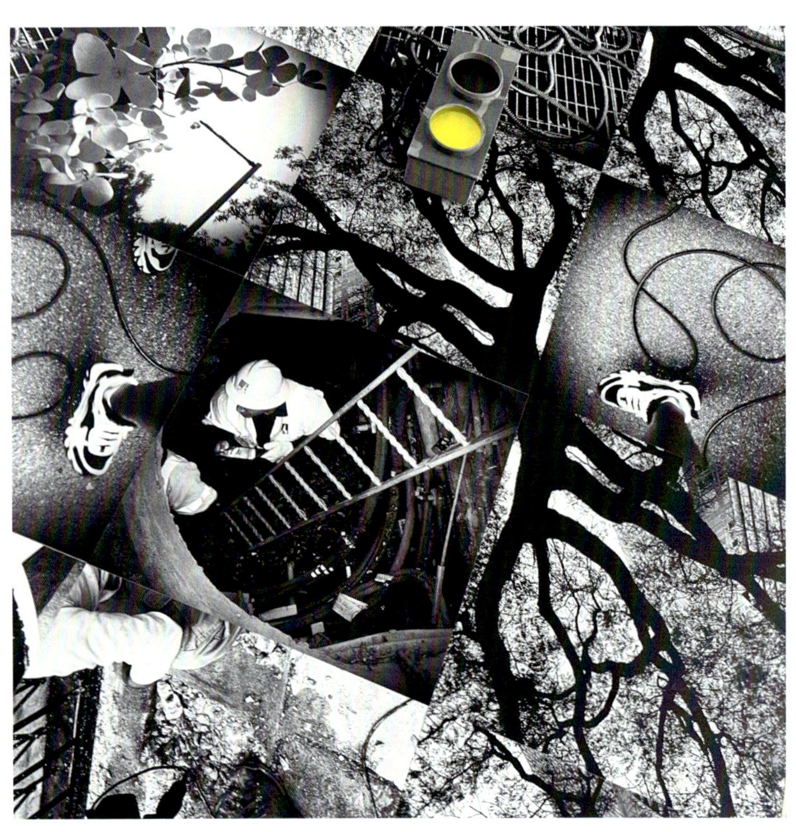

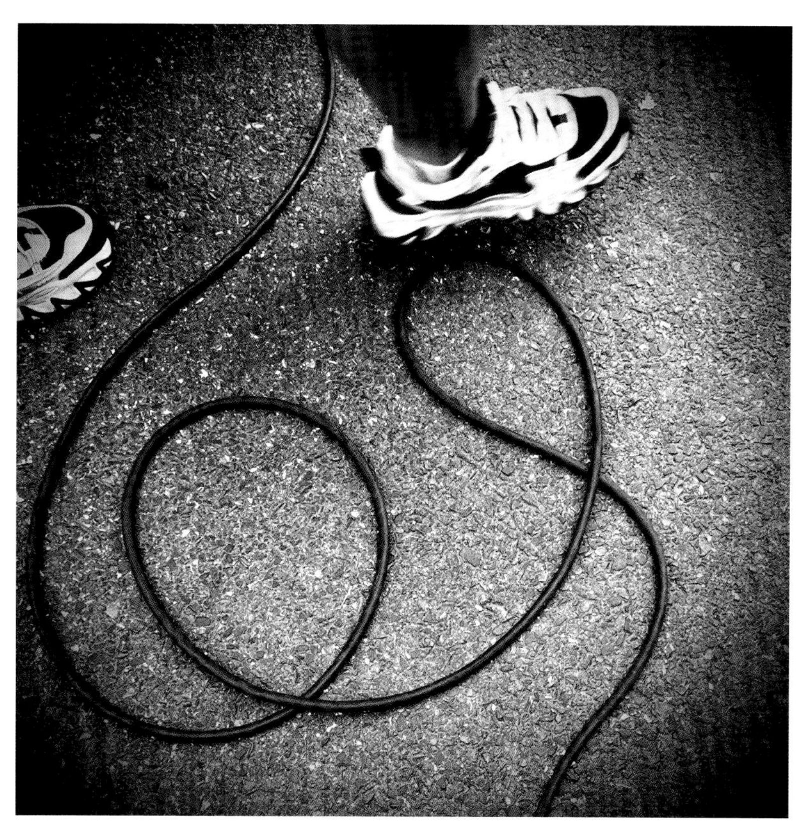

Tenderness

温柔

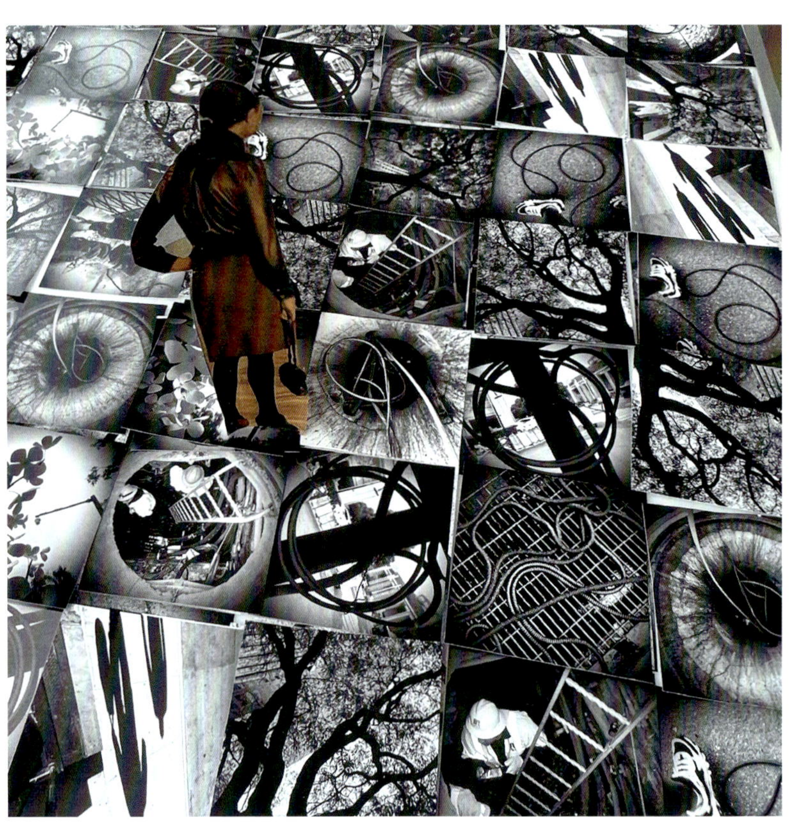

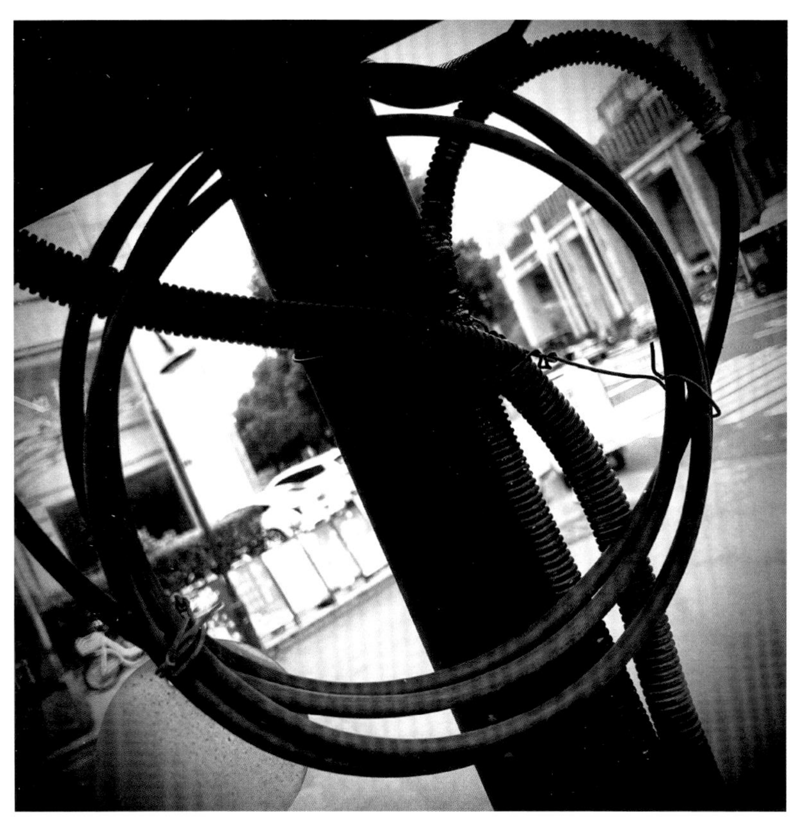

Ghost Town

鬼城

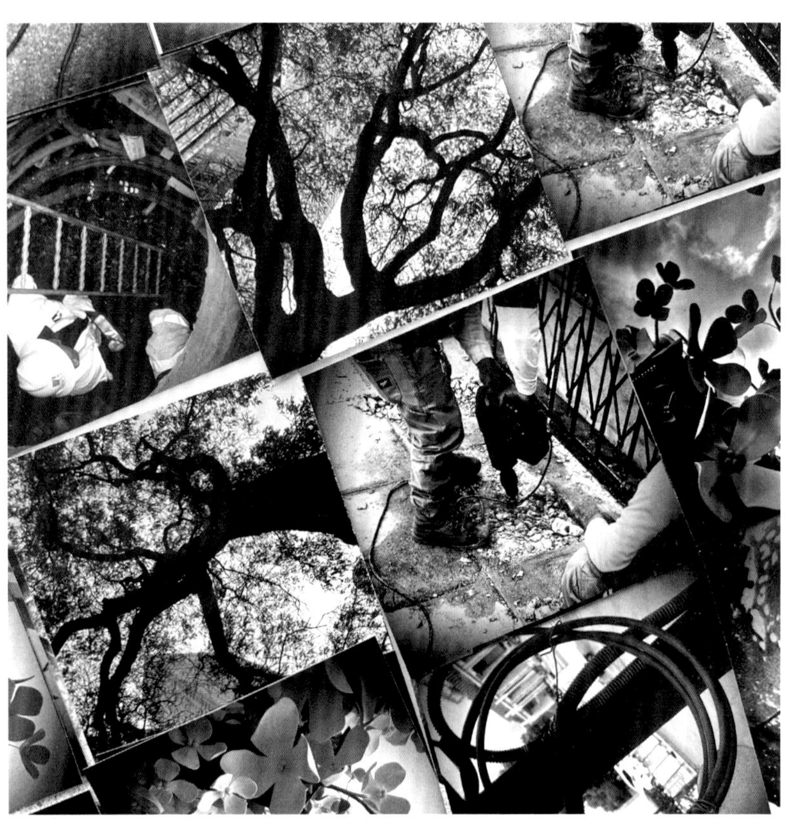

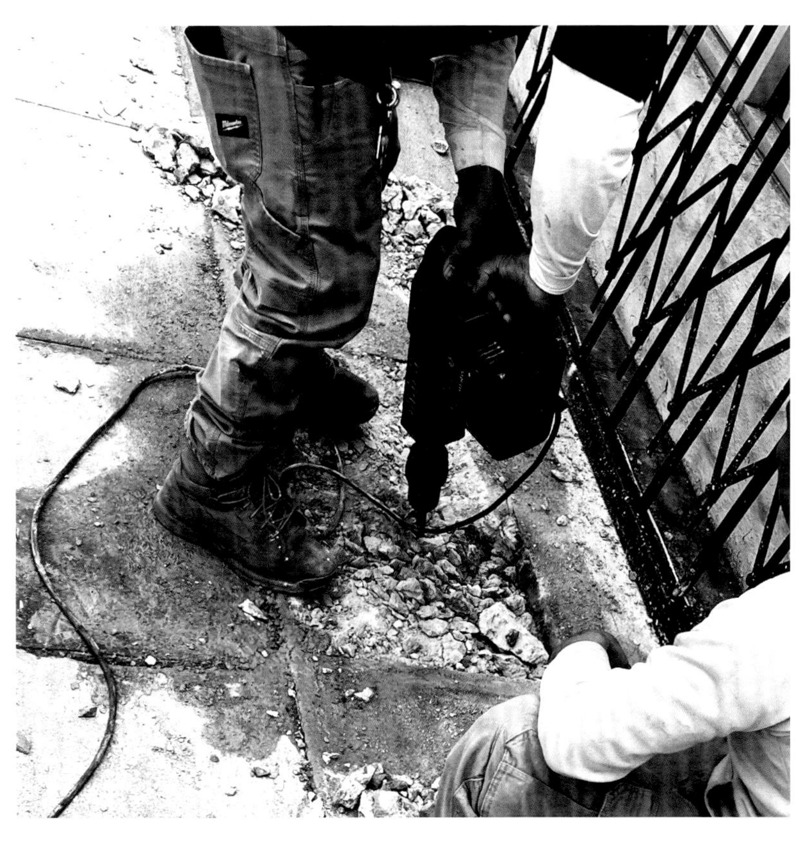

Santa Monica Boulevard

圣莫尼卡大道

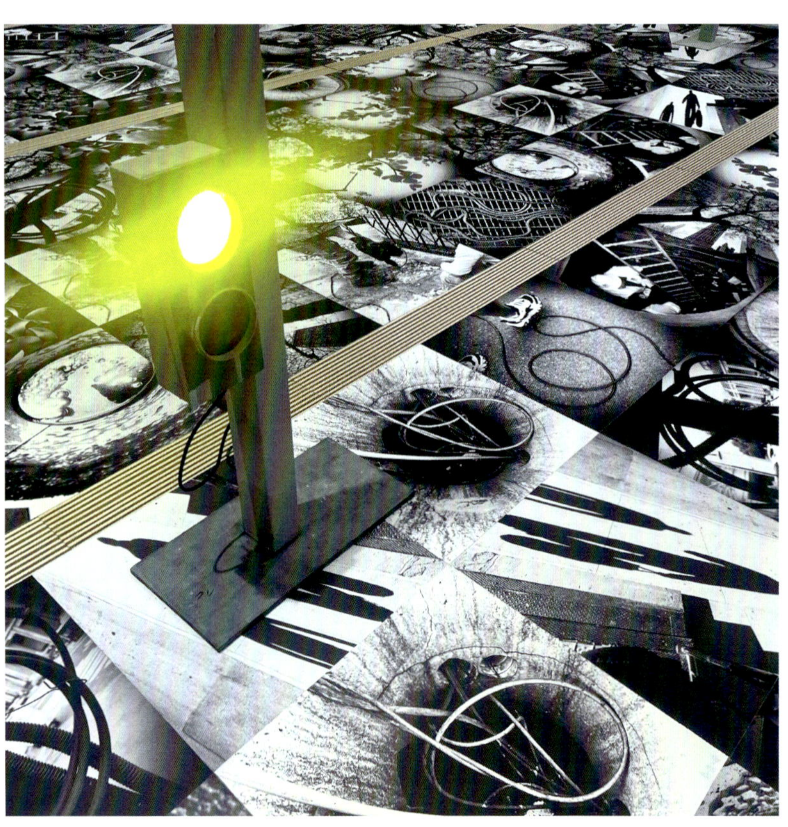

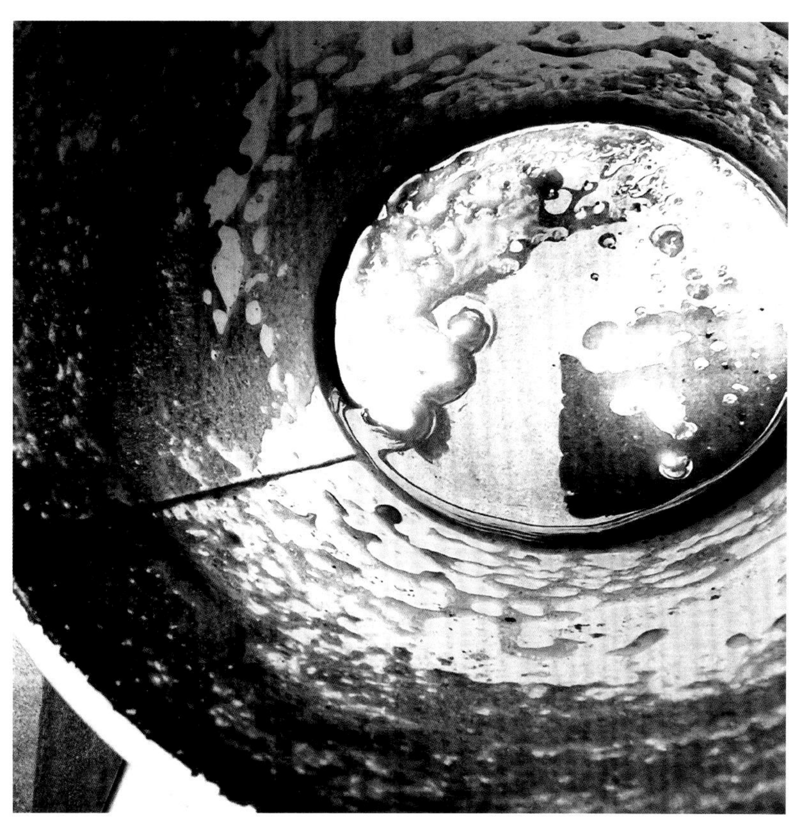

Telescope

望远镜

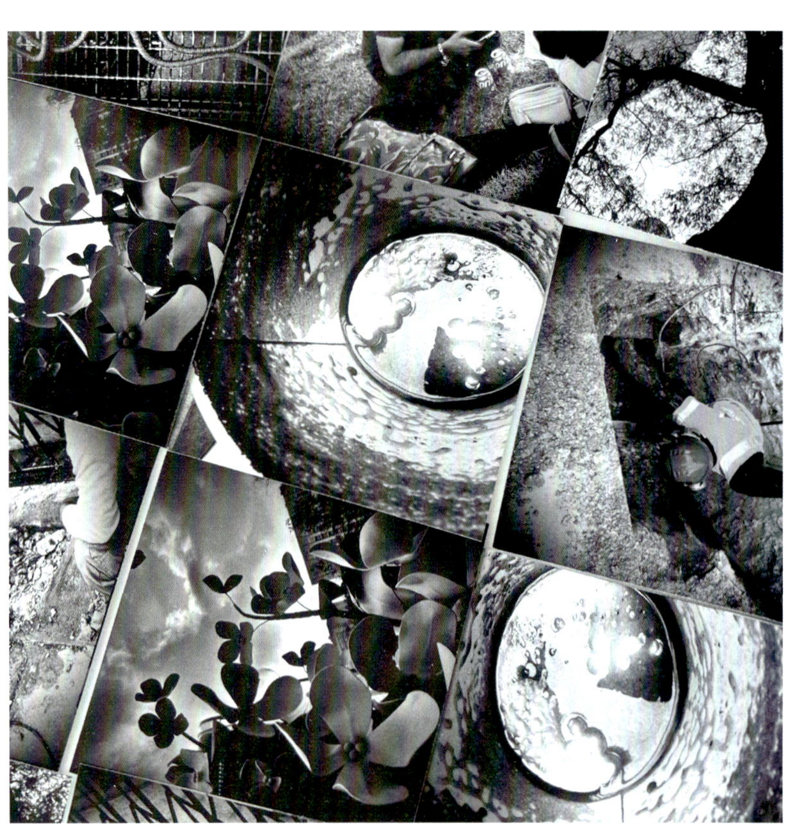

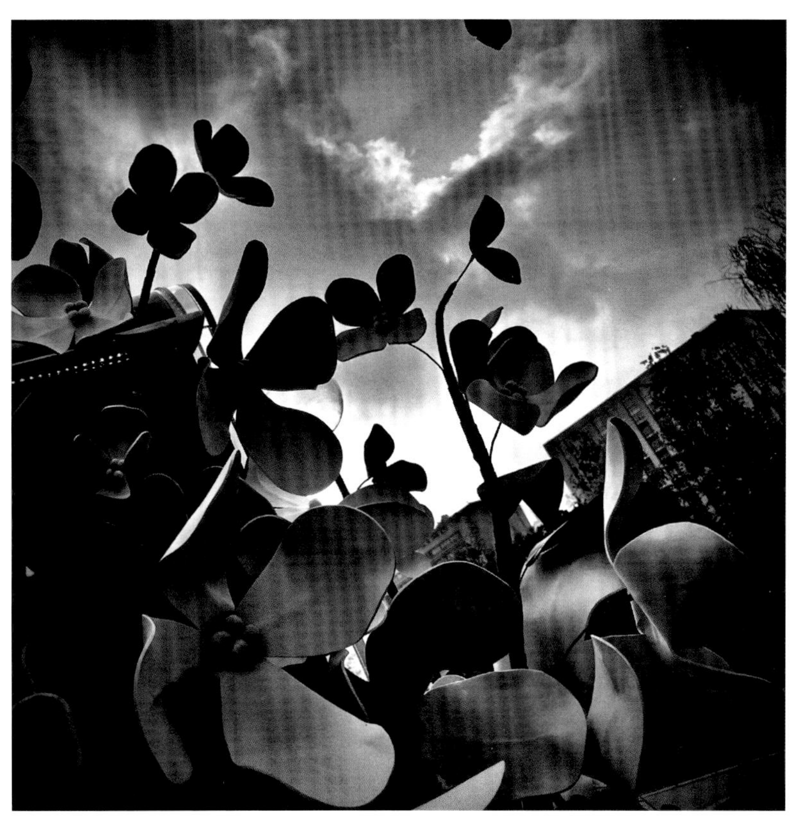

Patterns in the Dark

暗中的图案

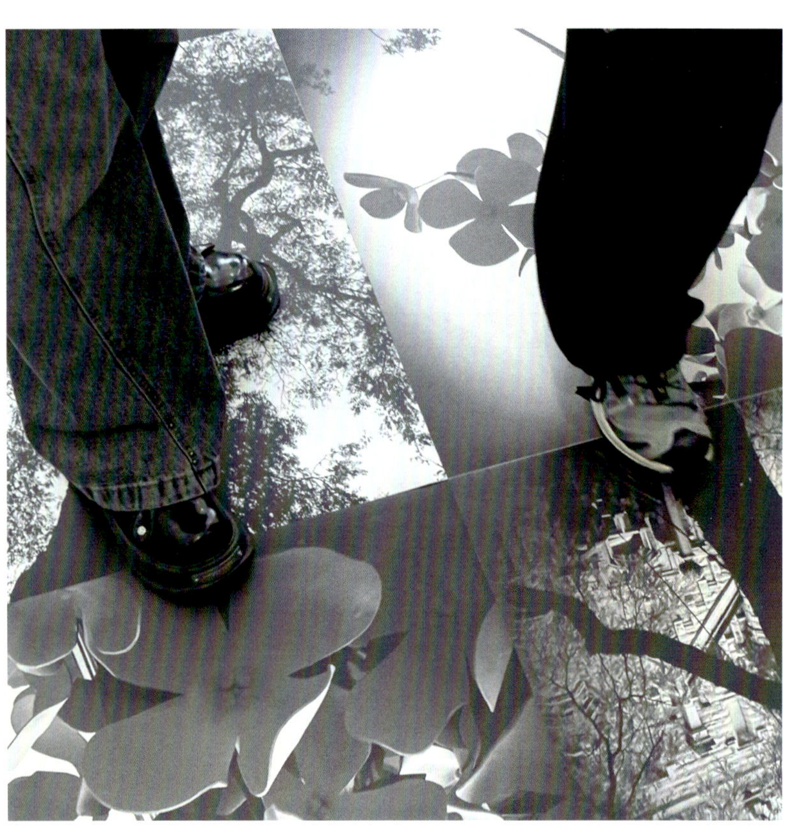

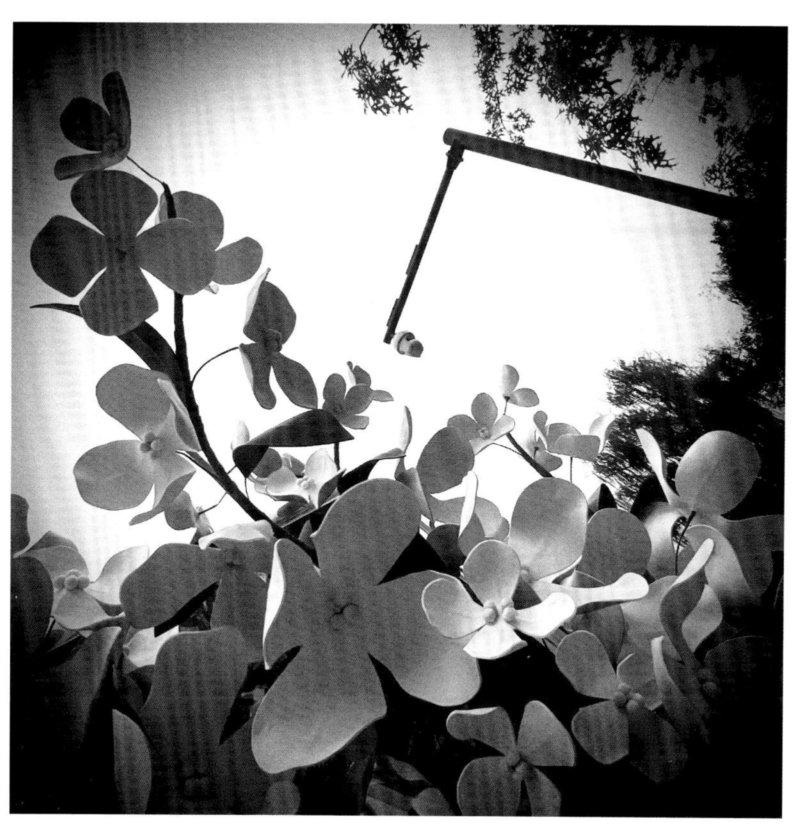

Sister Sinister

邪恶姐妹

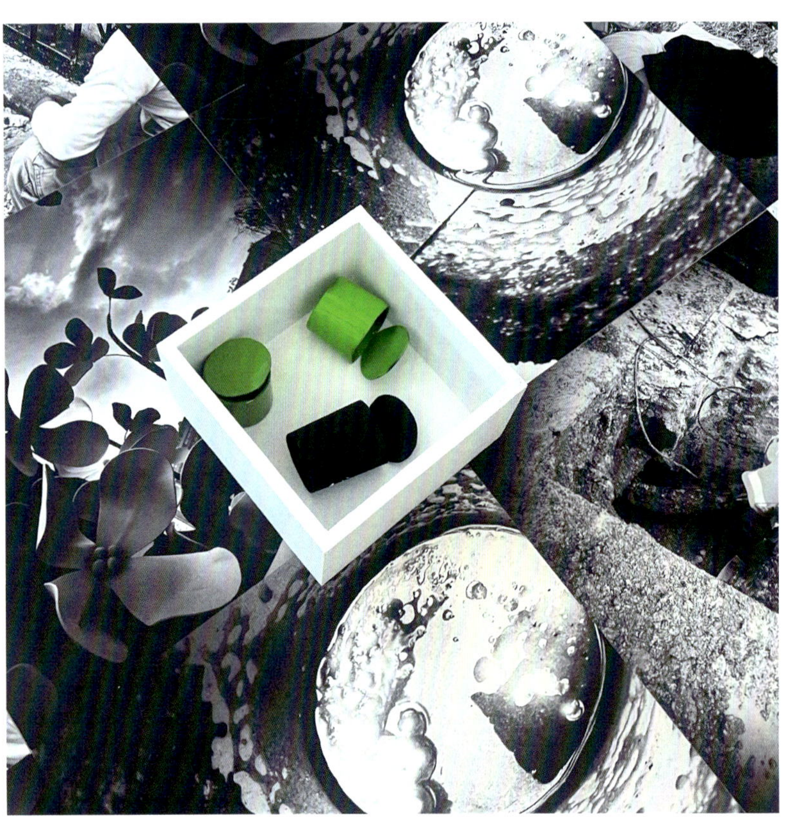

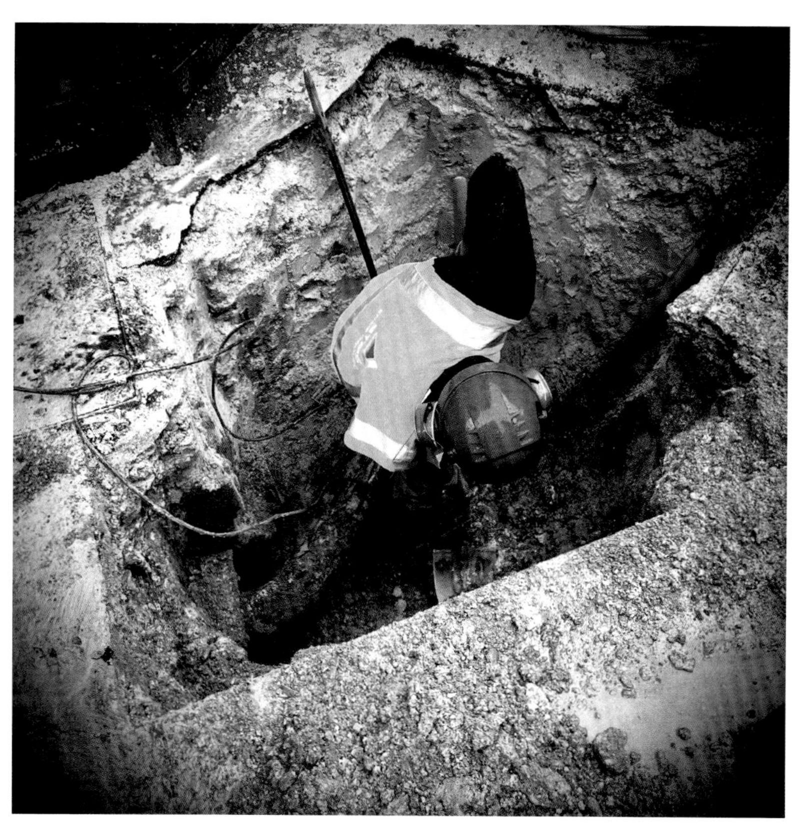

The Contrarian

反潮流者

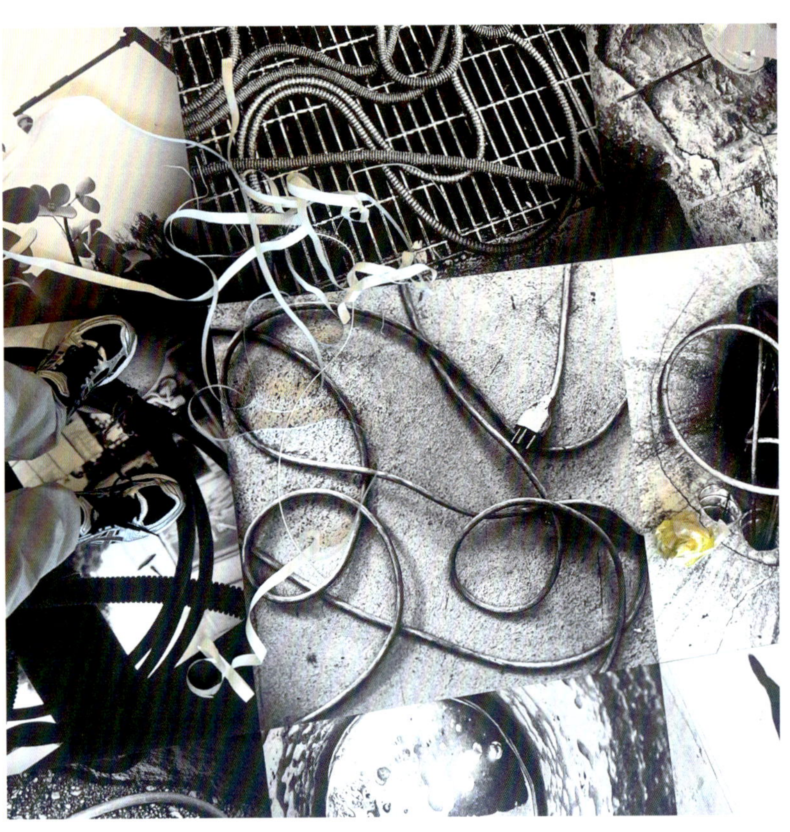

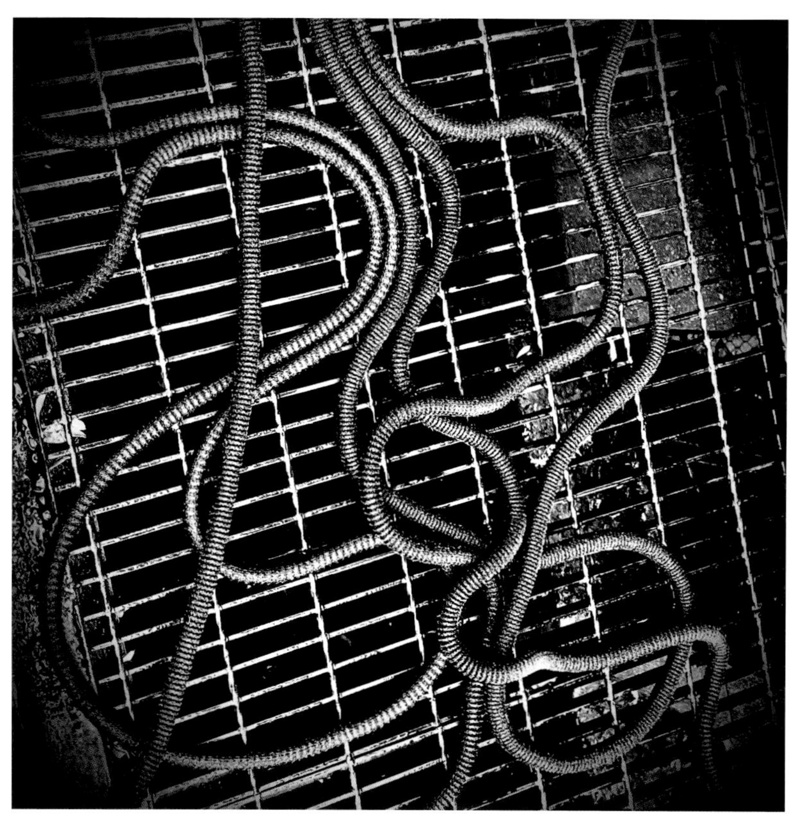

Living Creature

活物

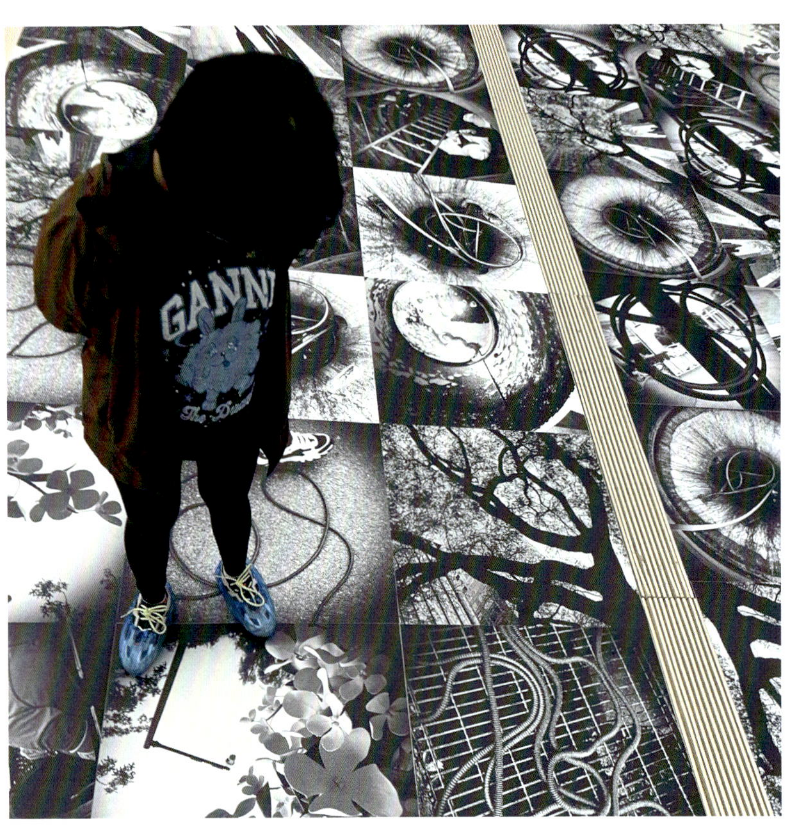

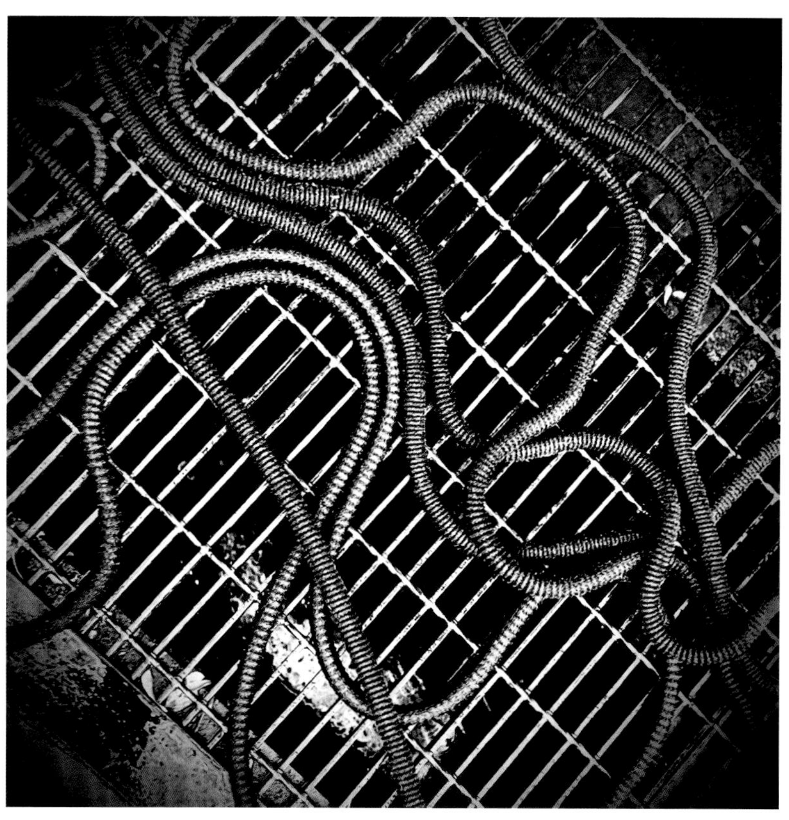

Sometimes Parallel

有时平行

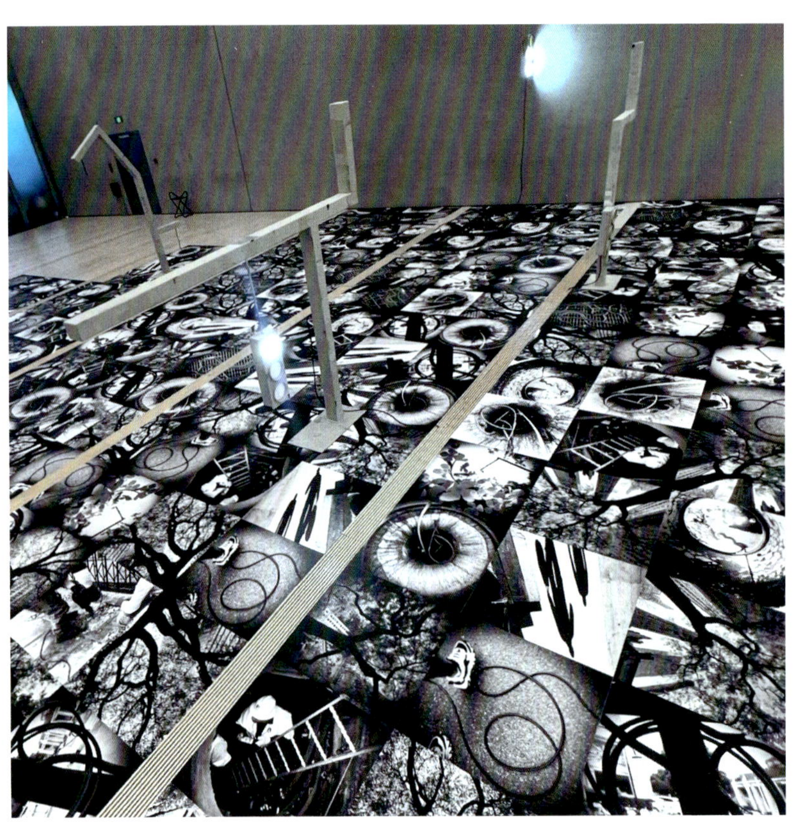

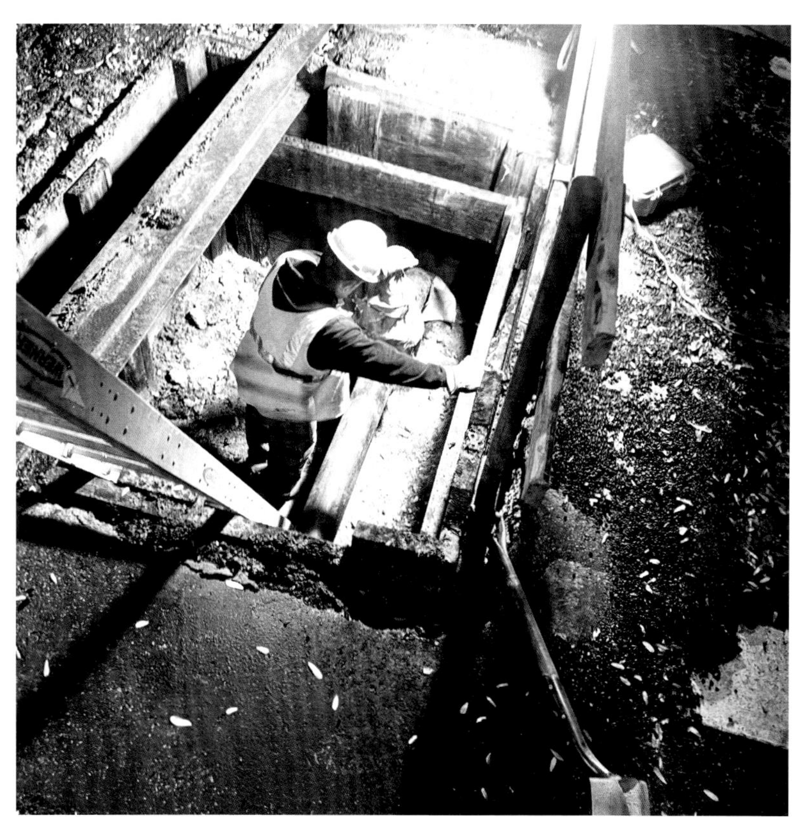

New Contributions

新的贡献

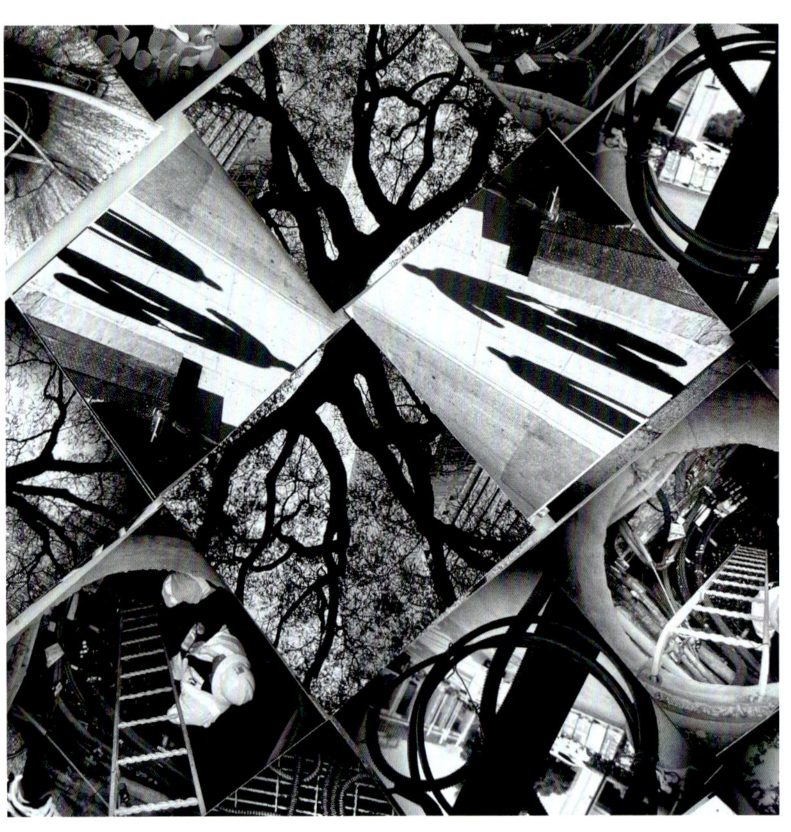

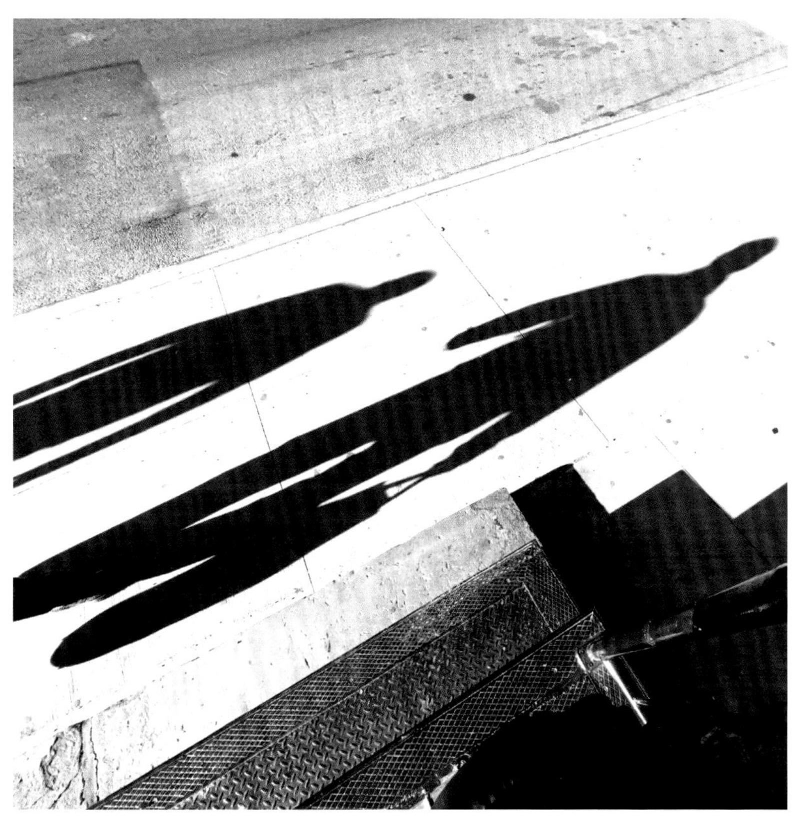

Cairo

开罗

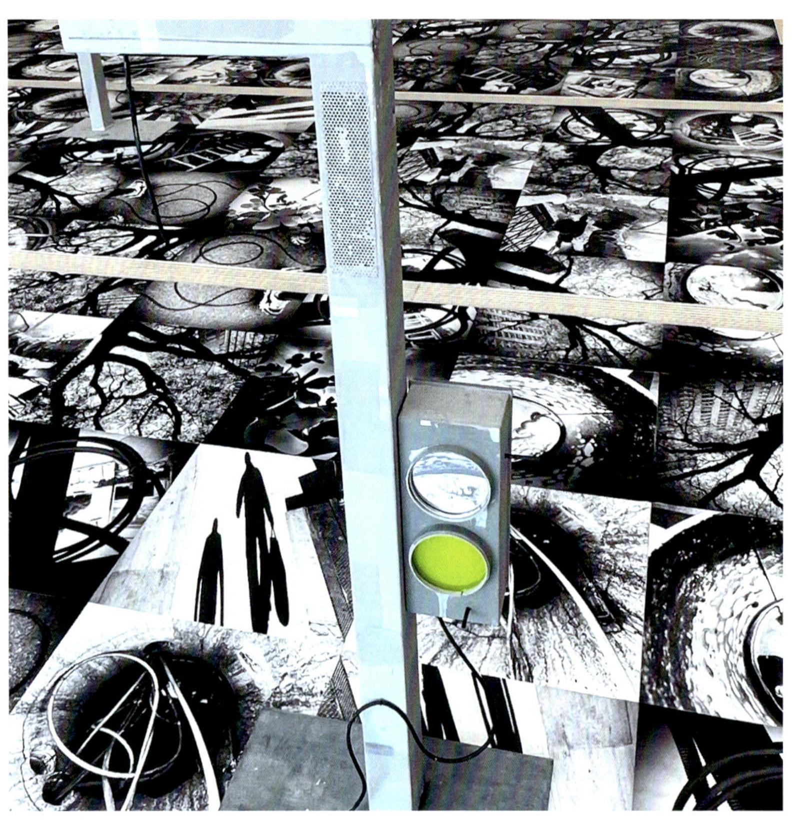

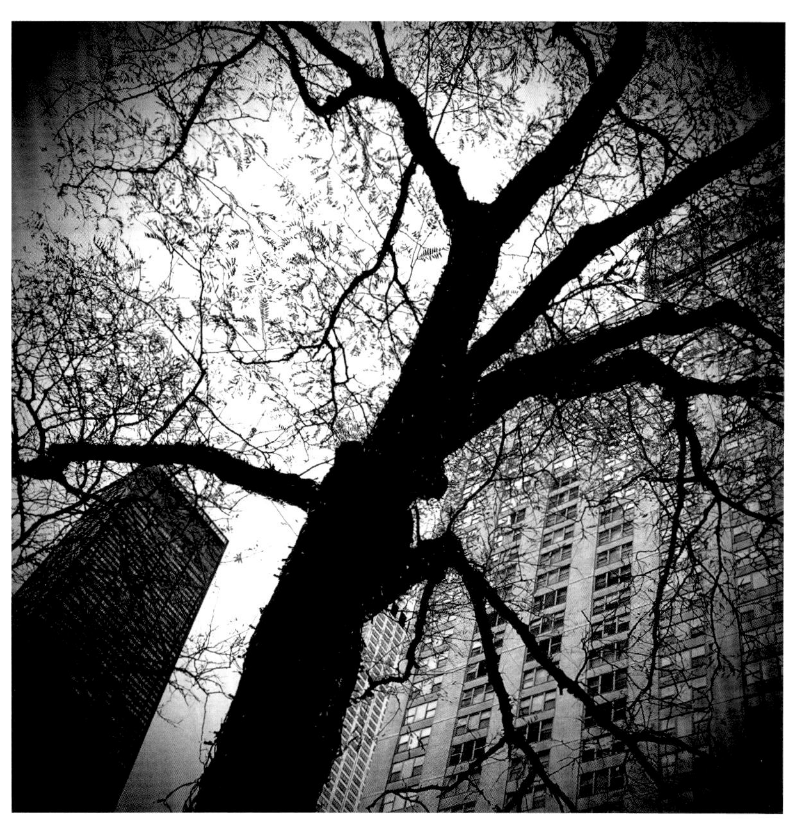

Higher Than Everything

高于一切

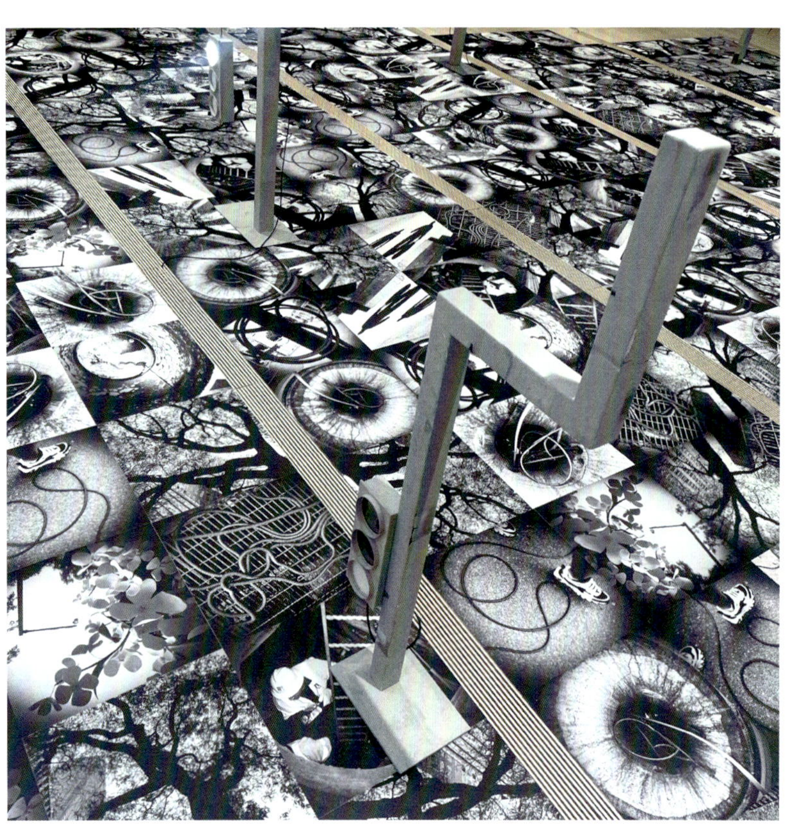

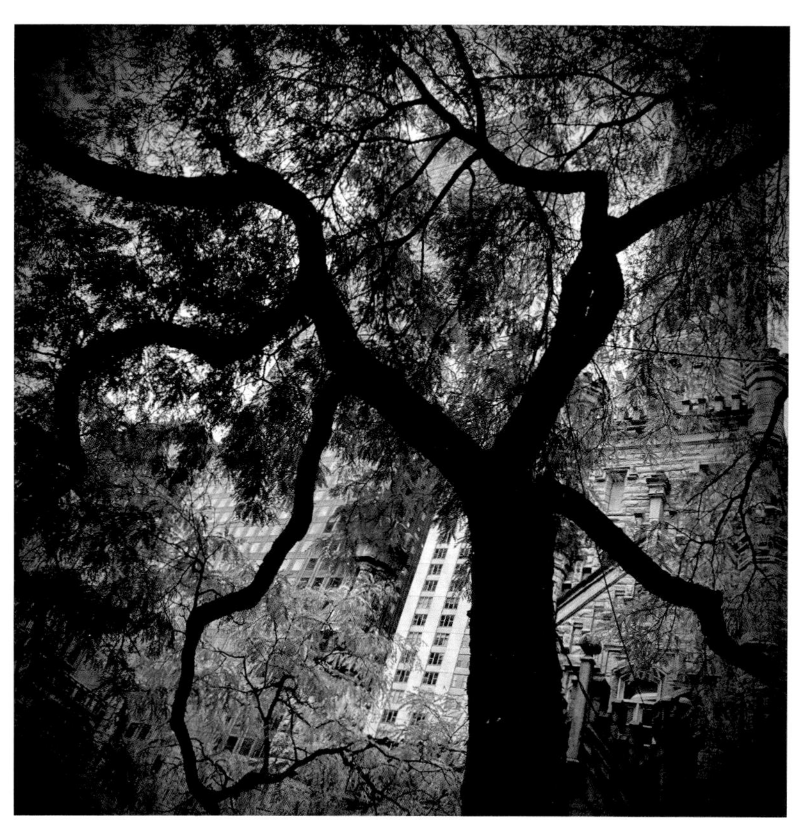

Fear-Free

无惧

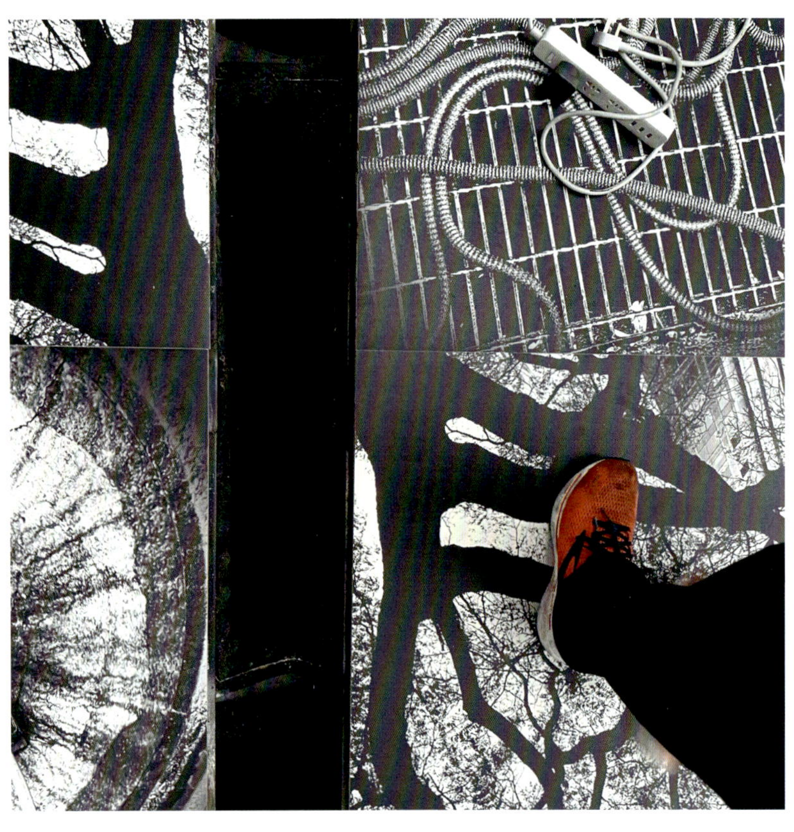

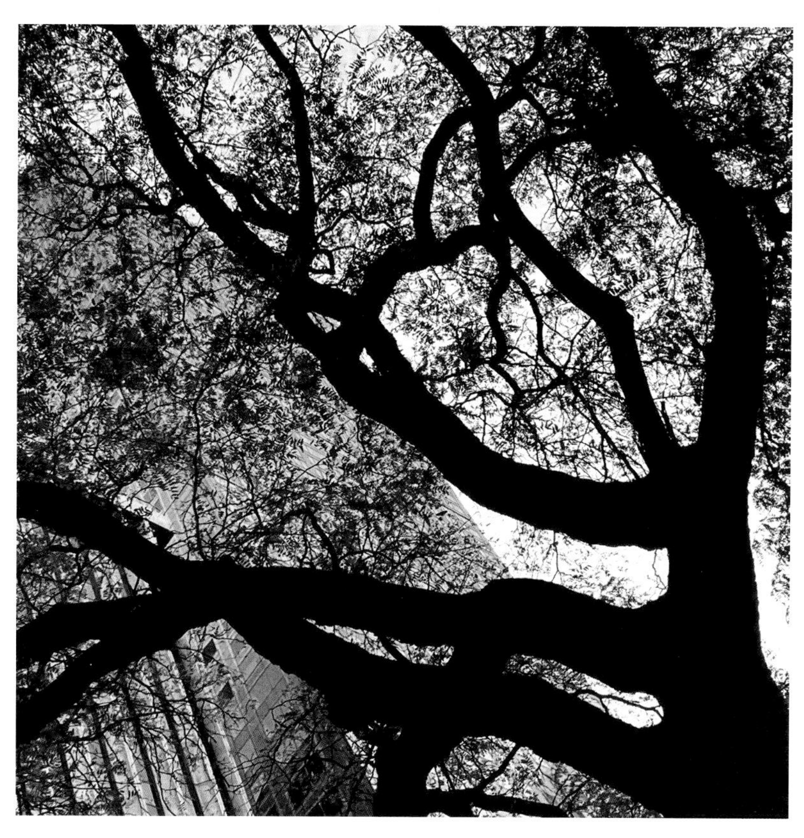

Lines One Can Follow

可以追随的线条

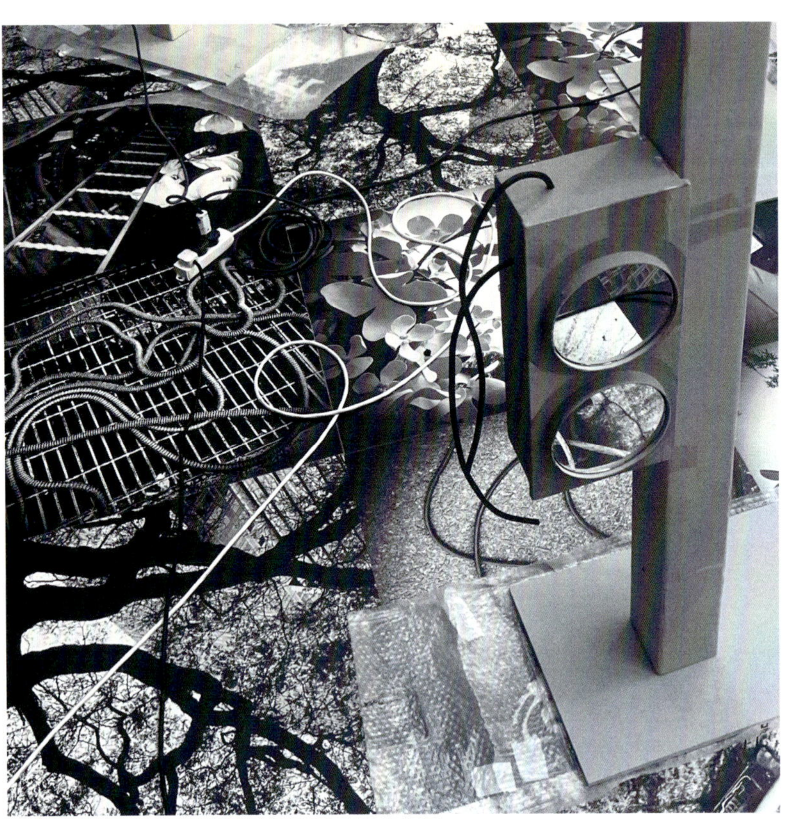

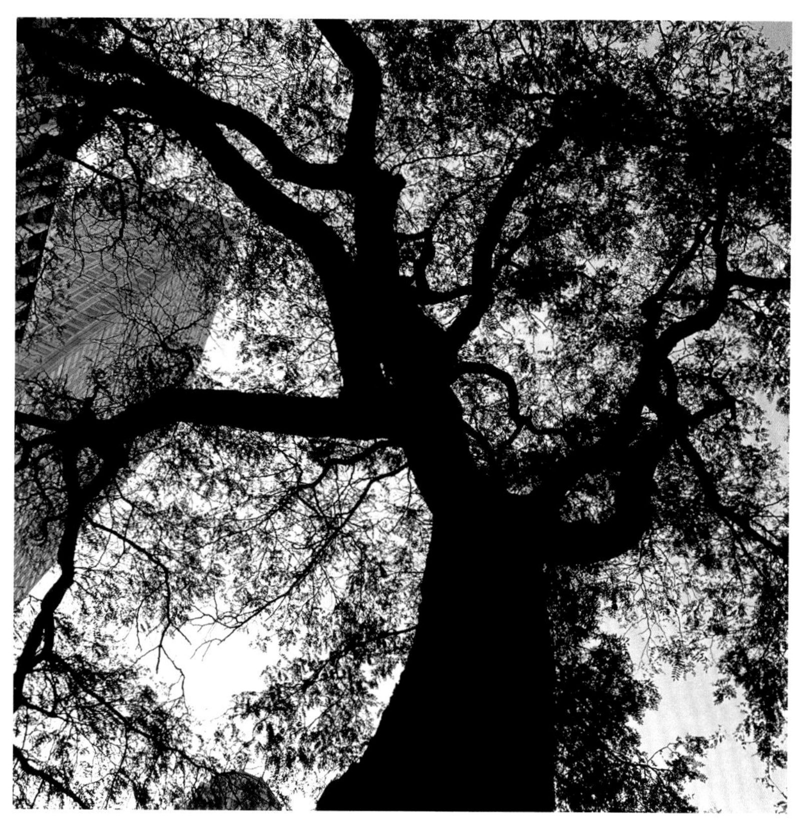

Map

地图

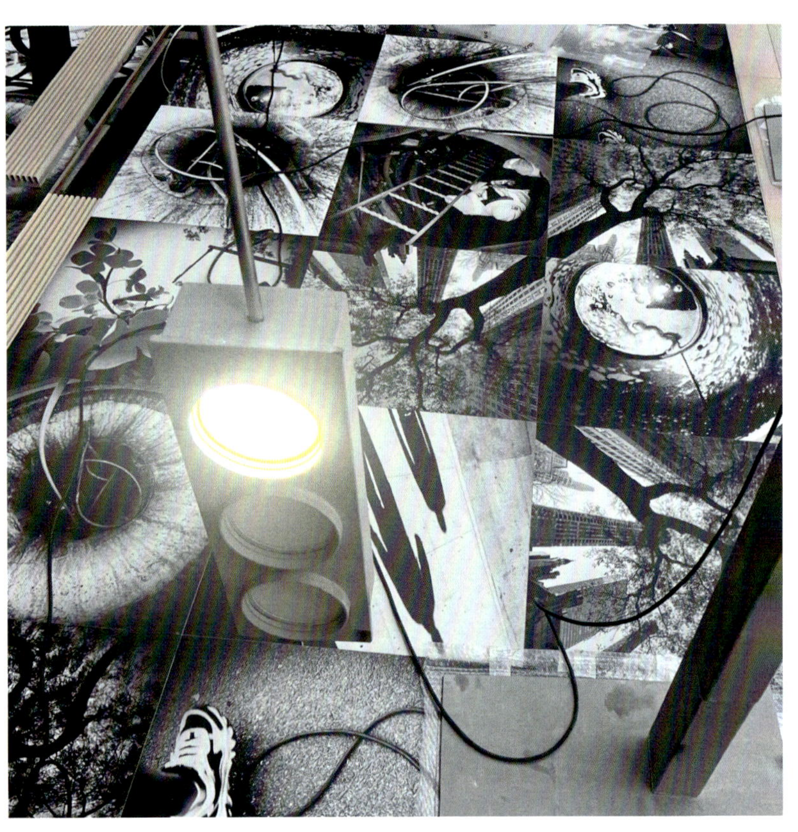

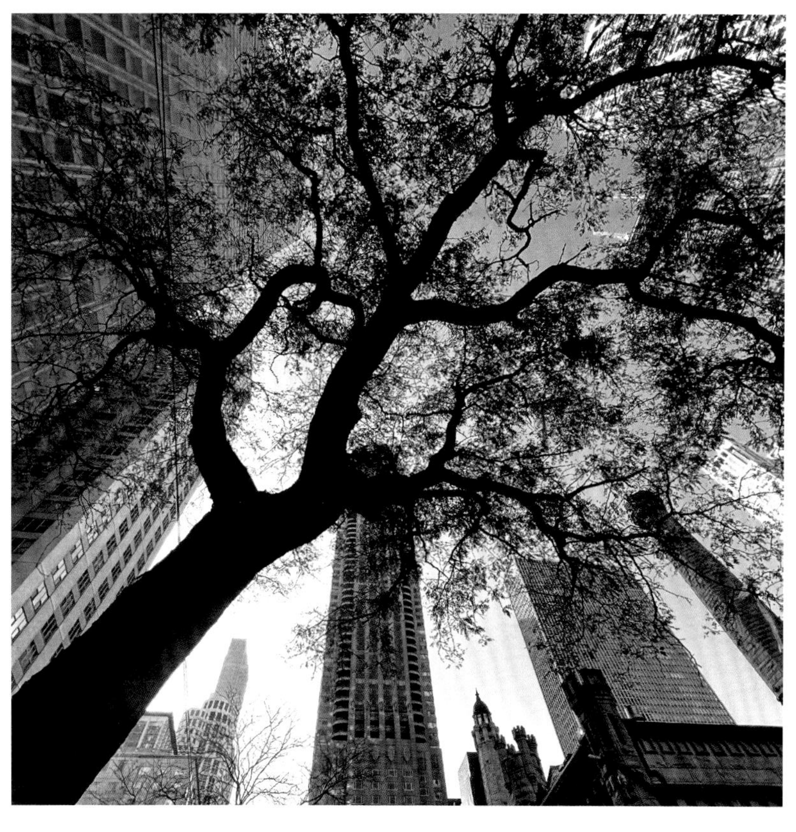

Summer, Fall, Winter, Spring

夏、秋、冬、春

Dunes Workshop
LI Yalun,
CHEN Feiyue

Dissolving the Ground

"The terrain is slippery and shifting, mined and undermined.
And this ground is, by essence, an underground."
— Jacques Derrida, *Limited Inc.*

The Flaneur in a Neoliberal Consumerist Landscape

"Empathy with the commodity is fundamentally empathy with the exchange value itself. The flâneur is the virtuoso of this empathy."
— Walter Benjamin, *The Arcades Project*

Heart-shaped lattes, pretzels, cocktails, streetlights, buses, high-rises, pedestrians, dogs, pigeons... black and white photographs of banal urban scenes weave into a rather unsettling neoliberal consumerist landscape. Walking through Peter Fischli's *Vertigo Vinyl Floor Pattern I, II, III* is a disorienting experience, reminiscent of a tourist stumbling through a metropolis.

This disorientation arises not only from the multitude of simulations within a city but also from the similarities across different urban scenes. Each image presents a familiar setting, yet its exact location remains ambiguous. Urban spaces no longer possess distinct localities or qualities; identifying specific places requires forensic scrutiny. In one photo, the Chinese characters on the wrapping paper of a straw may suggest a Starbucks in a Chinese city, but even this offers no certainty. In another image, we see the silhouette of the Eiffel Tower—but is it truly in Paris or the replica in Tianducheng near Hangzhou? The obfuscation in Fischli's work compels viewers to question the authenticity of places and reflect on their surroundings.

沙丘研究所
李雅伦、陈飞樾

溶解大地

"地域是滑动化的，被开采和削弱。而这片土地，本质上是地下。"
——雅克·德里达，《Limited Inc》

新自由主义和消费主义景观中的游荡者

与商品共情，根本上是与交换价值共情。游荡者正是这种共情的大师。
——瓦尔特·本雅明，《拱廊街计划》

心形拉花的拿铁、碱水面包、鸡尾酒、路灯、巴士、高楼大厦、行人、狗、鸽子……一系列平常的城市场景交织成一个令人不安的新自由主义和消费主义景观。穿行在彼得·费茨利的艺术作品《眩晕乙烯基地板图案 I, II, III》里是一种晕眩的体验，一如游客在大都市中跌跌撞撞穿行。

这种晕眩感不仅来自于大都市中各式各样的感官刺激，也来自于场景的不断重复。这组作品中，每个画面都展示了一个貌似熟悉的环境，却让人猜不透它具体拍摄于哪个地方。都市空间不再具有独特的地方特质；要确定任何具体地点都需要进行法医般的仔细检查。在一张照片中，吸管的包装纸上有中文字，这可能暗示它来自中国城市里的星巴克，但即便如此也无法确定。在另一张照片中，我们看到埃菲尔铁塔的剪影，但它真的在巴黎吗？还是只是杭州附近复制品的照片？这些作品迫使观众质疑地点的真实性，并反思我们周围的环境。

This vertiginous experience prompts deeper inquiries about placelessness in a globalized world, where unique urban characteristics are eroded by pervasive gentrified homogeneity. In a world increasingly dominated by McDonald's and Starbucks, how different are cities like Hangzhou and Zurich? Recently, spaces catering to China's new middle class have adopted predominant Western aesthetics—designed by globally renowned star architects, constructed with imported materials, and populated with international brands.

The anthropologist Marc Augé used the term *non-lieux* (non-place) to describe transitional spaces devoid of local history or social relationships. These spaces—airports, subways, chain coffee shops, etc.—are often temporary and anonymous, where people pass through without forming meaningful connections or experiences. With globalization, consumerism, and urbanization, people increasingly value efficiency, leading to the proliferation of such non-places. Like many urban dwellers around the world, Peter Fischli often finds himself immersed in this homogeneous landscape, captured through his camera and laid out on the museum floor at BY ART MATTERS.

In the 19th century, industrialization created modern cities, previously unseen in the slow-paced, tight-knit rural communities. This bustling environment, replete with stimuli, led to a blasé attitude[1]—a detached indifference shielding urban dwellers from sensory overload. Untangled from small, confined communities, urbanites gained freedom; yet this freedom was not always comforting. Even when surrounded by crowds, they still felt lonely and lost. The flâneur emerged in this expanding metropolis; for Baudelaire and Benjamin, this urban wanderer is the product of modernity—an observer

1 Georg Simmel, *The Metropolis and Mental Life*, in *The Sociology of Georg Simmel*, Free Press, 1950, pp. 409–424.

这种晕眩的体验引发了对全球化世界中“无地方性”的更深层次思考。在一个日益被麦当劳和星巴克主导的世界中，杭州和苏黎世的城市究竟有多不同？尤其是近年来，中国“新中产阶级”的空间是高度西方化的——由明星建筑师设计，使用进口材料，充斥着国际的品牌、商店和商品。

人类学家马克·奥热以“非场所”（non-lieux）去描述这种与当地的历史、社交关系缺乏关联的过渡空间，以及这些当代世界中，缺乏身份感、历史感或社会互动的空间。这些空间通常是短暂的、匿名的，人们经过它们时不会形成有意义的联系或体验。创造这个词的人类学家奥热认为，在全球化、消费主义和城市化的影响下，人们越来越看重效率和功能性，这样的“非场所”也因此越来越多。像所有全球化都市的居民一样，费茨利也常常处在这种同质化中。他用镜头捕捉它们，并把它们摊开呈现在天目里美术馆的地板上。

在19世纪，工业化创造了现代城市，也制造了一种新的群体——都市人。相比于乡村慢节奏的熟人社会，复杂都市中多样的外部刺激使都市人产生齐美尔所称的“腻烦态度”[1]，他们用漠然、无感的态度来保护自己过载的精神。相比于紧密联系在一起的乡土人情社会，都市人对于人际关系的态度总是有所保留，也使他们获得了更多的个体自由以及独特性。当然这种自由并非舒适的，即便无时无刻不处在人群中，他们仍然时常感到孤独和迷失。对于波德莱尔和本雅明来说，游荡者正是在这些快速生长的大都市中涌现的现代性的产物——一个以悠闲、好奇但又情感上疏离的态度在城市中漫游的观察者。

---

1 格奥尔格·齐美尔，《大都市与精神生活》，收录于《格奥尔格·齐美尔社会学》，自由出版社，1950年，第409－424页

endowed with leisure, curiosity, and perceptiveness. Fischli always seems to possess the keen eye of a flâneur when moving through a city, observing and documenting everyday life and public spaces from a distance. In 19th-century Paris, when the Haussmannization of the city regulated urban mobility through modern city planning, the freedom of the flâneur, along with Guy Debord's notion of *dérive*,[2] became strategies to create encounters that restructure urban experience. Today, the flâneur's domain extends beyond arcades and streets to subways, airports, and shopping malls. In metropolises where uniformity prevails, discovering unexplored terrain becomes increasingly challenging. Yet in *Vertigo Vinyl Floor Pattern I, II, III,* we see Fischli as the contemporary flâneur, giving his attention to mundane objects. We rediscover a focus on the overlooked—the passers-by, other urban inhabitants, from animals and trees to vehicles—and, most intriguingly, the ground plane.

Destabilized ground

"We move about over this ground as over a flimsily covered abyss."
— Martin Heidegger, An Introduction to Metaphysics

Looking up at a small patch of sky framed by skyscrapers, gazing down at a pedestrian crossing from a second-floor window, or observing a streetscape reflected in a pane of glass—the constant shift in perspectives creates disorientation, which is intensified by the tiled placement on the floor. Viewers are forced to confront the surface beneath their feet with newfound attention. What was once solid, continuous ground becomes fragmented by a multitude of perspectives, scales, and orientations.

---

2 A spontaneous and unstructured journey through urban spaces, where one immerses in the environment and experiences the city through senses and emotions. This practice encourages participants to reconsider the city as they experience it.

费茨利不像游客那样匆忙地“打卡”名作和景点，他总是展现出游荡者敏锐的眼光，在穿行城市时观察并记录日常生活和公共空间。在十九世纪的巴黎，当奥斯曼的现代城市规划限制了城市的流动，游荡者的自由，以及之后德波提出的“漂移”[2] 概念，成为重构城市体验的策略。如今，游荡者的领域已从街道扩展至地铁、机场和购物中心。在同质化的都市中，发现尚未被探索的地带变得愈加困难，但在《眩晕乙烯基地板图案I,II,III》的照片中，我们看到作为当代游荡者的费茨利对被忽视的日常事物的关注，对于路人、动物、树木、车辆，以及对地面的观察。

不稳定的地面

“我们在这片大地上移动，仿佛在一个薄薄覆盖的深渊上行走。”
——马丁 · 海德格尔，《形而上学导论》

向上看被高楼框住的一小片天空，从二楼窗户向下看斑马线，透过玻璃向外看街道的景致……视角的不断变化带来了迷失感，这组艺术作品在地板上的网格化铺设将这种迷失感推向了极致。观众被迫以一种全新的注意力来面对他们步行的地面。曾经坚固、连续的地面被多种视角、尺度和方向打破。在这片不稳定的地面上，观众的视角不断变化——从地下到地上，向下看、向上看，透过镜头和反射看，仿佛行走在不稳定的地景上。晕眩感是显而易见的，地面不再是坚固、可靠的表面，而是一个不断移动、不稳定的图像层，迫使观众重新思考他们的位置和方向。

2　即兴而主观地穿越城市空间的方式，将城市空间通过个人的经历剪切重组。这一策略使空间陌生化，产生邂逅的可能。“漂移”试图找回现代城市所缺失的不完整性、短暂性和创造性。

On this destabilized ground, viewers are constantly shifting and sliding—from underground to above ground, looking down and up, through lenses and reflections, as if walking on unstable terrain. Vertigo becomes palpable. The ground is no longer dependable but a shifting layer of images that compel the viewer to continually reposition and reorient themselves.

Heidegger spoke of the ground as a concealed abyss, a metaphor for the instability of metaphysical structures. This metaphor takes on a literal dimension in Fischli's photographs, which reveal the hidden world beneath the surface—escalators descending underground to perhaps a subway platform; the gaps in the grates covering the pavements; the roots of trees; and opened manholes with mysterious, snake-like power cables. These images serve as reminders of the hollow ground beneath every city and the flows of its infrastructure. *Vertigo Vinyl Floor Pattern I, II, III* dissolves the ground, offering a glimpse into this subterranean world, with its labyrinthine networks of tunnels, roots, and cables. It is perhaps closer to the true concept of 'ground'—the foundation that supports all life above.

Fischli's fascination with the subterranean is not new. In his earlier work *Kanalvideo* (1992), created with David Weiss, he explored the hidden sewage systems of Switzerland through abstract, endless loops of footage. This interest in what lies beneath the surface continues in the *Vertigo Vinyl Floor Pattern I, II, III,* where the ground is revealed as a permeable membrane. This theme is addressed directly in his new video work, exhibited at BY ART MATTERS, in which the subway becomes the focus. The subway is not merely part of a vast infrastructural web supporting a city; it is also a continuous stream of experiences connecting all global metropolises.

海德格尔将“地面”描述为一个“被遮蔽起来的深渊”，这是对支撑形而上学结构的不稳定性的隐喻。在费茨利的照片中，这一隐喻被赋予了具体的维度，揭示了地表下隐藏的世界——通向地铁站的自动扶梯、人行道上的铁栅盖、树木的根和冠、或者更为神秘的景象：井盖打开着，蜿蜒着的电缆从里面伸出来。这些图像提醒着我们，城市的大地其实是中空的，基础设施在其间流动与循环。《眩晕乙烯基地板图案I, II, III》解构了地面，提供了一瞥这个地下世界，展现出隧道、根系和电缆的迷宫网络。这也许更接近“地面”的真实概念——支撑着所有地上生命的基础。

费茨利对地下的迷恋并不新鲜。在他早期与大卫·威斯合作创作的《Kanalvideo》（1992年）中，他探索了瑞士隐藏的下水道系统，将其展示为抽象、无尽的影像循环。这种对地表下的迷恋在《眩晕乙烯基地板图案 I, II, III》中得以延续；地面被揭示为一种可渗透的膜。这一兴趣更直接地反映在他在天目里美术馆展出的新的视频作品中，该作品以地铁本身作为主题。地铁不仅是连接城市的巨大网络的一部分，也代表了一种连续的体验，一种在全球所有大都市的地铁中相似的感受。

漂浮

现代主义时代和国际风格在许多方面已经“抹去了”地球的物理和文化基础。[3] 随着乡土建筑让位于同质化的城市景观，我们不仅失去了与地方的联系，也失去了日益难以捉摸的“扎根感”。也许更具破坏性的是社交媒体，它深入渗透在我们生活的方方面面。

---

[3] 在现代主义建筑中，Tabula Rasa 是一种重要的手段，它忽视场地上物理、文化和历史层面的现状。“Tabula Rasa”是一个拉丁语短语，意为“一块干净的板子”。

Floating groundlessly

The modernist era and the International Style have, in many ways, wiped clean the physical and cultural ground.[3] As vernacular architecture succumbs to homogenized urban landscapes, we lose not just a connection to place but also a sense of identity. Groundedness is increasingly elusive. Perhaps more disruptive is the prevalence of social media, which deeply permeates all aspects of our lives.

The square crop and grid format of the photos in *Vertigo Vinyl Floor Pattern I, II, III* reference social media posts. On Instagram or TikTok's infinite scroll of images, a vast amount of content crowds the same space. With a flick of the thumb, one can leap from a production line in a factory in Dongguan to an influencer on a beach in Hawaii. This scrolling interaction allows users to teleport between geographical locations. The constant stream of information on the screen creates a sense of weightlessness, leaving the user unmoored from specific, grounded locations, as if floating in the air.

In 1968, the Apollo 8 spacecraft captured the famous Earthrise photograph from the Moon. Earth was no longer seen as the ground or the environment, but had shrunk into an image of a planet. In 1989, David Harvey introduced his renowned concept of time-space compression in *The Condition of Postmodernity*, describing how advancements in communication and transportation had condensed the world into a continuously connected marketplace. In 1991, the World Wide Web was born.

---

3 Tabula Rasa is a Latin phrase meaning a clean slate. In Modernist architectural theory, it refers to the approach to a site that disregards existing physical, cultural and historical contexts in design and starts with a clean slate.

《眩晕乙烯基地板图案 I, II, III》中的方形裁剪和网格格式的照片影射了社交媒体的发布方式。在 Instagram 或抖音的"照片墙"或者"瀑布流"中，大量的内容拥挤在同一空间——手指轻轻上划，界面向下滚动，你可能刚刚看到的是东莞某个工厂的流水线直播，下一秒又和某位网红一道，站在夏威夷的沙滩上。这种"向下滑动看到更多"的内容模式使得用户在地理意义的各个地方之间快速切换。屏幕上不断流动的内容让人感到头晕目眩，在无尽的图片流中滚动，让用户产生了一种无重感，似乎脱离了任何特定的地点，而在空中漂浮。

1968年，阿波罗八号飞船从月球拍摄了著名的"地升"照片。地球不再是"大地"或者"环境"，而是缩小成如今标志性的一颗小蓝球。1989年，马克思主义者大卫·哈维在《后现代的状况》中提出了他著名的"时空压缩"一说。通讯和交通科技的进步被资本的全球化扩张的欲望所驱动，贸易不再惧怕距离和时差，以至于整个地球变成了一个联通不断的市场。1991年，万维网诞生。

几十年后，超越物理城市景观，另一层公共空间由数字设备和互联网形成，现在它主导了我们的生活。这一层广阔的非物质公共基础设施将我们瞬间传送，抹去所有地理限制，创造了一个脱离现实世界的连接网络。观看者很难不把费茨利的这件作品放置到网络状况及后现代状况中去，或者说，很难无视掉这层语境。一个持续存在的问题似乎埋在这些照片之下——"我们现在在哪里？"这是一个对所有人而言既具象又隐喻性的问题。

在《附近的消失》一书中，中国人类学家项飚使用"附近的消失"这一术语，来描述基于地理和社区的联系如何逐渐被更远距离、更抽象的关系取代。我们对大洋彼岸的新闻和热点事件保持密切关注，

Decades later, beyond the physical urban landscape, another layer of public space has been created by digital devices and the internet, one that now dominates our lives. This layer of expansive, immaterial public infrastructure teleports us and erases all geographical constraints, creating a web of connections detached from the tangible world. It is impossible to ignore the context of networks and the postmodern condition when viewing Fischli's work. A persistently underlying question seems to be embedded in these photographs—"Where are we now?" This is both a literal and metaphorical question, one addressed to everyone.

In *The Nearby: A Scope of Seeing*, Chinese anthropologist Biao XIANG introduces the term "the disappearance of the nearby" to describe how connections based on geographic proximity and community have gradually been replaced by more abstract relationships. We pay close attention to global news yet may remain unaware of the lives of those around us. We search for restaurants through rankings rather than encountering local places on foot. Increasingly mediated by devices, the internet, and algorithms, we float in a virtual realm—one characterized by smooth transactions devoid of friction and barriers.

From ground to floor: a massive interior

"Junkspace is overripe and undernourishing at the same time, a colossal security blanket that covers the earth in a stranglehold of seduction…"

"Continuity is the essence of Junkspace; it exploits any invention that enables expansion, deploys the infrastructure of seamlessness: escalator, air conditioning, sprinkler, fire shutter, hot-air curtain... It is always interior, so extensive that you rarely perceive limits; it promotes disorientation by any means (mirror, polish, echo)..."
— Rem Koolhaas, *Junkspace*

却可能对身边的人的生活知之甚少。我们通过排名搜索餐厅，而不是在日常散步时偶遇街边的小店。我们习惯于通过设备、互联网和算法这些非物质的中介来观察世界，而它们抹去了物理世界中的距离感。一方面，城市正在失去其特征，变得越来越没有人情味和归属感；与此同时，都市居民选择宅在家中，通过虚拟的互联网与世界相连。"附近"意味着摩擦与障碍，而自由市场追求的是减少交易摩擦。

从大地到地板——巨大的室内空间

"垃圾空间既过于成熟又缺乏养分，是一条覆盖地球的庞大安全毯，紧紧束缚着它，散发着诱惑的气息……"

"连续性是垃圾空间的本质；它开发了各种能够进行扩张的创意，调动了无缝衔接的基础设计；自动扶梯、空调、自动喷淋、防火隔板、热风帘… 它只有室内，极其广大让你触不到边缘；它用各种方式扰乱方向感（镜面、抛光、重复）…"
——雷姆 · 库哈斯，《垃圾空间》

自17世纪现代性萌芽以来，又随着科技和资本主义的发展，人类似乎越发迅速地把世界给缩小了。在这个过程中，一个不太经常被谈论但十分根本的观念转化，在于人类对生存环境的理解由置身其中变为从外部审视。列维 · 斯特劳斯认为，像地球仪这样的微缩物的出现，其最重要的意义在于颠覆了人类理解事物的方式。我们不再需要一步一步地去探索，通过摸索来逐渐了解整体，而是能够一眼看到全貌。如果说前现代的世界曾是广袤而未知的领域，人类被浩瀚宇宙所笼罩，探险者不断向前迈进，而远方的总会不断涌现出新的地平线，那么，

Since the 17th century, with the development of technology and capitalism, humanity has seemingly accelerated the process of shrinking the world. During this period, a conceptual shift occurred in how we perceive our environment—moving from being immersed in it to observing it with an externalized viewpoint. For Lévi-Strauss, the advent of miniatures, such as globes, fundamentally altered the way humans understand the world. We no longer need to explore the terrain; instead, we can see the entirety at a glance. The pre-modern world is a vast and unknown territory enveloped by the immense universe, where explorers continuously forge ahead as new horizons endlessly emerge in the distance. In modernity, technological advancements have increasingly internalized our conception of the world. Humanity no longer stands upon the earth—the Earth becomes an object within our grasp. The distant horizon has disappeared, and everything on Earth seems to be controlled.

The transformation of the ground into a floor marks a profound shift from exteriority to interiority. The floor, as a surface, belongs to a controlled environment, separated from the natural world. The use of vinyl material in Fischli's work hints at this process of interiorization, where the external world is subsumed into an ever-expanding interior realm. Modern materials like concrete, steel, glass, and plastic fuel this interiorization, enabling the construction of massive structures—shopping malls, casinos, and airports, all with highly regulated interiors. Vinyl is of particular interest here in shaping the interior. This synthetic surface is often used to replace natural materials like wood or marble due to its affordability, durability, and, most importantly, its wide range of colors and patterns. While it imitates the patterns of natural materials, its artificiality can be spotted in the repetition of surface patterns, echoing the repetitiveness of consumerist imagery that Fischli captures. The floor is a surface that can be endlessly reconfigured and repurposed. In this vast interior, the ground loses its rootedness and stability, becoming a malleable plane within a constructed environment.

观测技术的进步和观念的转变已经让这个世界越来越“内部化”。人类不再站立在大地上——当我们手握地球仪，就好似化身为一个漂浮在宇宙中的巨大神灵，而地球变成了一个易于把玩的物件，被我们尽收眼底。远方消失了，地球上的事物似乎都被打上了已知或可知的烙印。

费茨利对地面的转化，揭示了从外部性到内部性的深刻转变。地板作为一种表面，属于一个受控的环境，与自然世界大有不同。费茨利使用的乙烯基材料暗示了这种内在化的过程，外部世界被吸收进了一个不断扩展的内部领域。现代材料如混凝土、钢铁和玻璃，促成了购物中心、赌场、机场等大型结构的建造，这些结构创造了高度受控的内部空间。乙烯基材料尤其值得注意，它广泛用于替代天然材料如木材或大理石，因其成本低、耐用性强、图案丰富。虽然它模仿了天然材料的图案，但在表面图案的重复中可以发现其人工性质，这种人工性与费茨利捕捉的消费主义图像的重复性产生了共鸣。地面，曾经象征着自然与无控制的力量，现在被地板取代，成为一个可以被无休止地重新配置和再利用的平面。在这个巨大的内部空间中，地面失去了作为扎根感或稳定性的象征，转而成为一个可塑的平面，化身为被构建的环境的一部分。

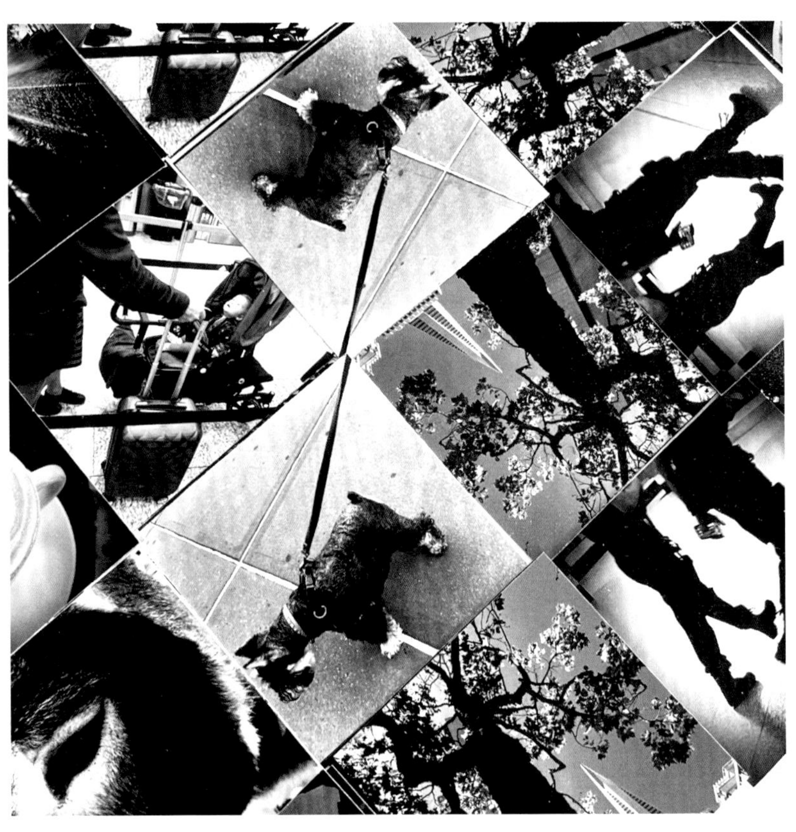

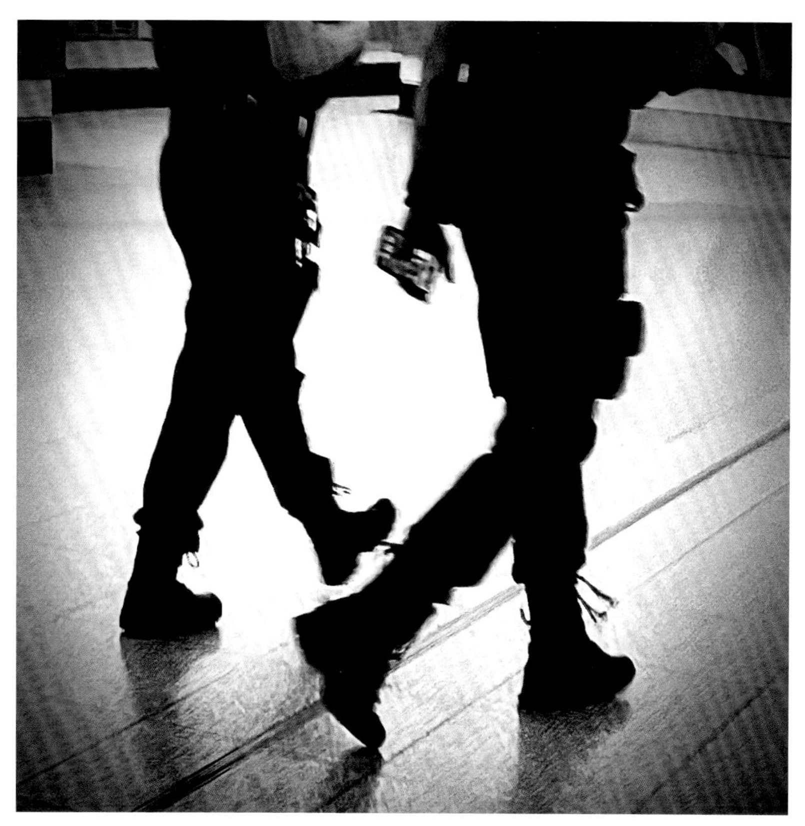

The Letter M

字母M

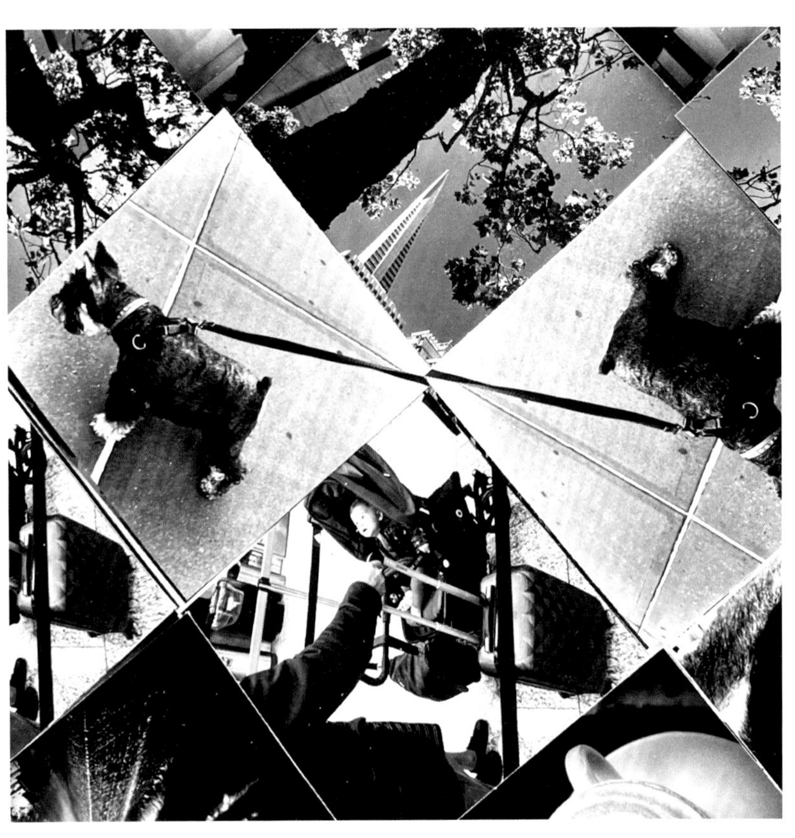

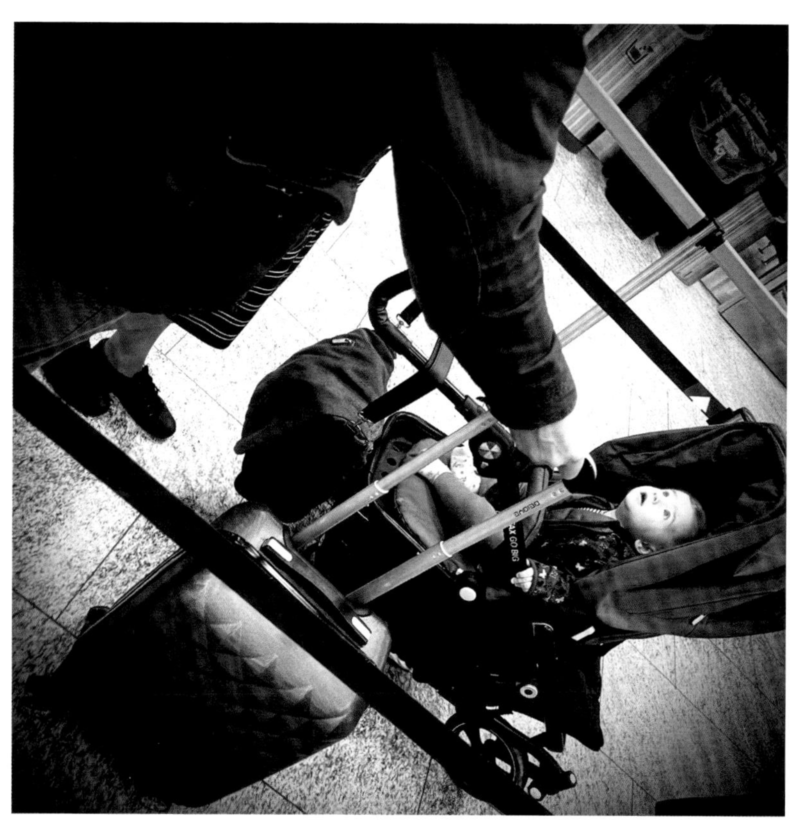

Miracle

奇迹

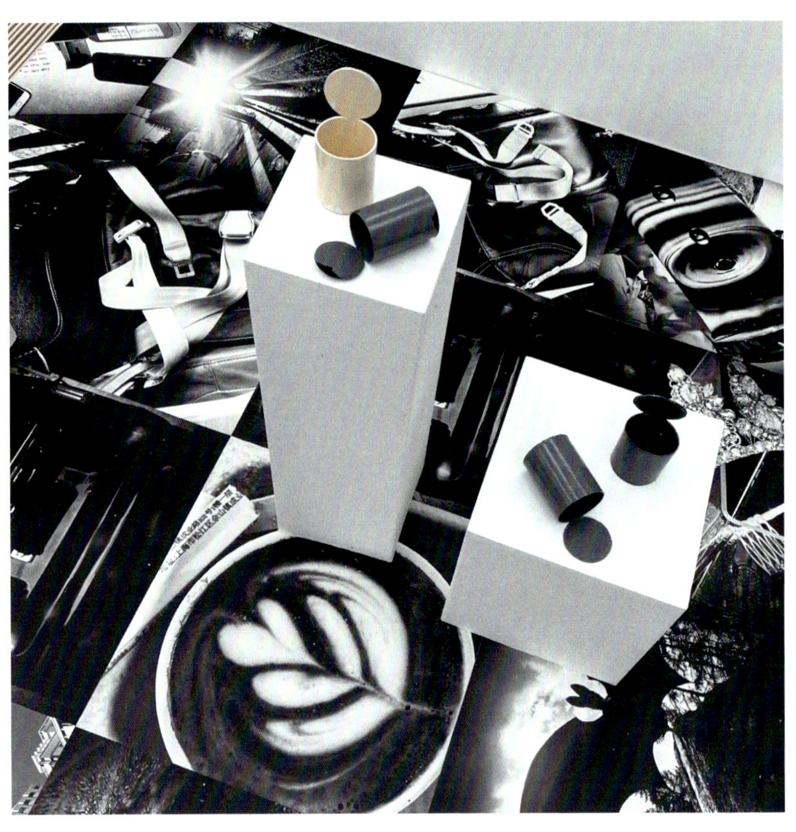

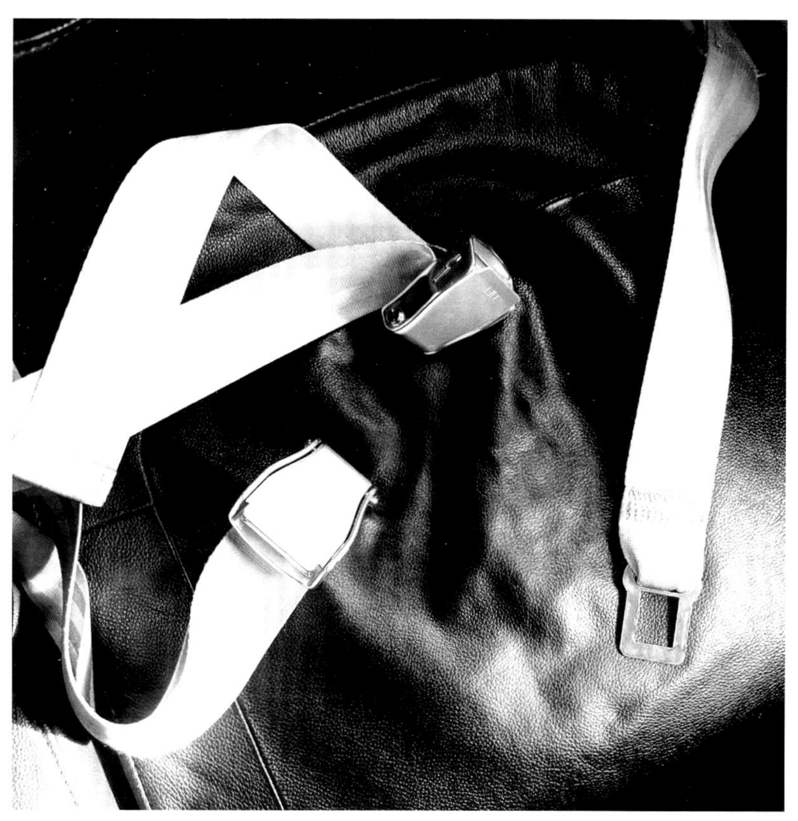

Outline

轮廓

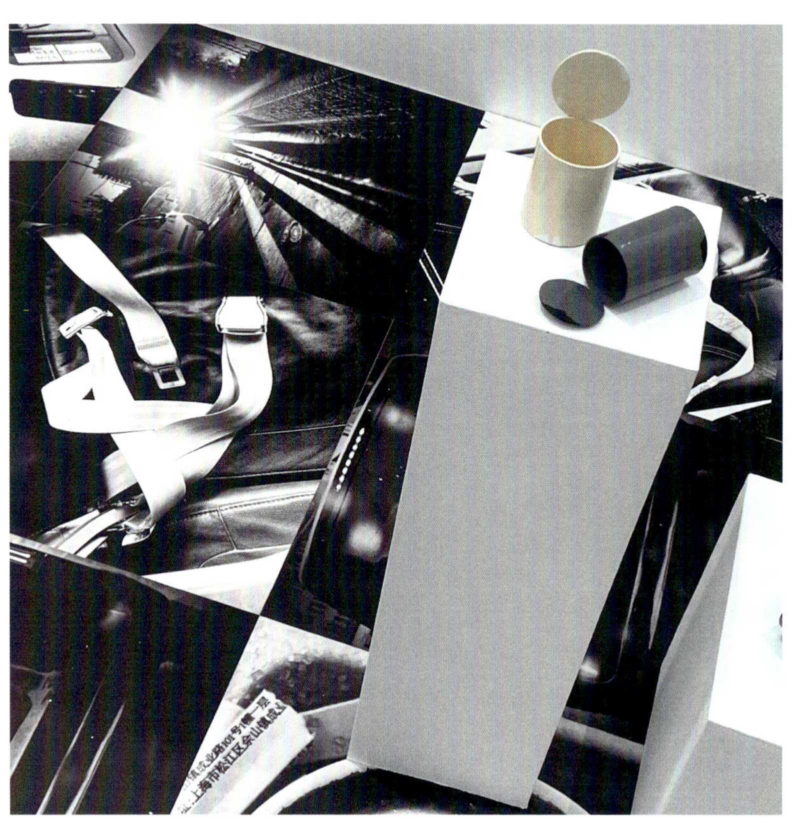

成业路101号
上海市松江区佘山镇

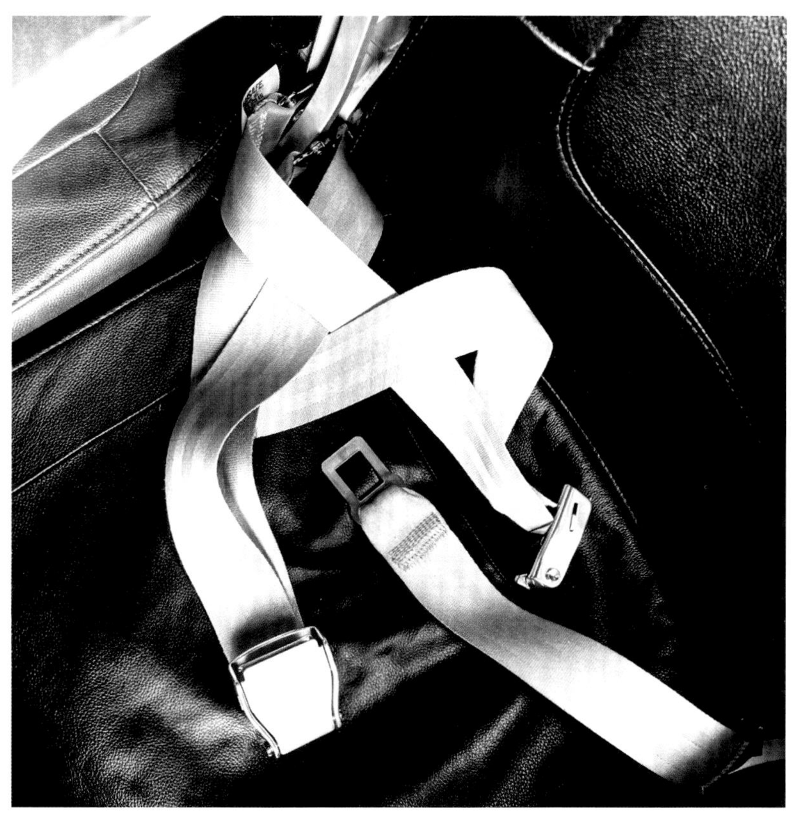

Futureproof

未来保证

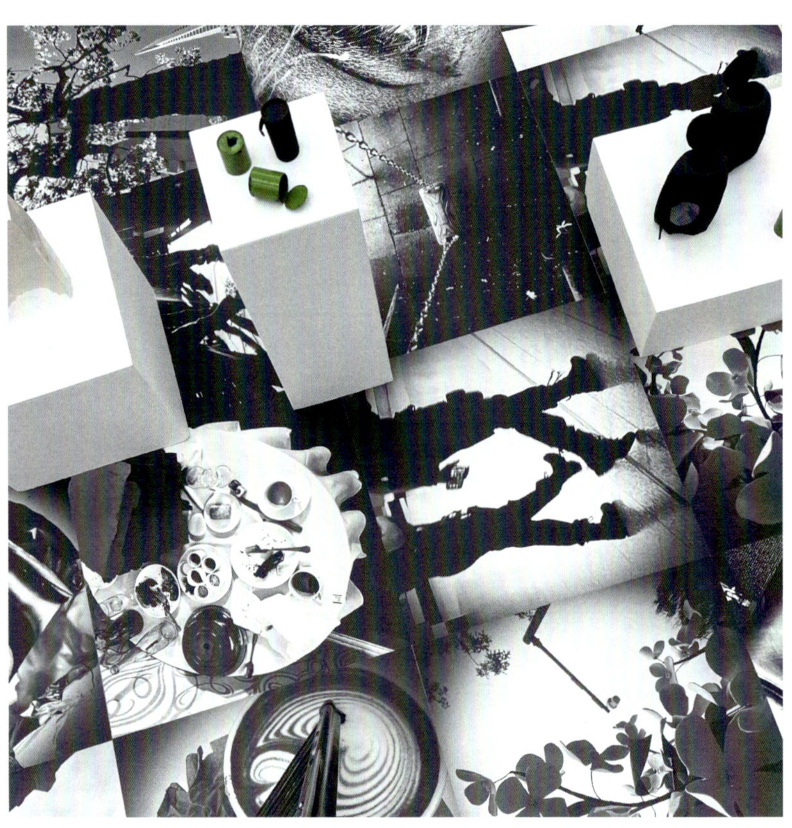

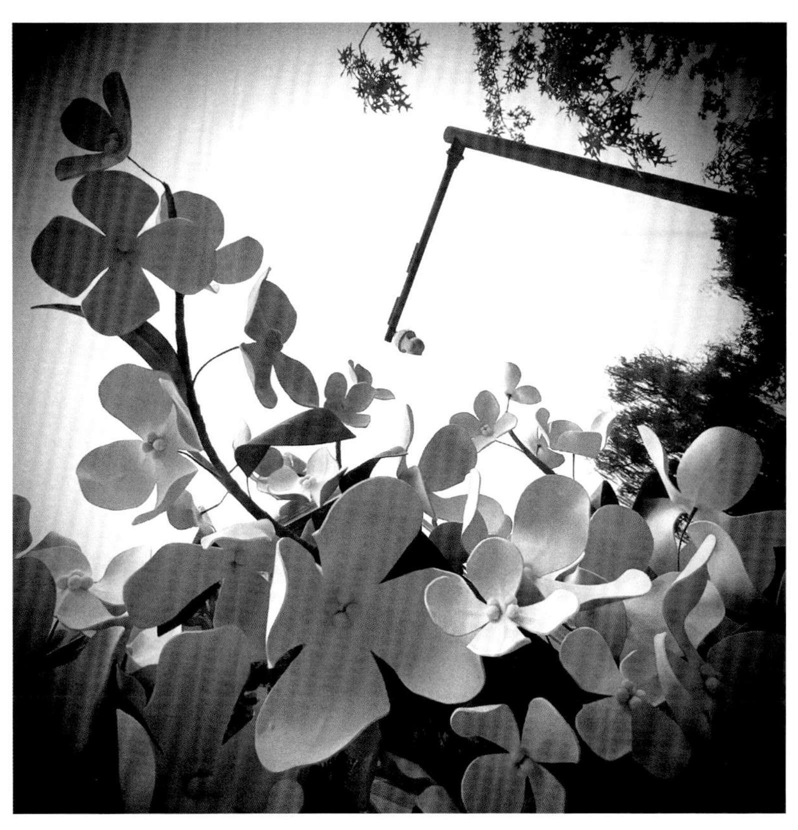

Zigzagging

之字形

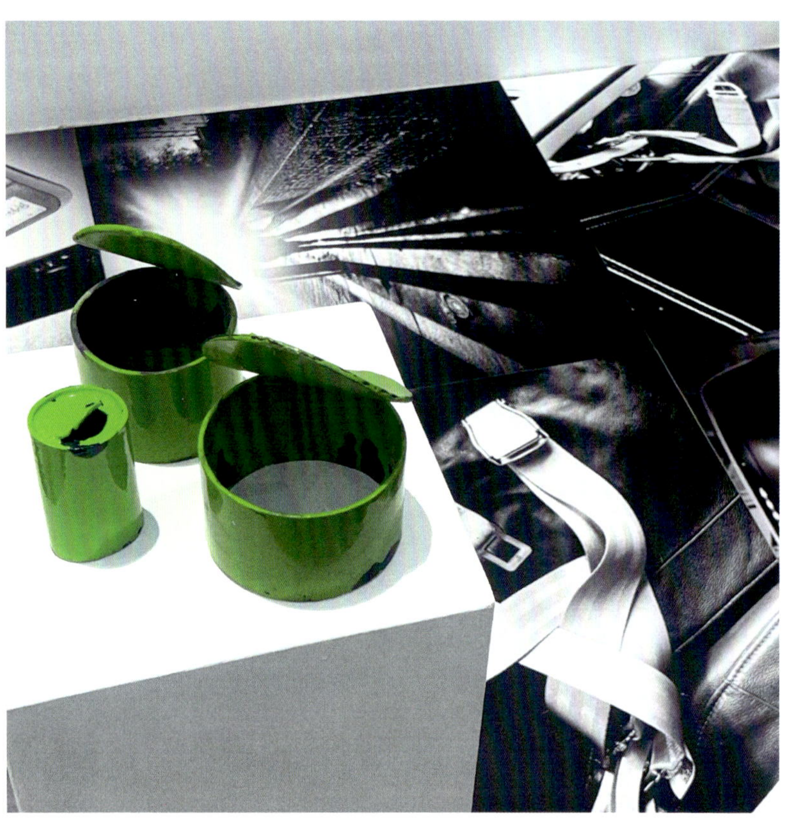

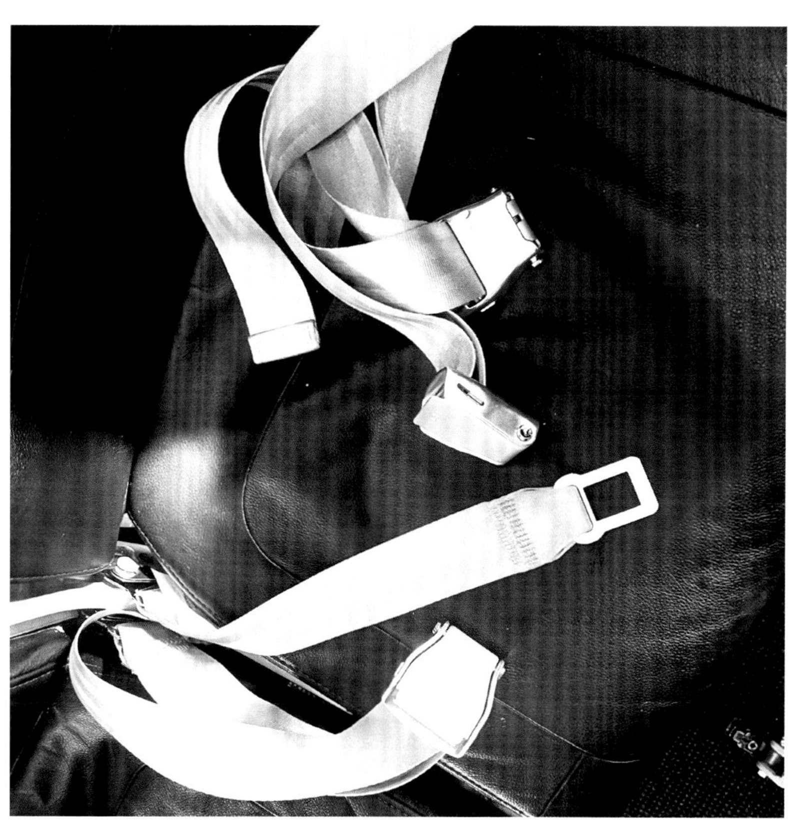

Trading Secrets

交易秘密

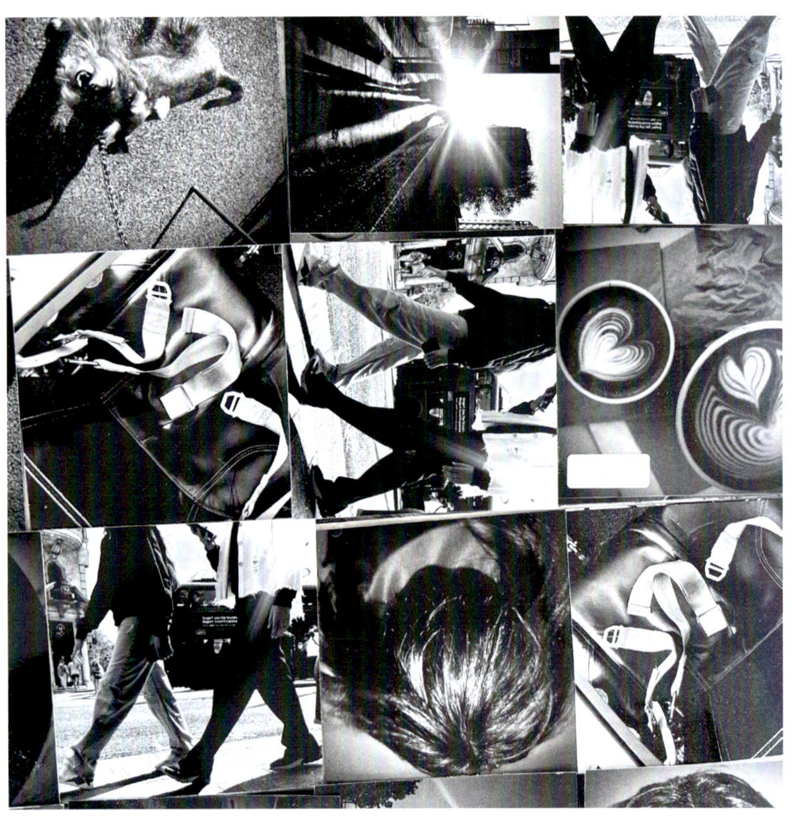

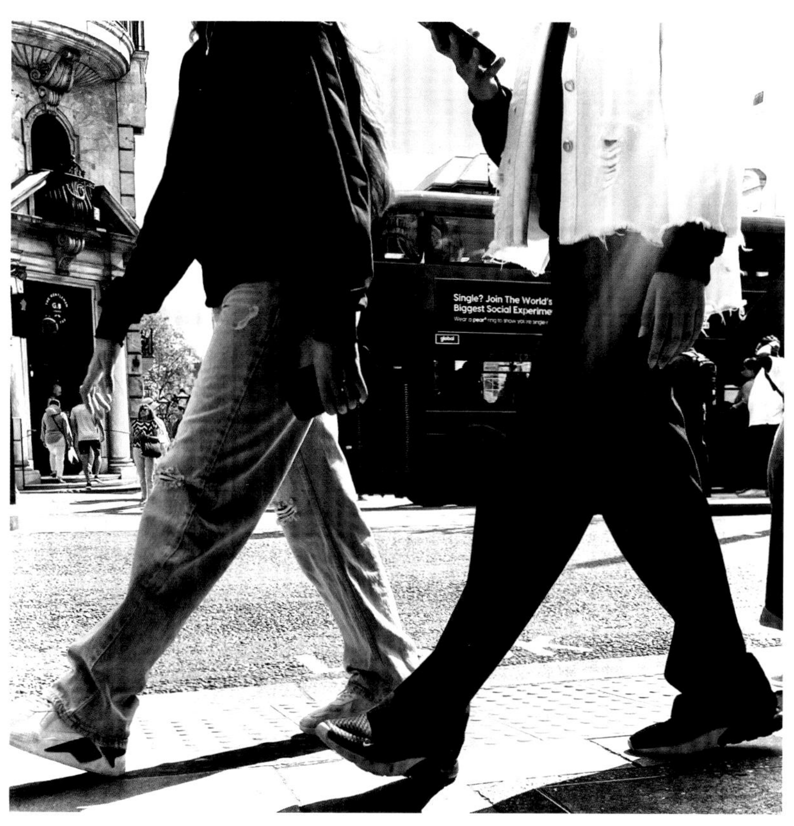

Join the World

加入世界

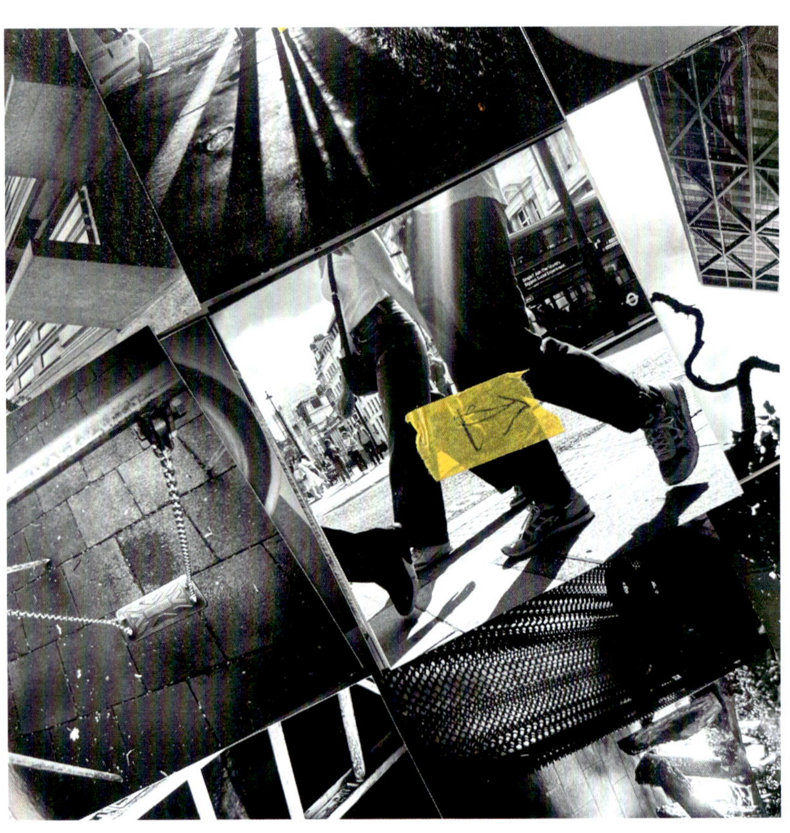

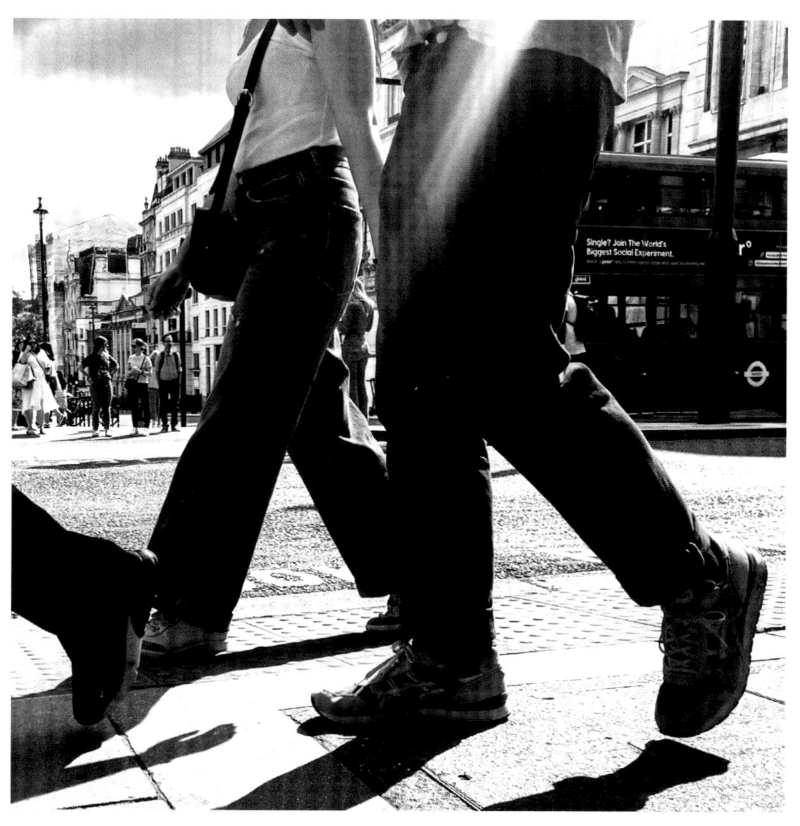

Social Experiment

社会实验

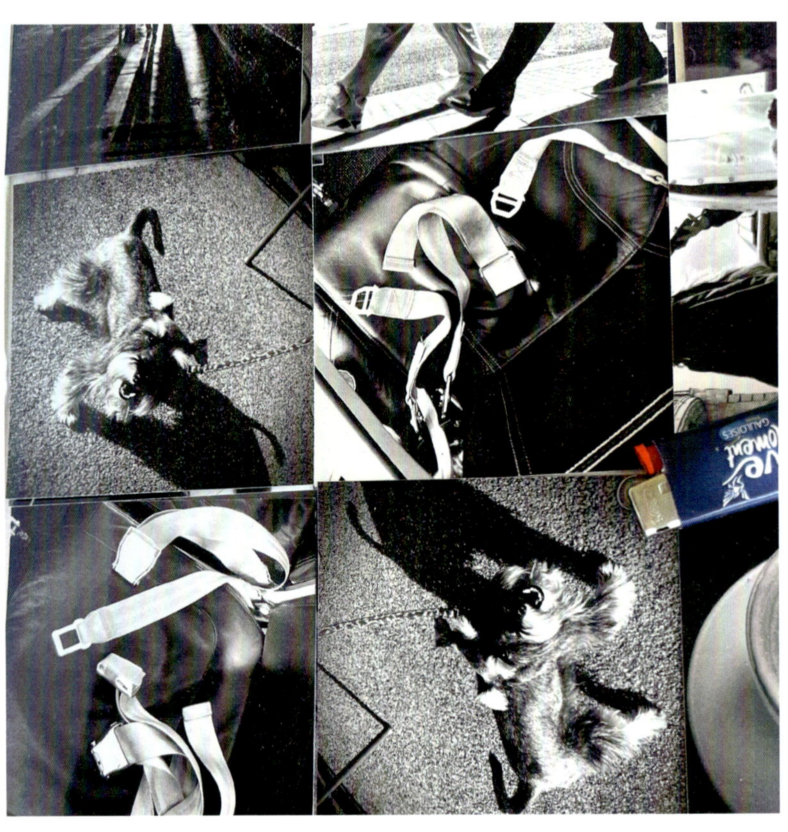
GAULOISES

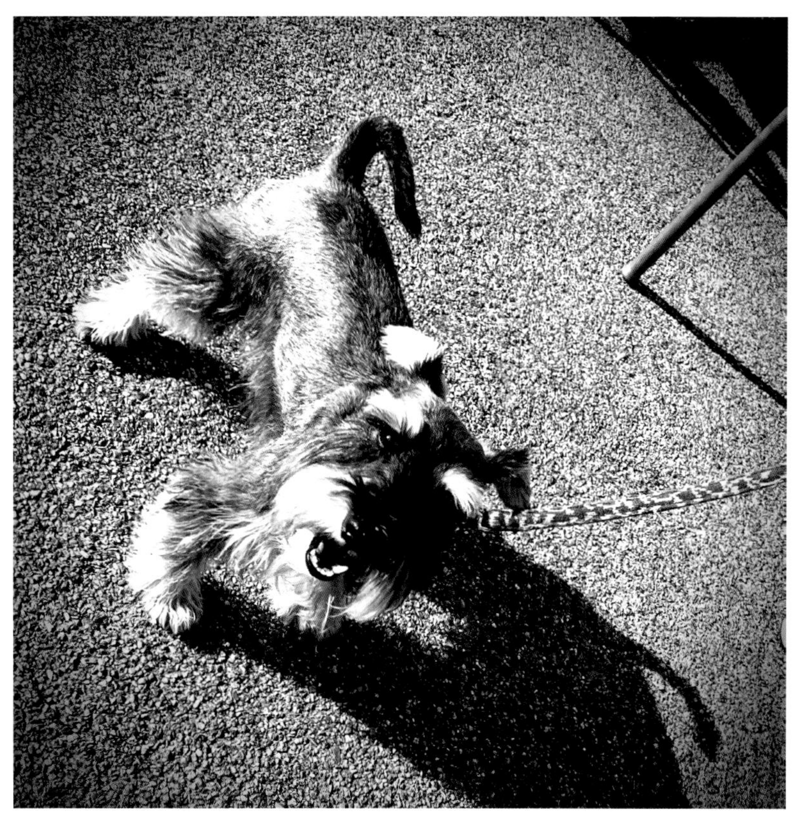

Jack

杰克

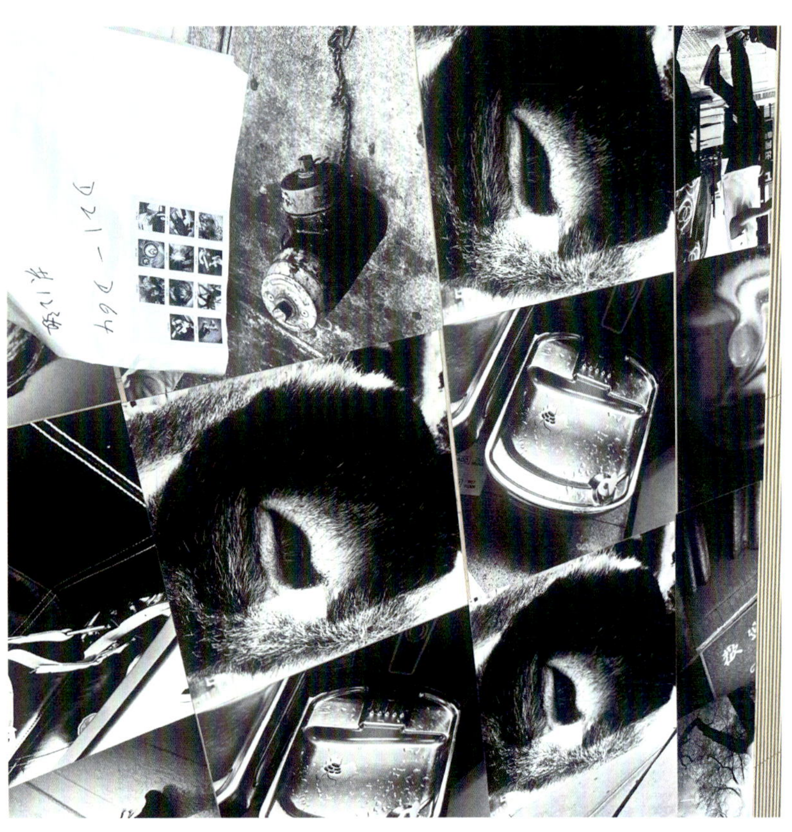

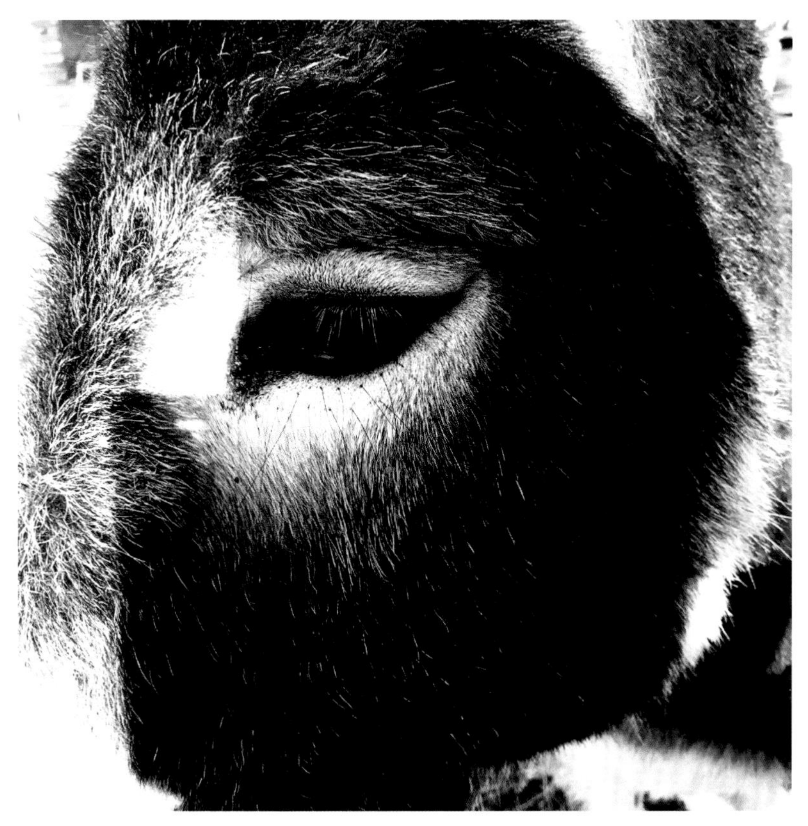

The Oracle

神谕者

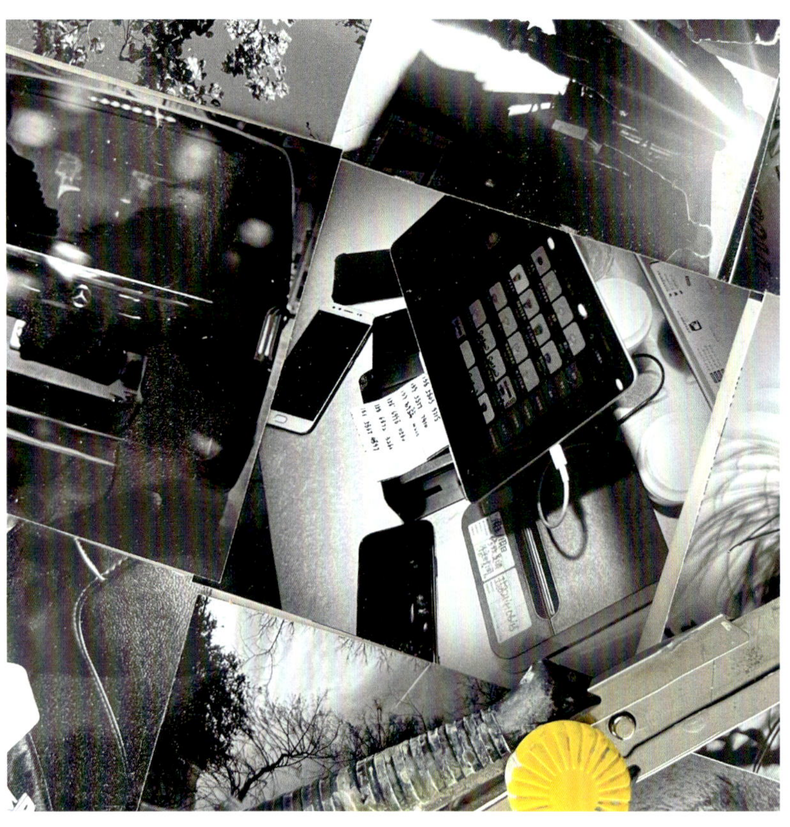

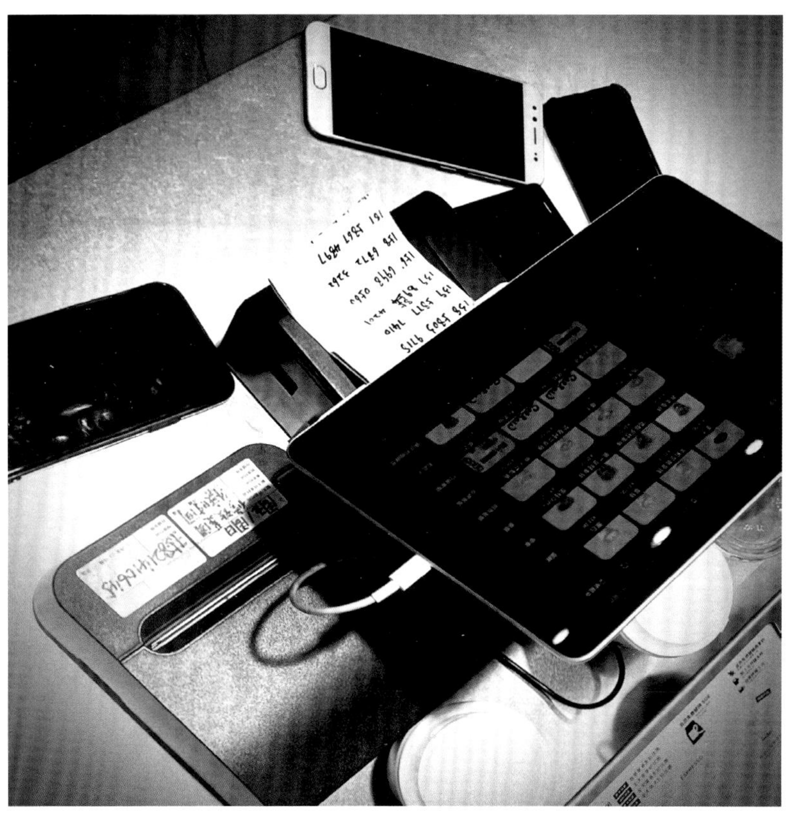

The Power of Unfair Advantage

不公平优势的力量

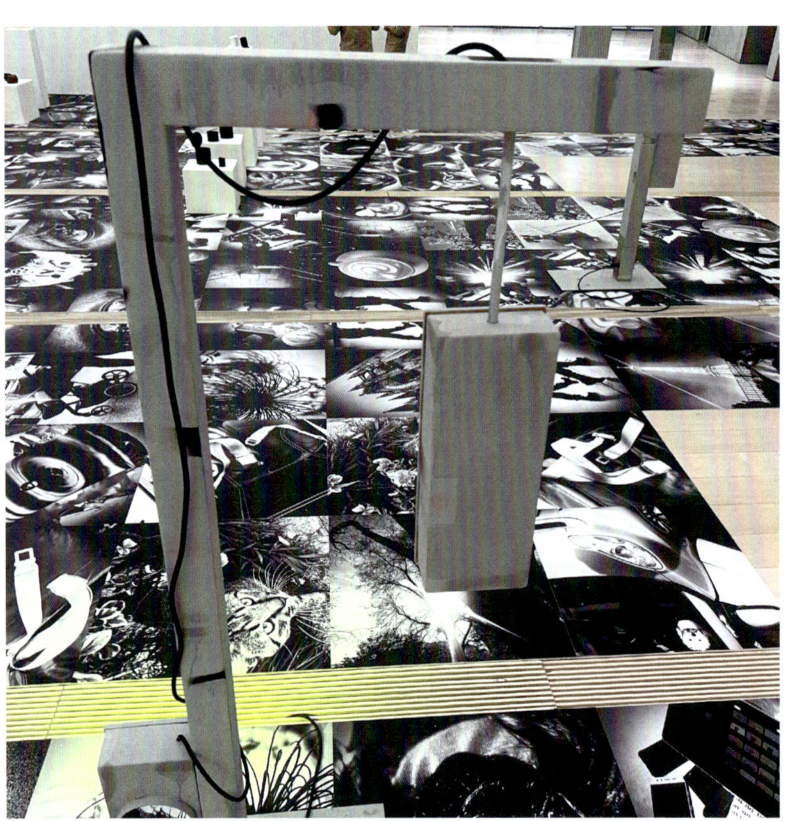

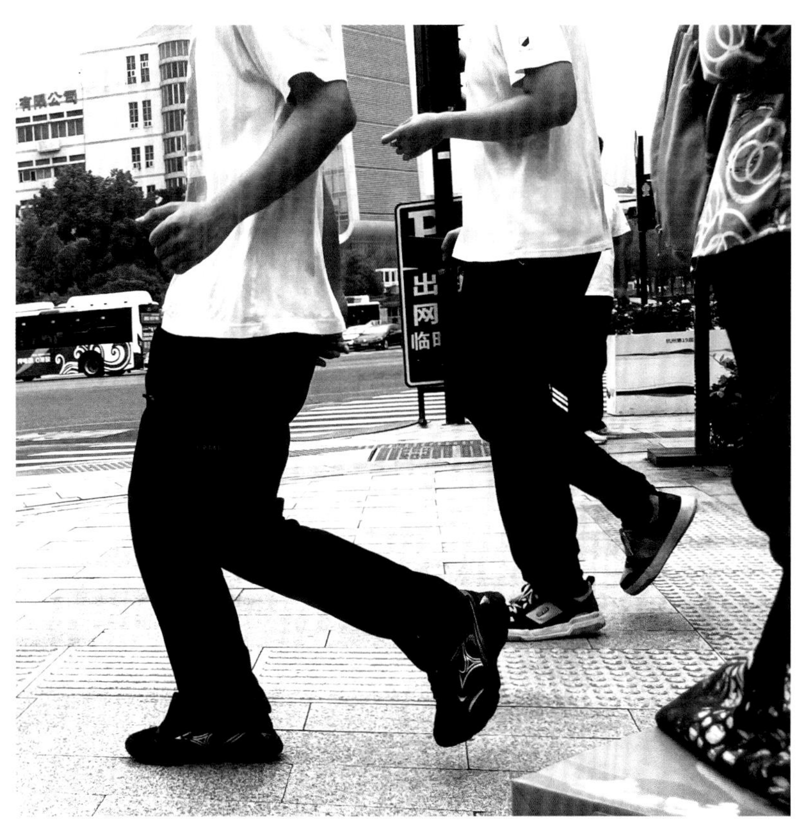

Experiment

实验

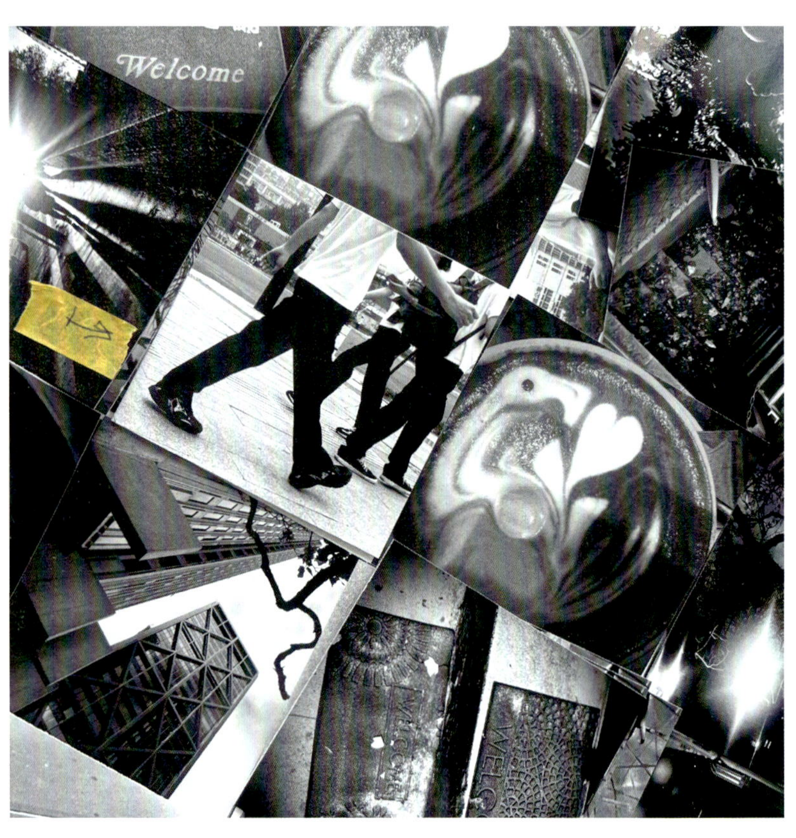
Welcome

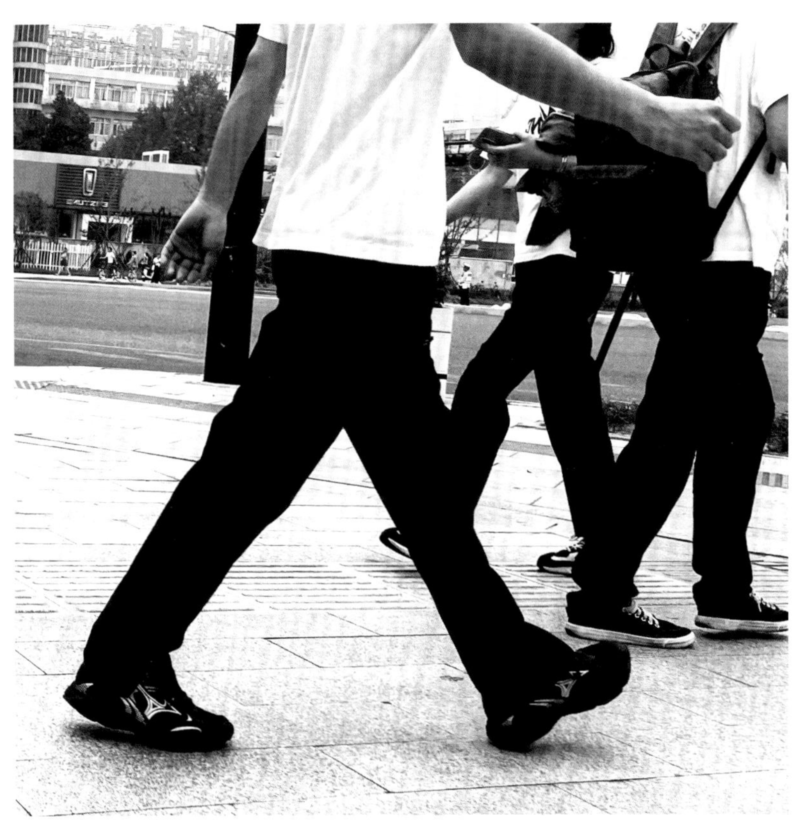

Alphabet

字母表

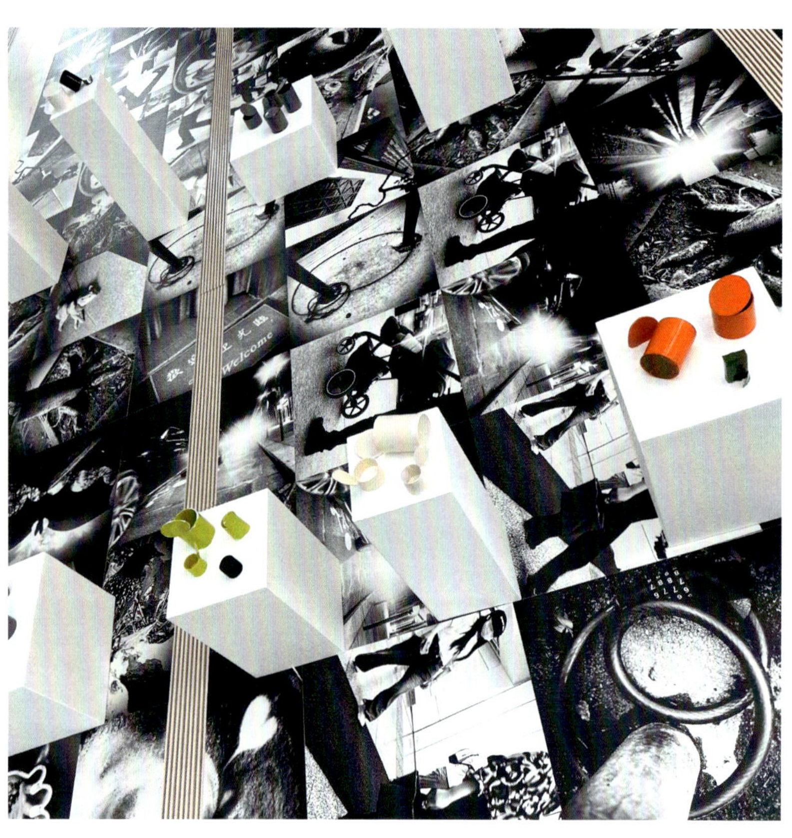
Welcome

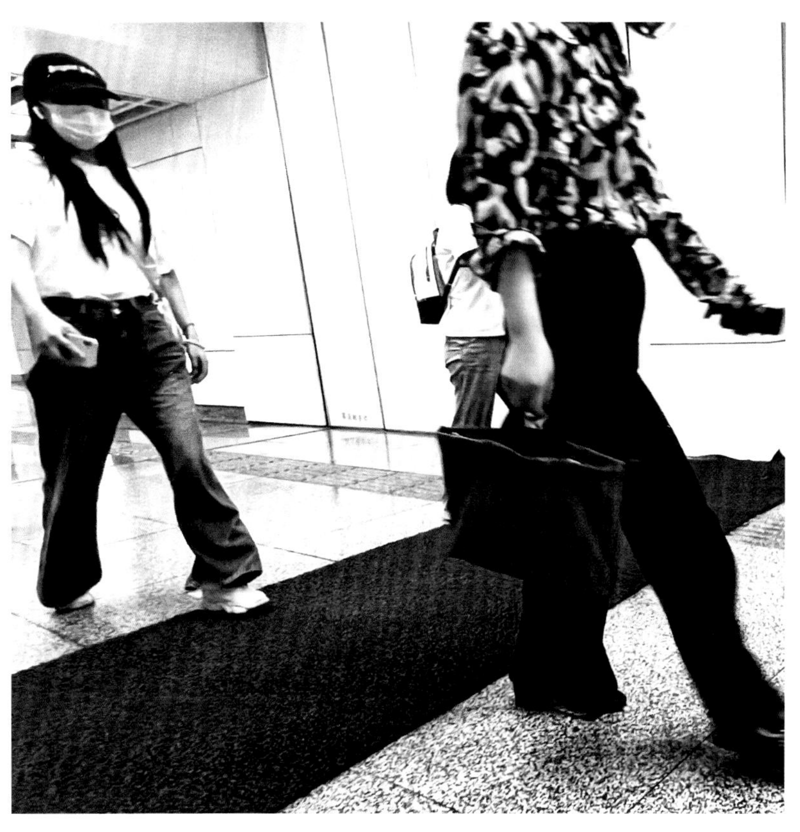

My Favourite

我的最爱

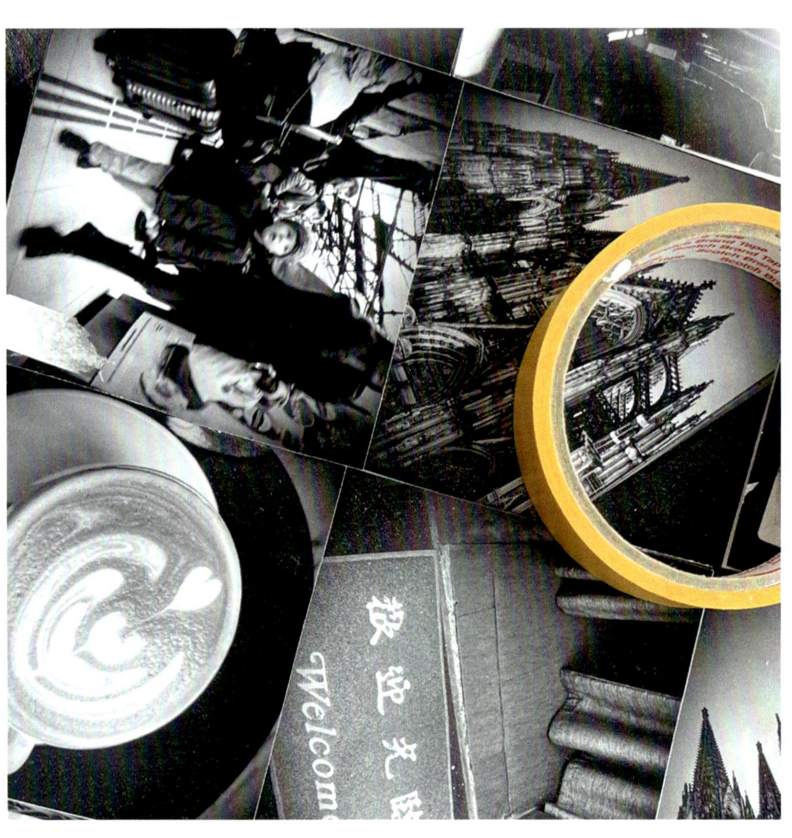
欢迎光
Welcom

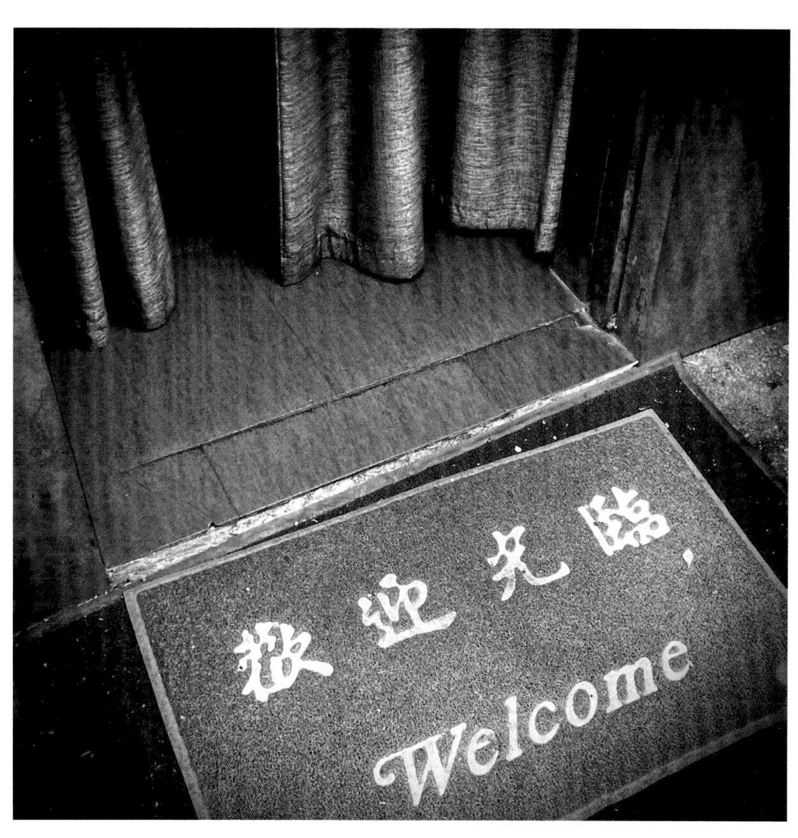

Moon

月亮

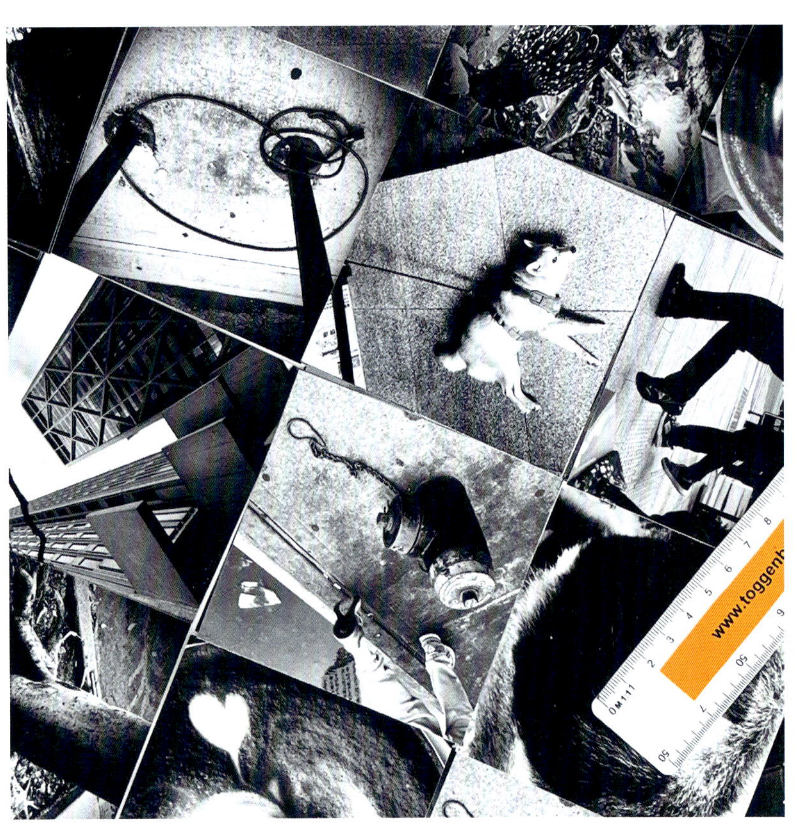

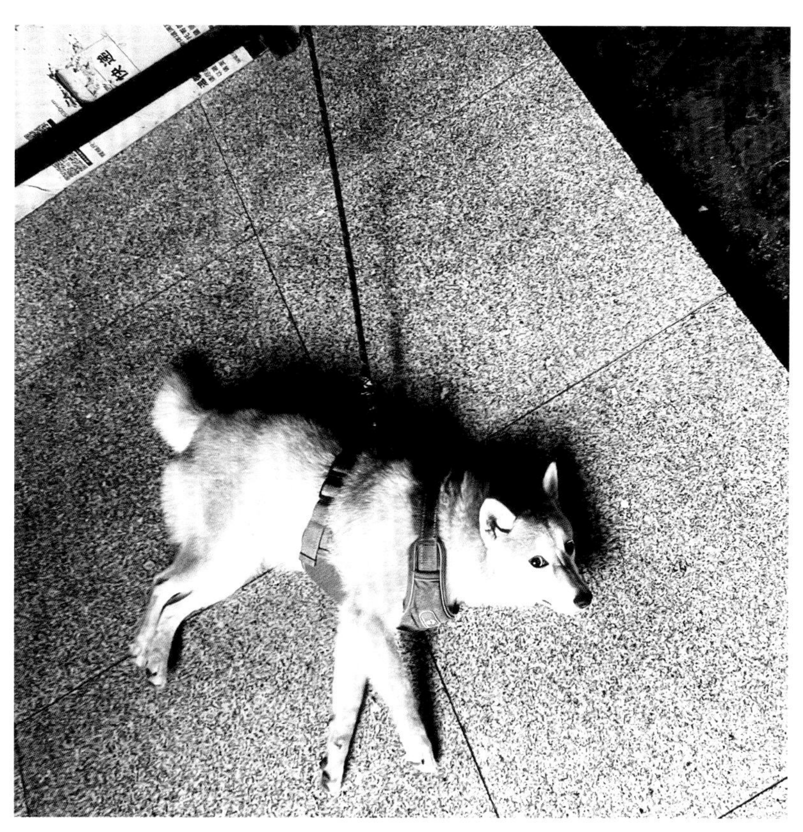

Prevent and Reverse

预防与逆转

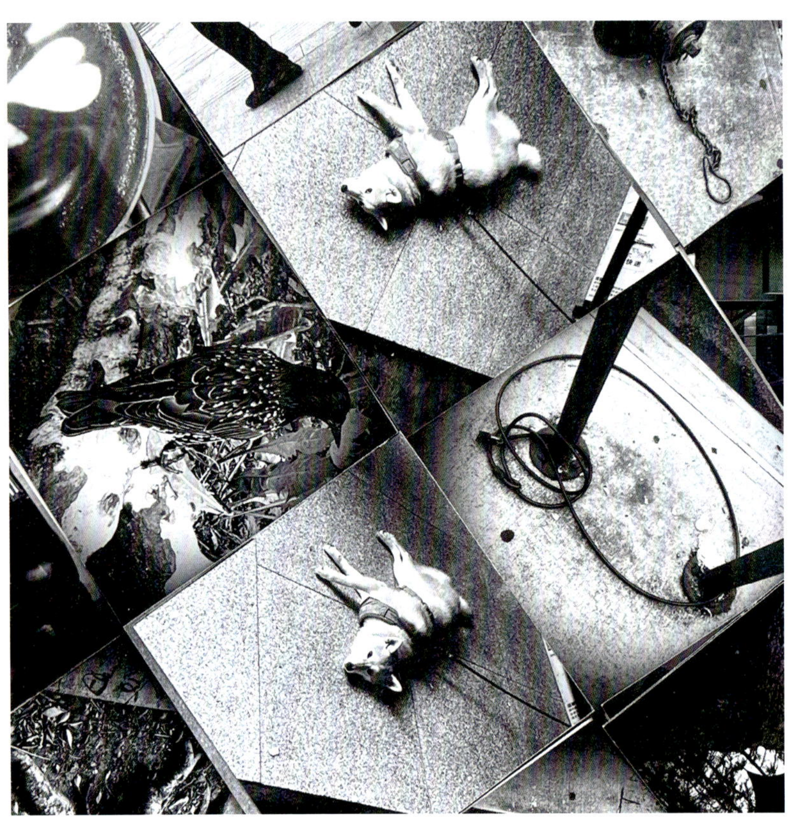

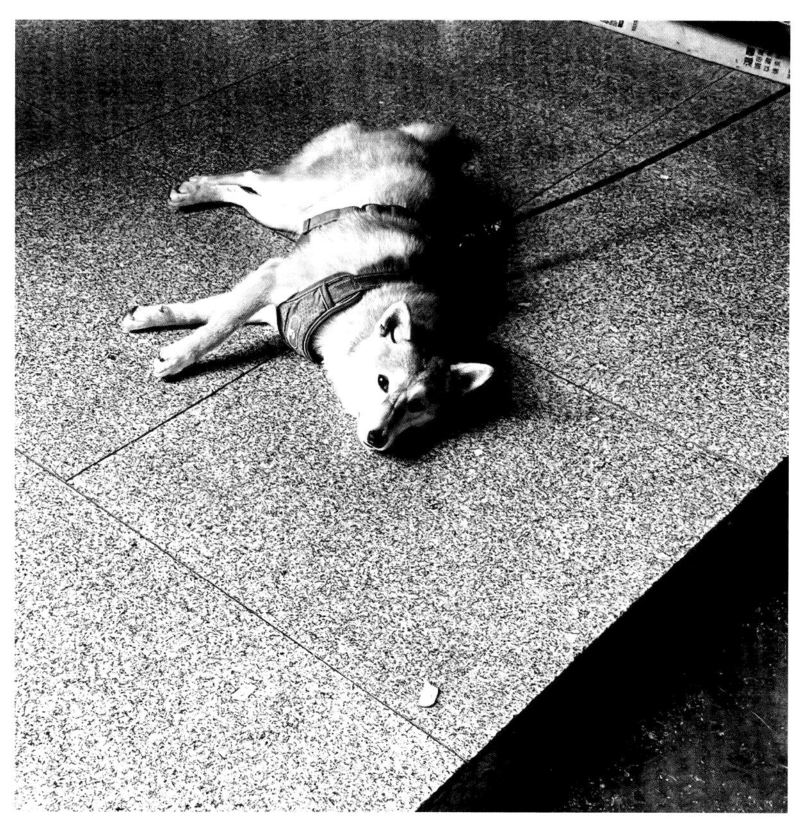

Zodiac Sign

星座

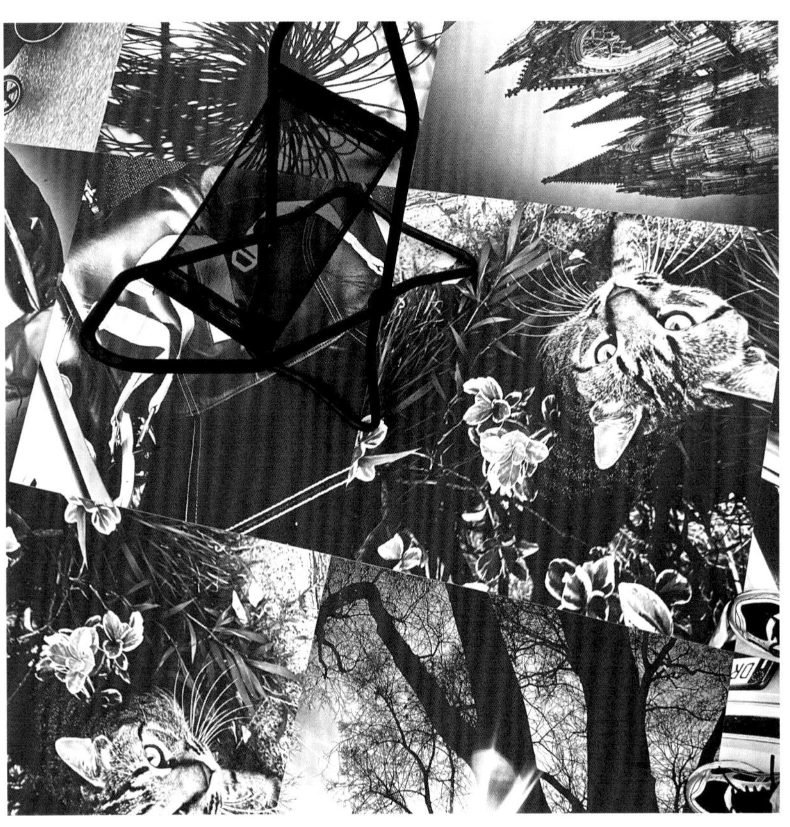

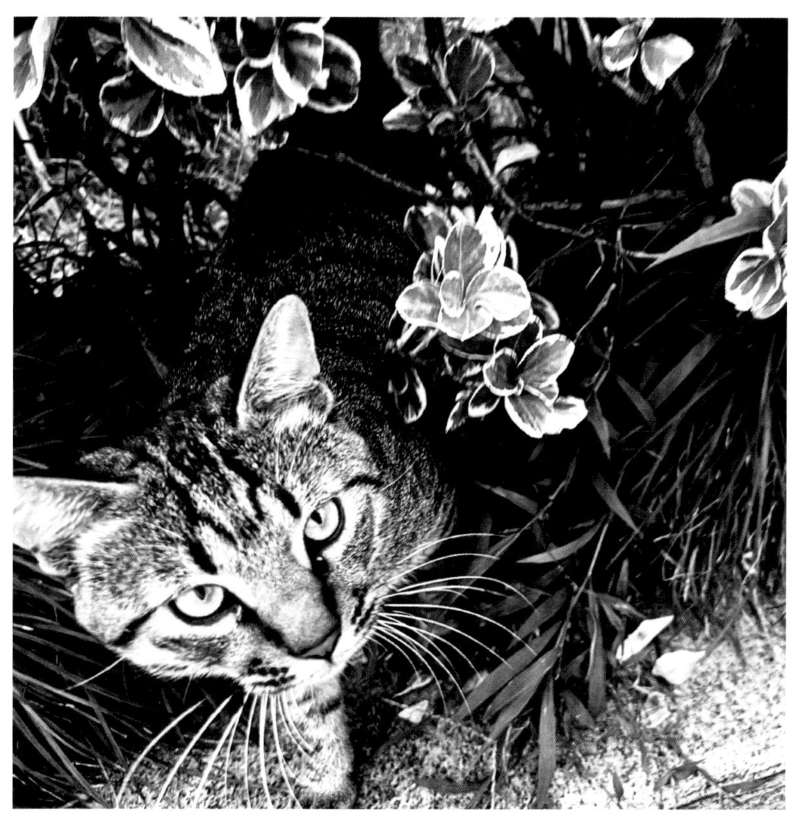

Everything

一切

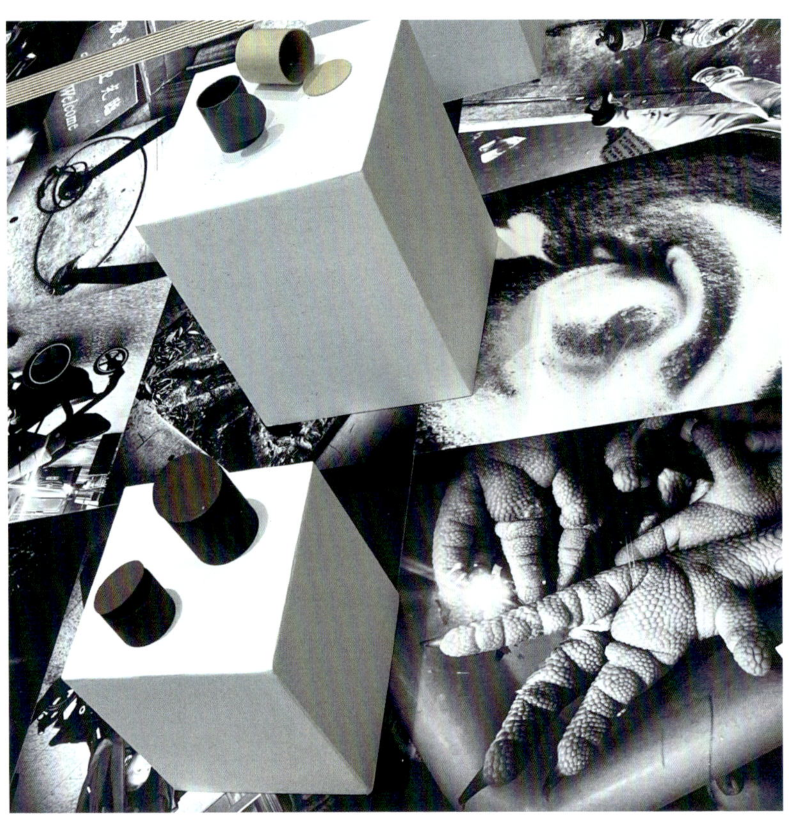
Welcome

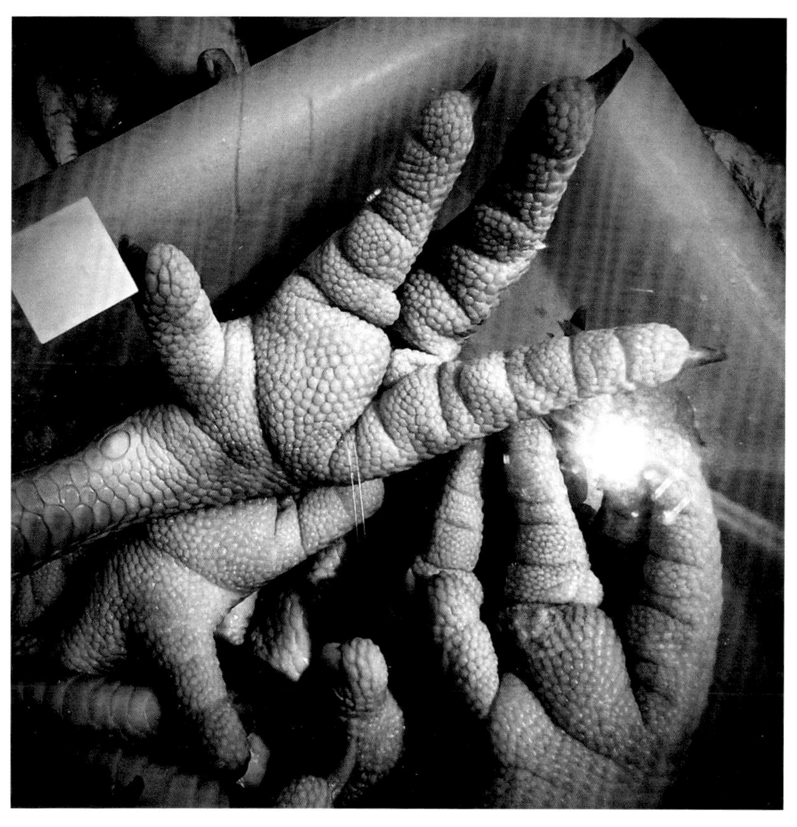

Toy

玩具

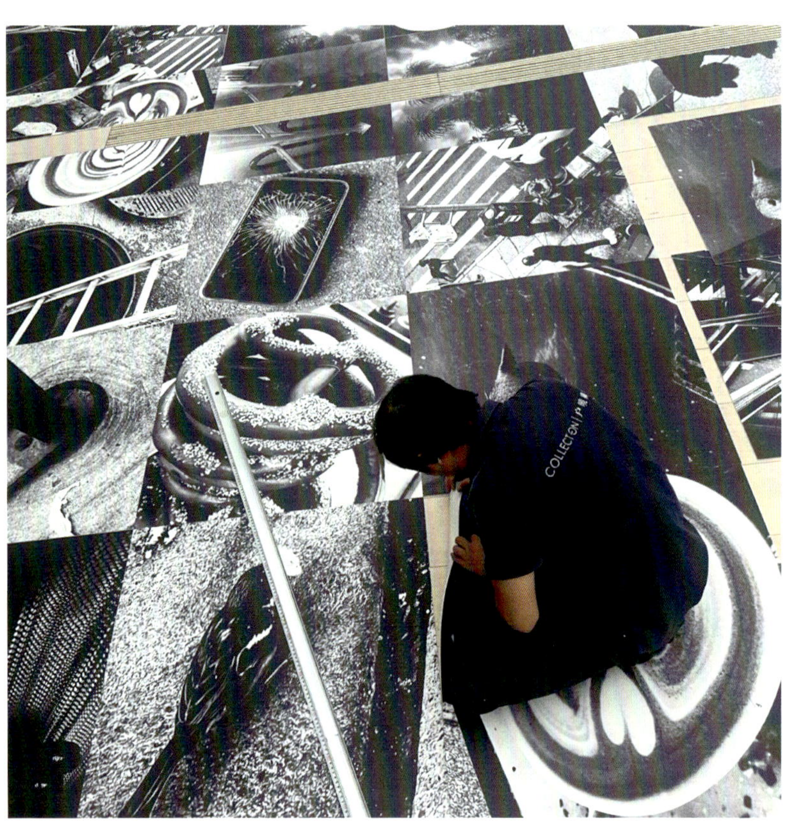
COLLECTION

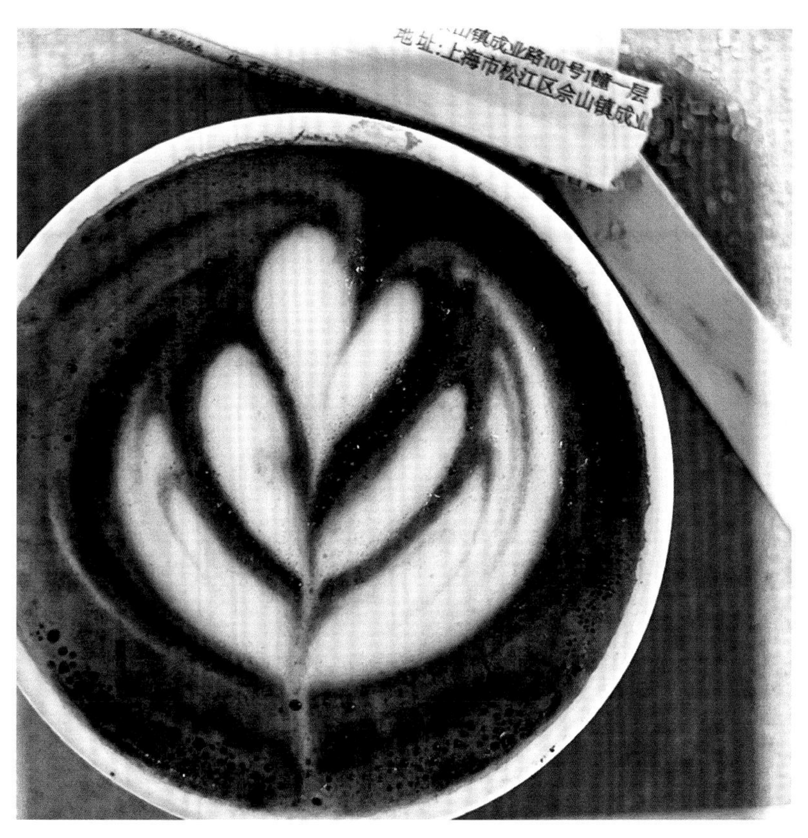

The Remarkable Truth

显著真相

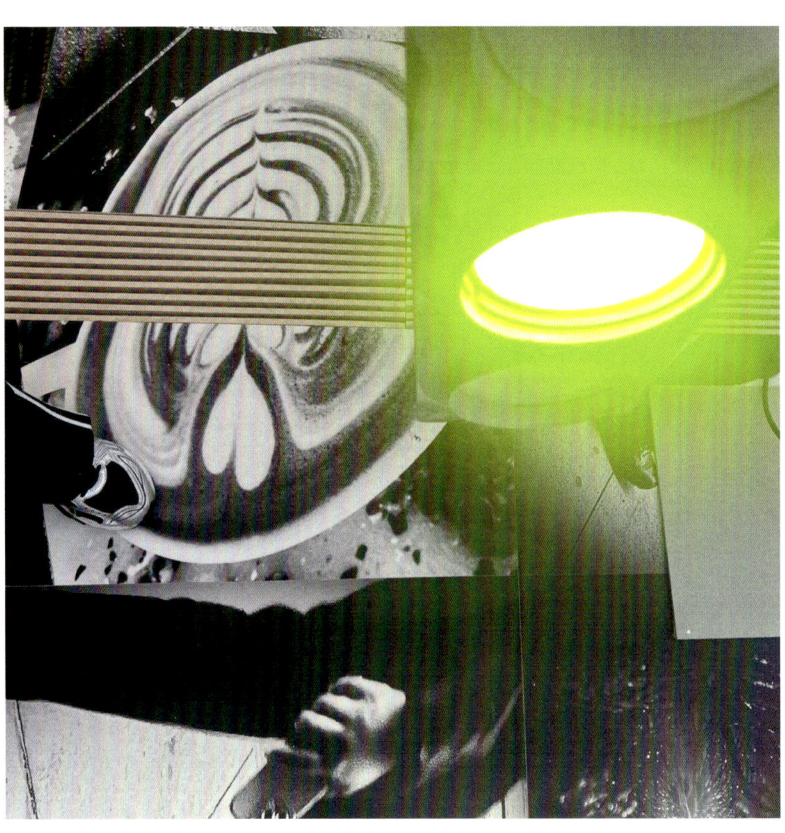

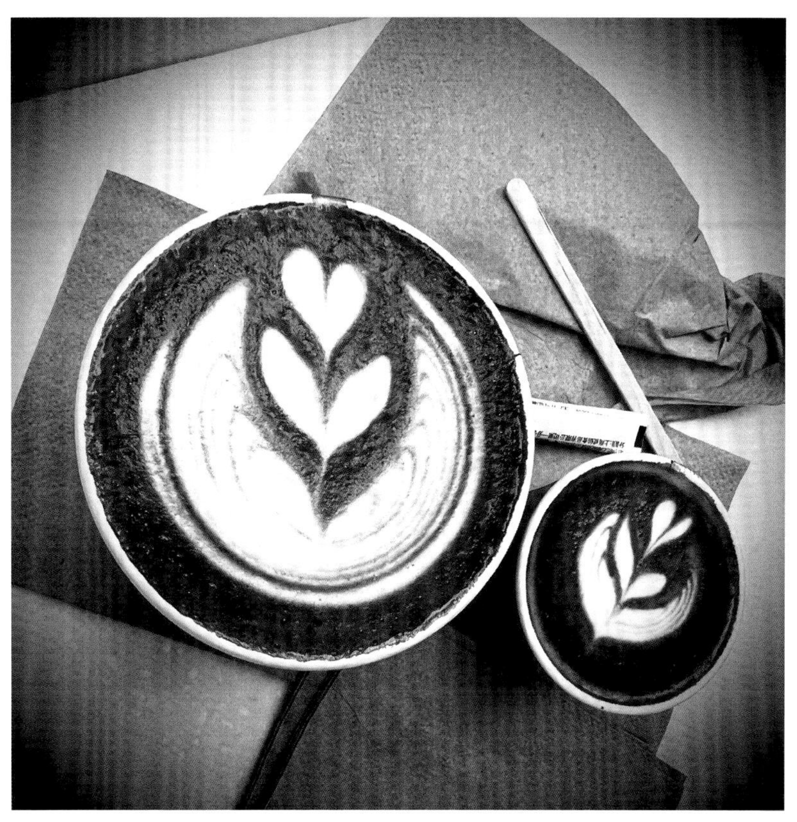

Chain Reaction

连锁反应

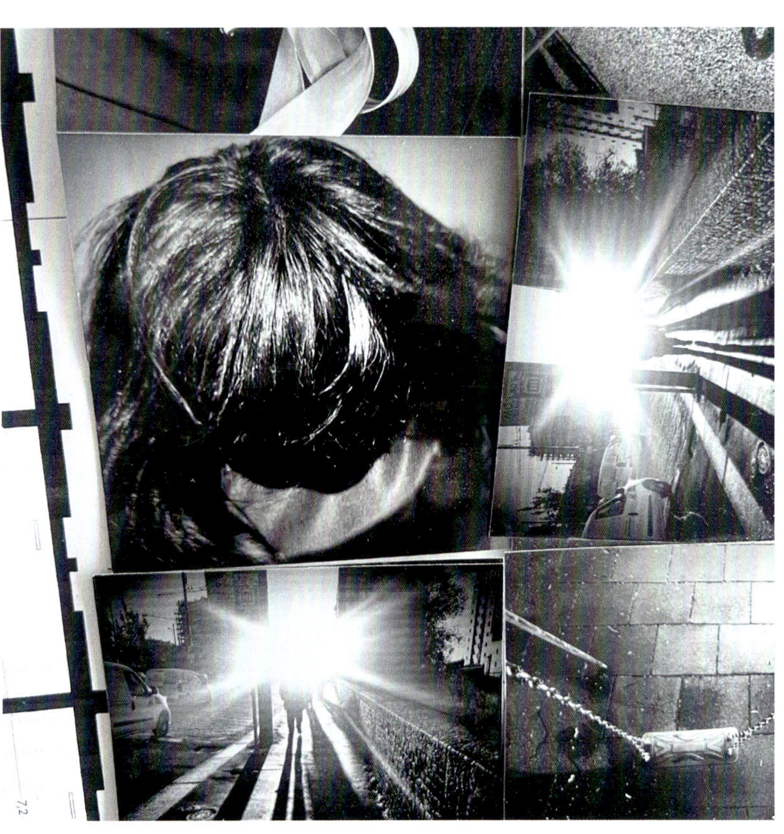

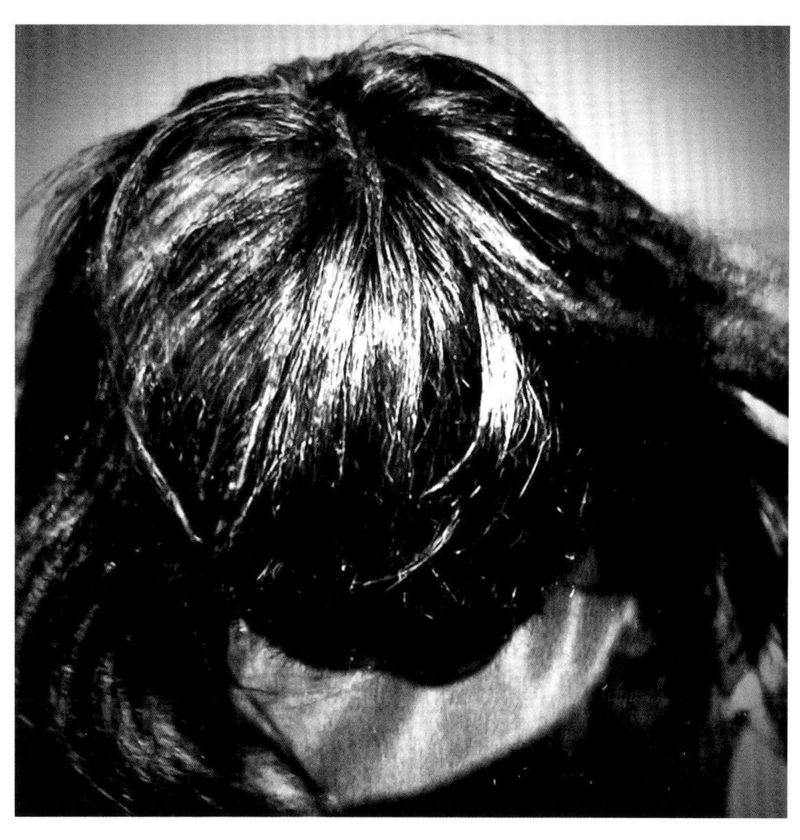

A Stolen Image

被偷的图像

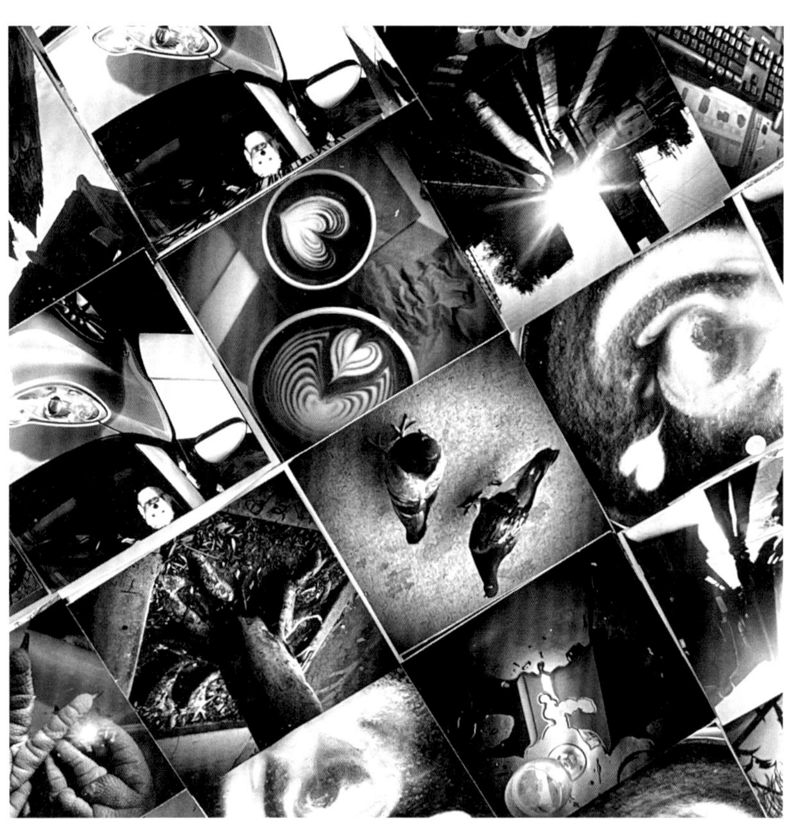

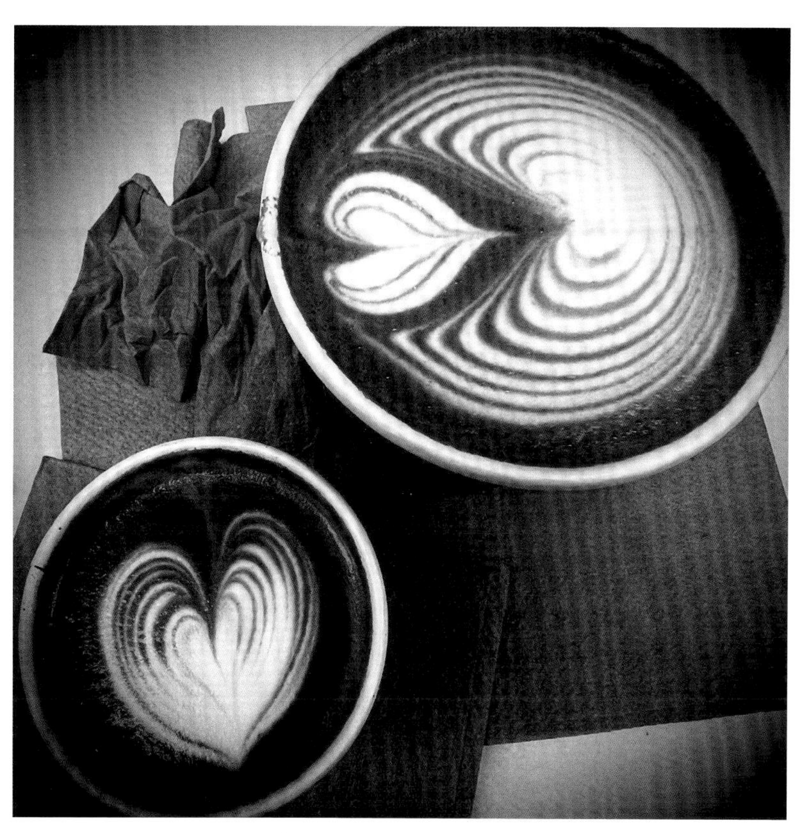

Matrix

矩阵

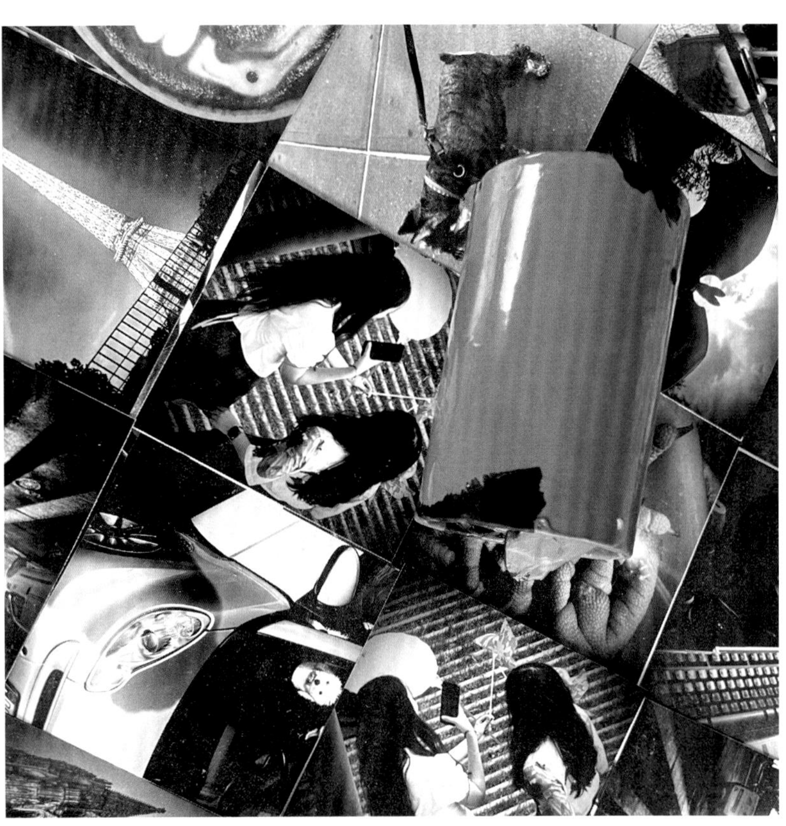

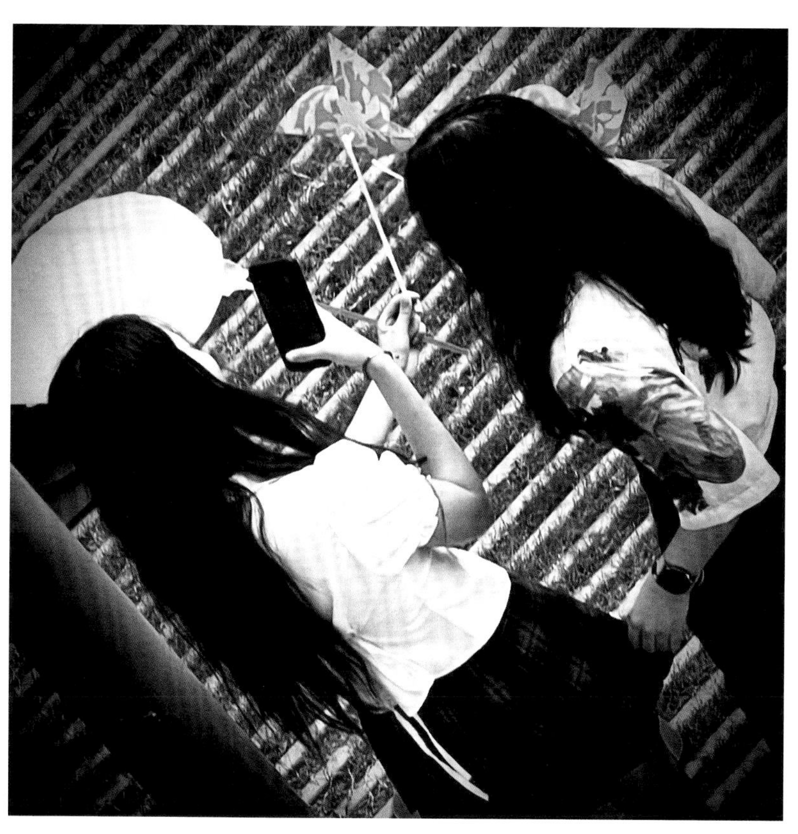

The Three Wishes

三个愿望

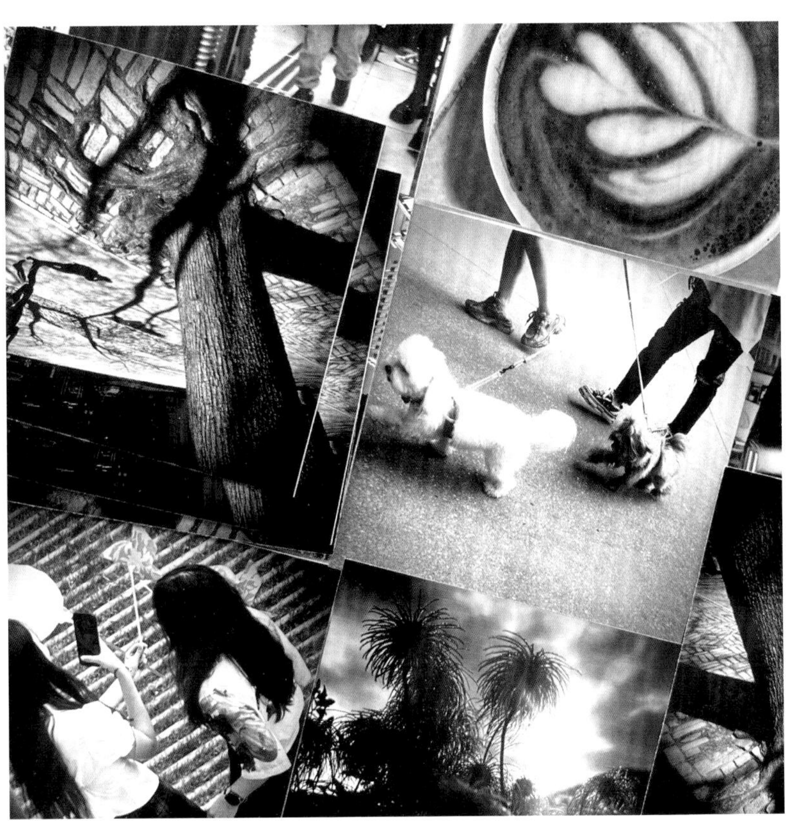

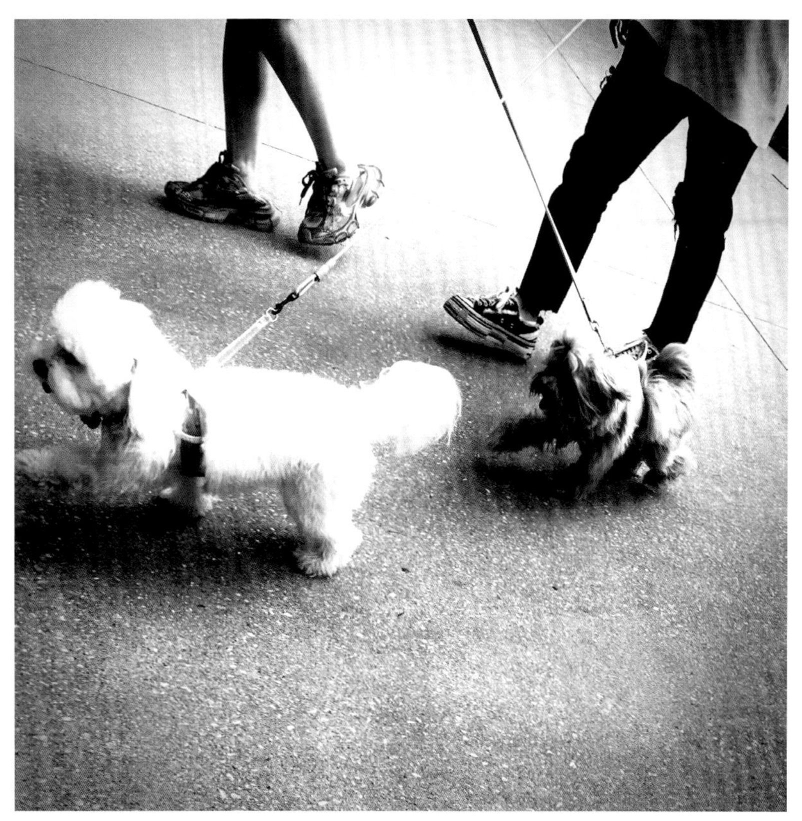

Traffic

交通

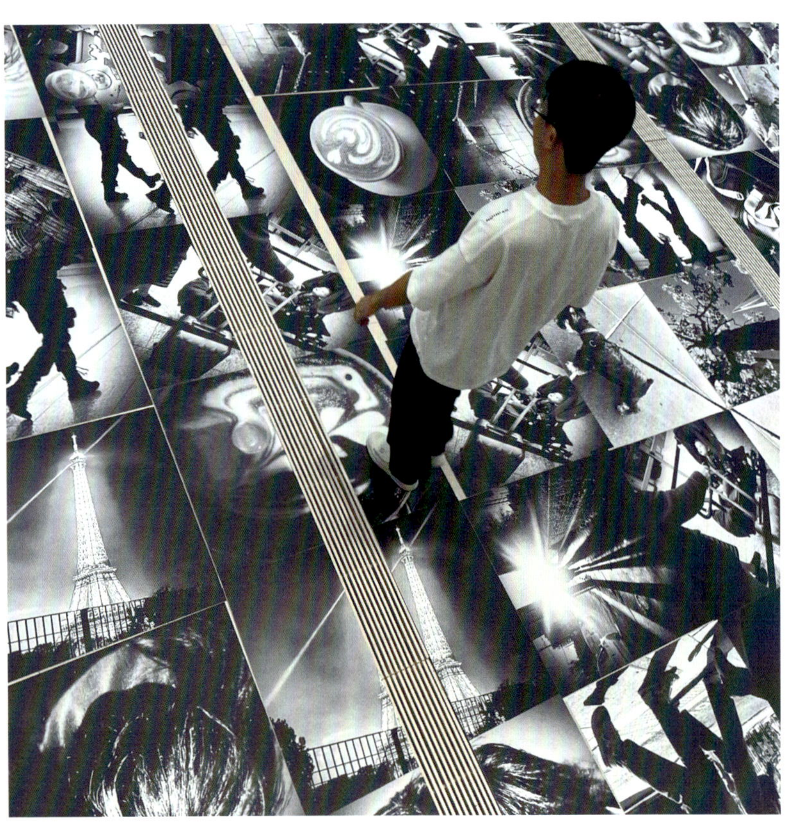

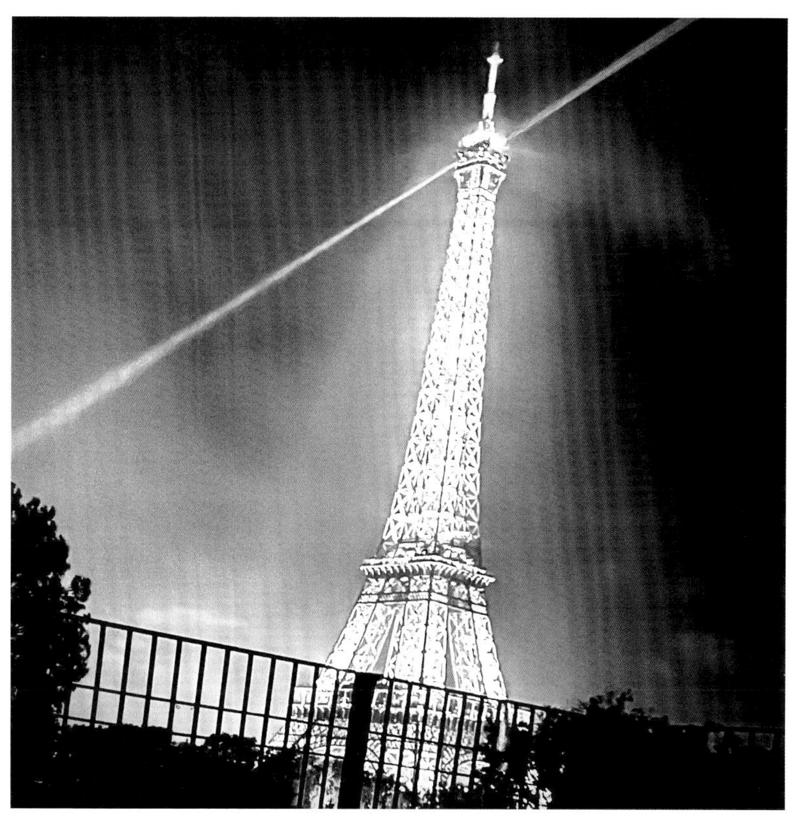

Paris

巴黎

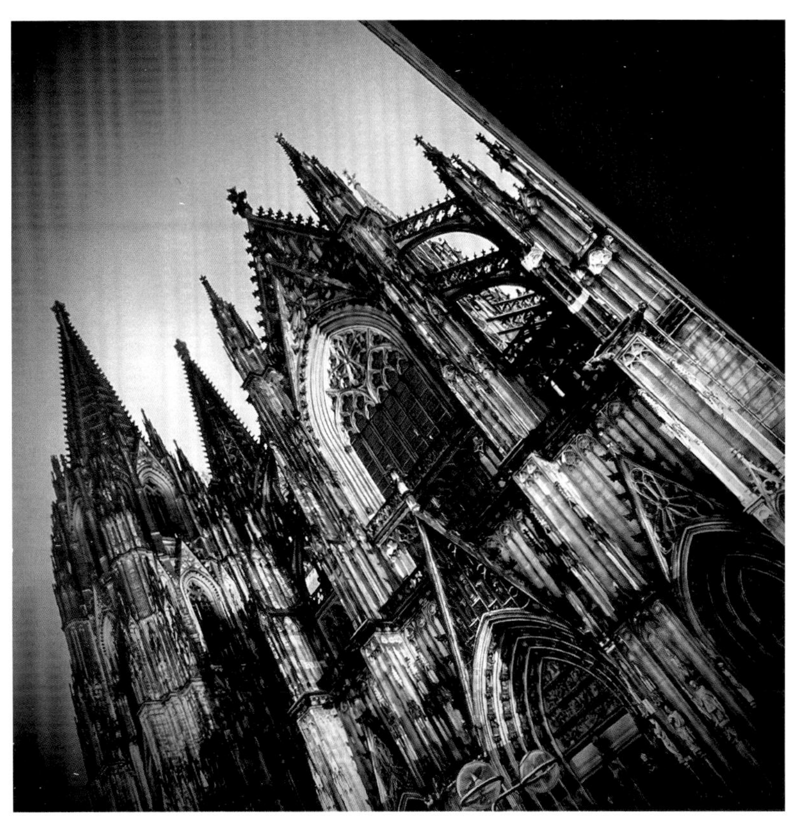

Cologne

科隆

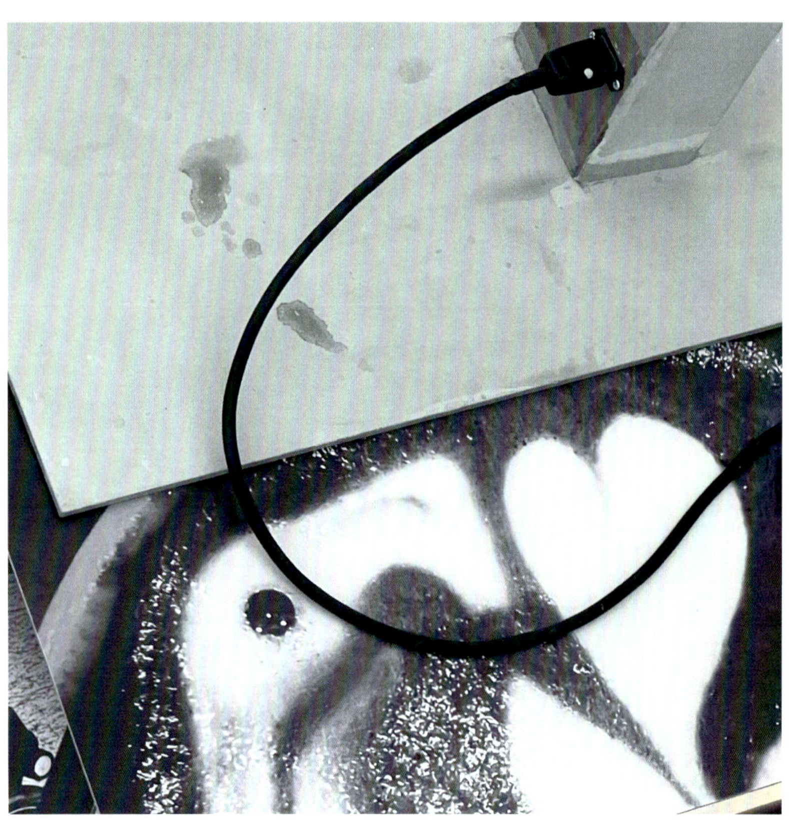

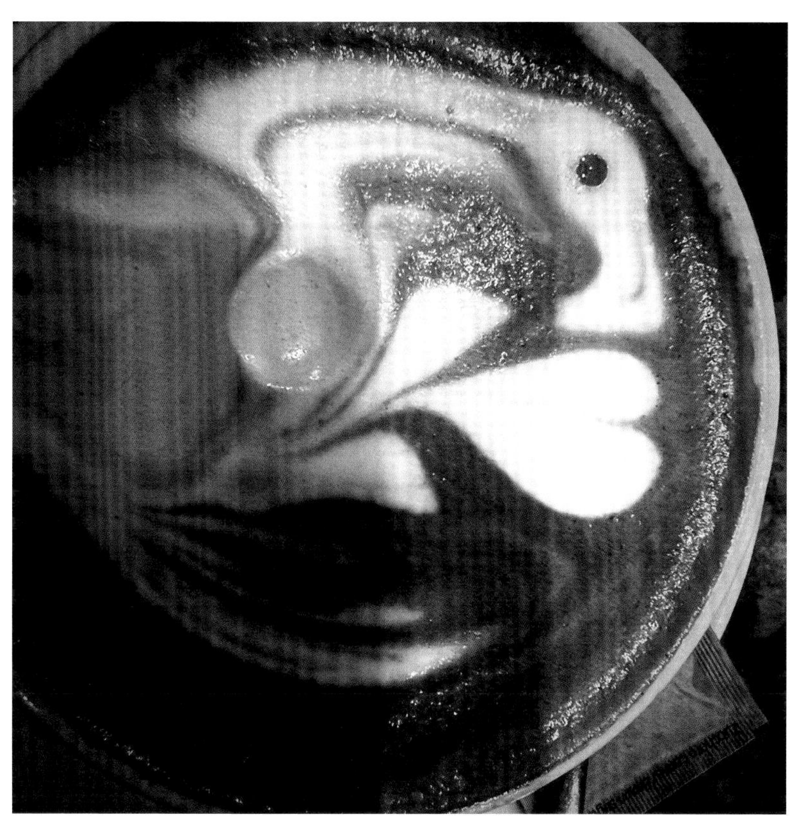

Zoom

缩放

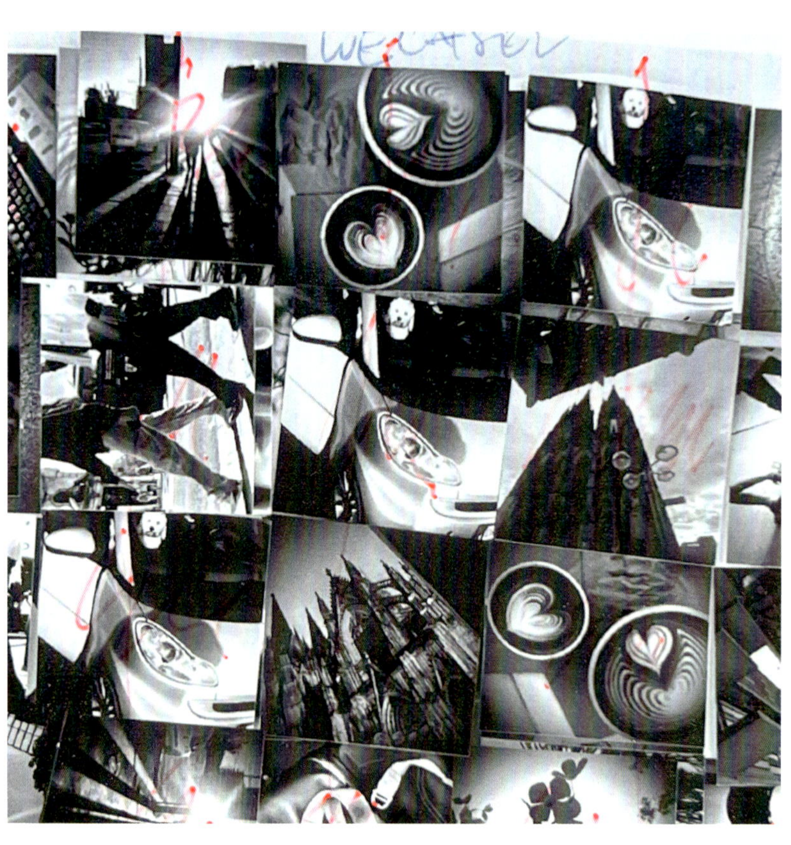

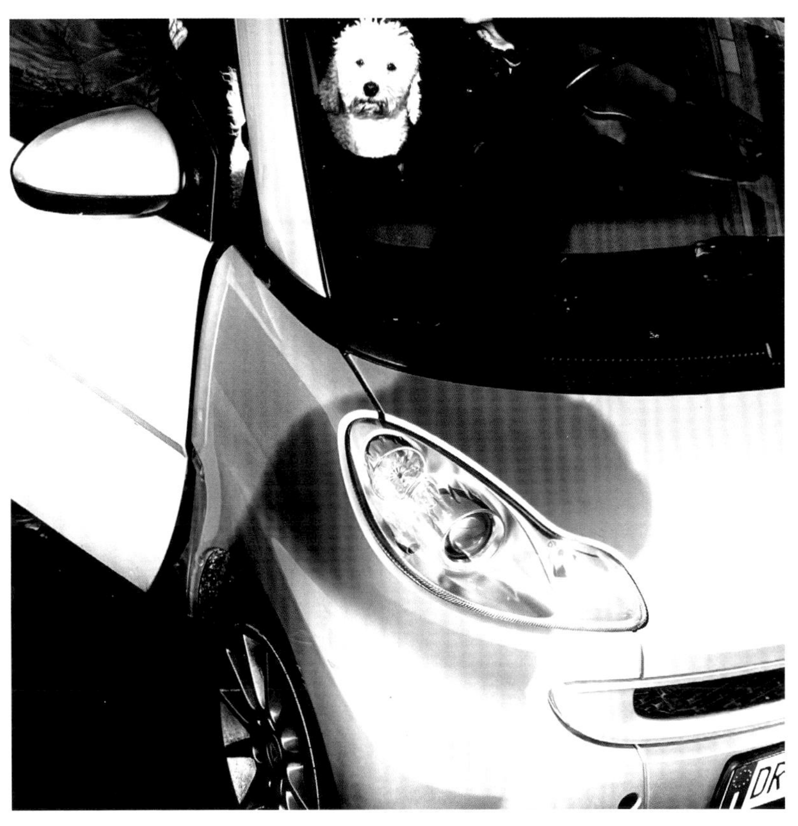

Mute Moment

静默时刻

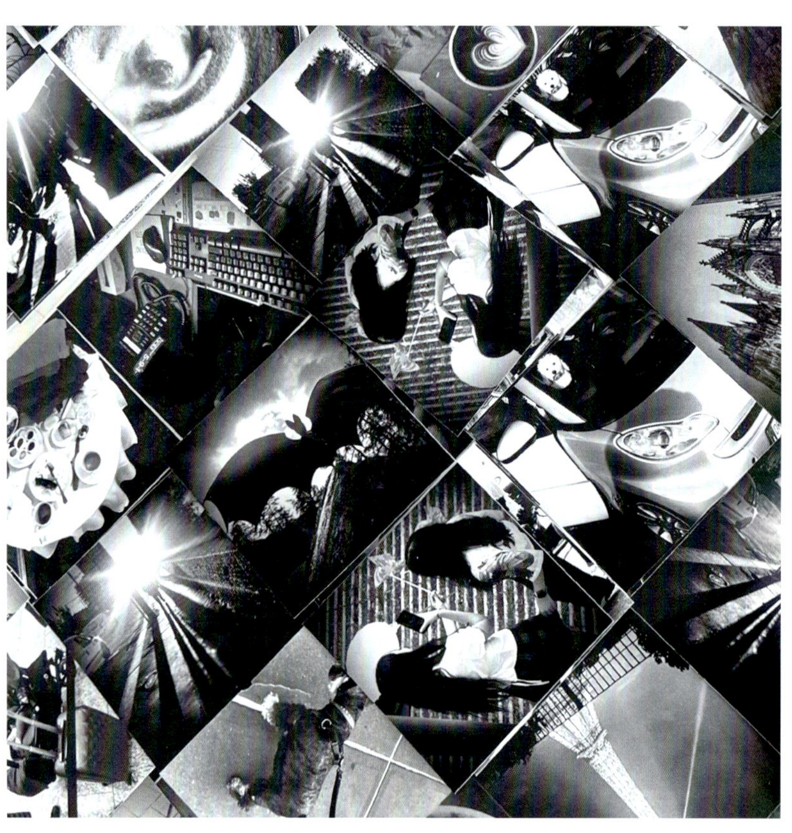

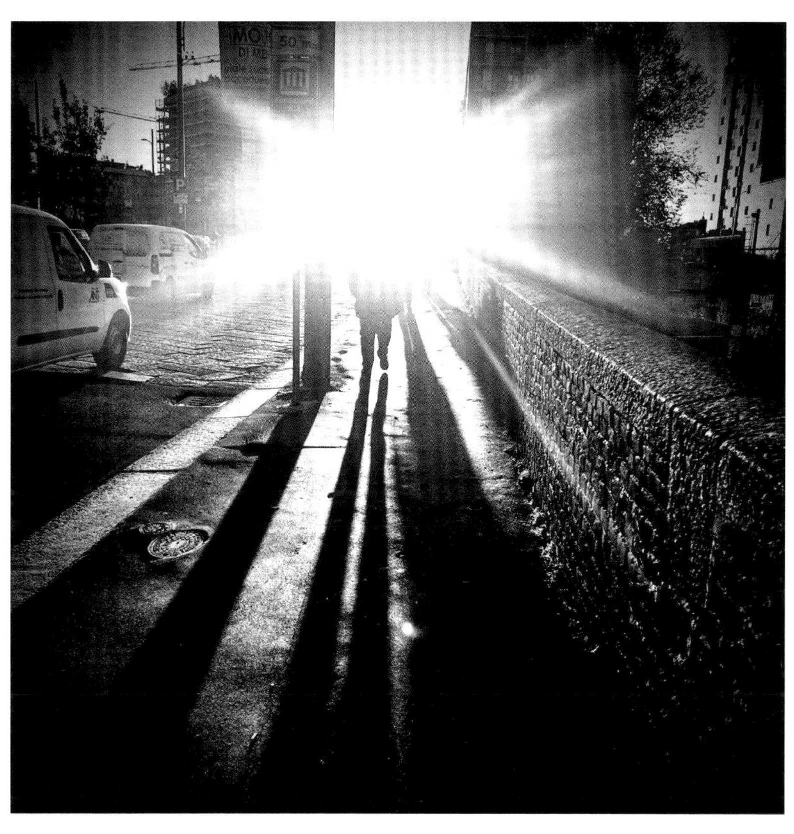

Torching the Apparatus

点燃装置

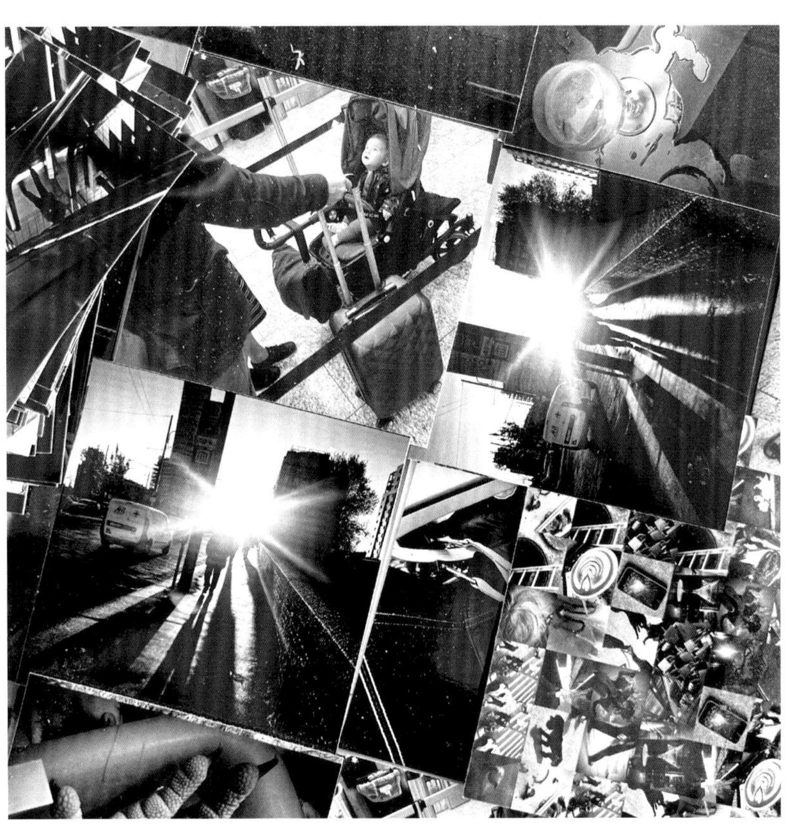

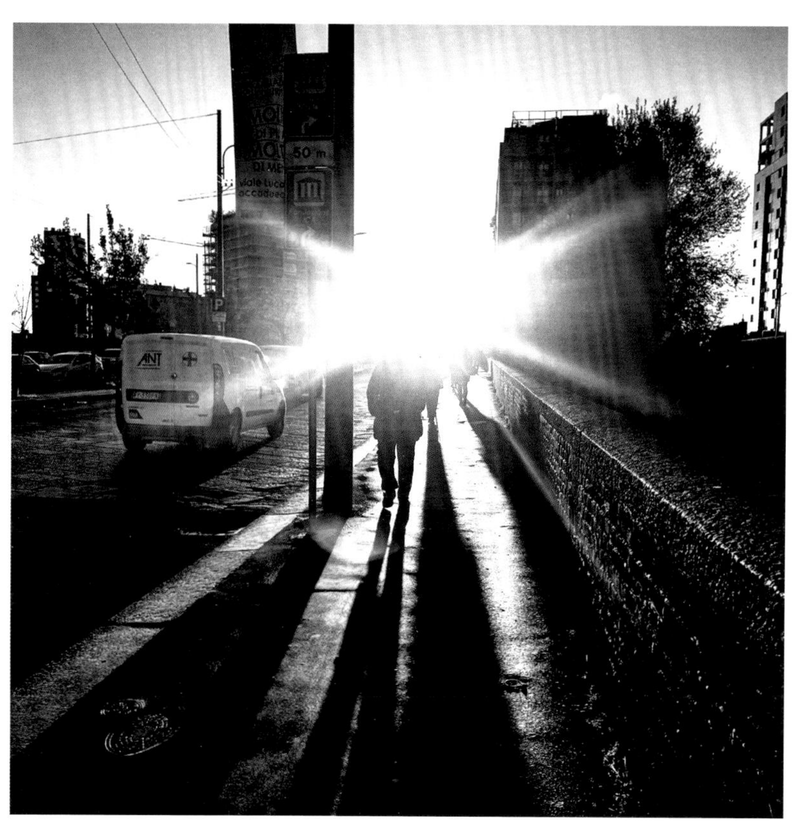

Slow Motion

慢动作

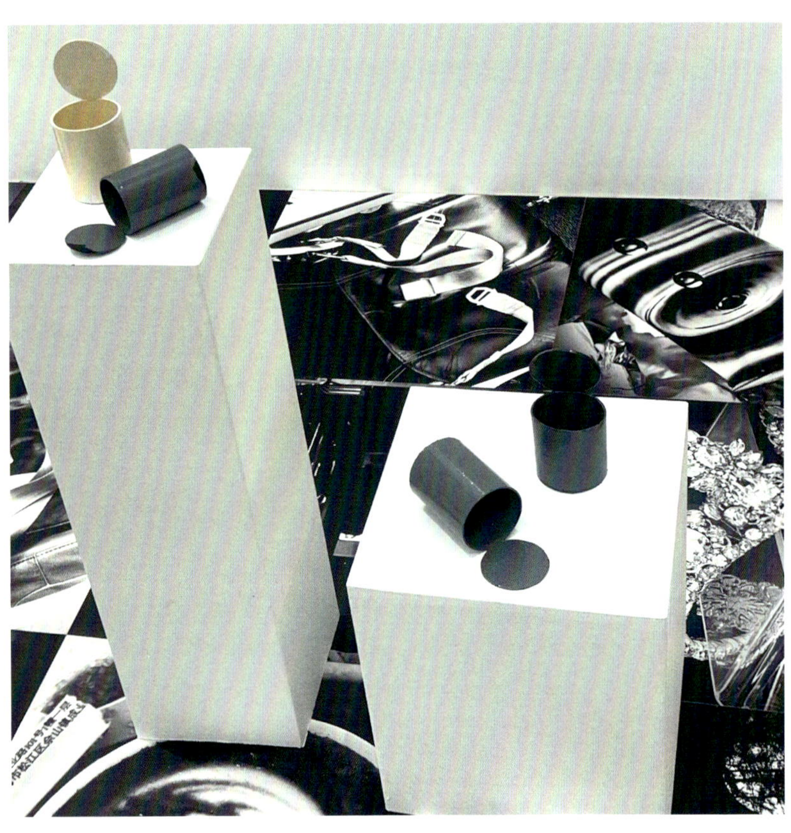

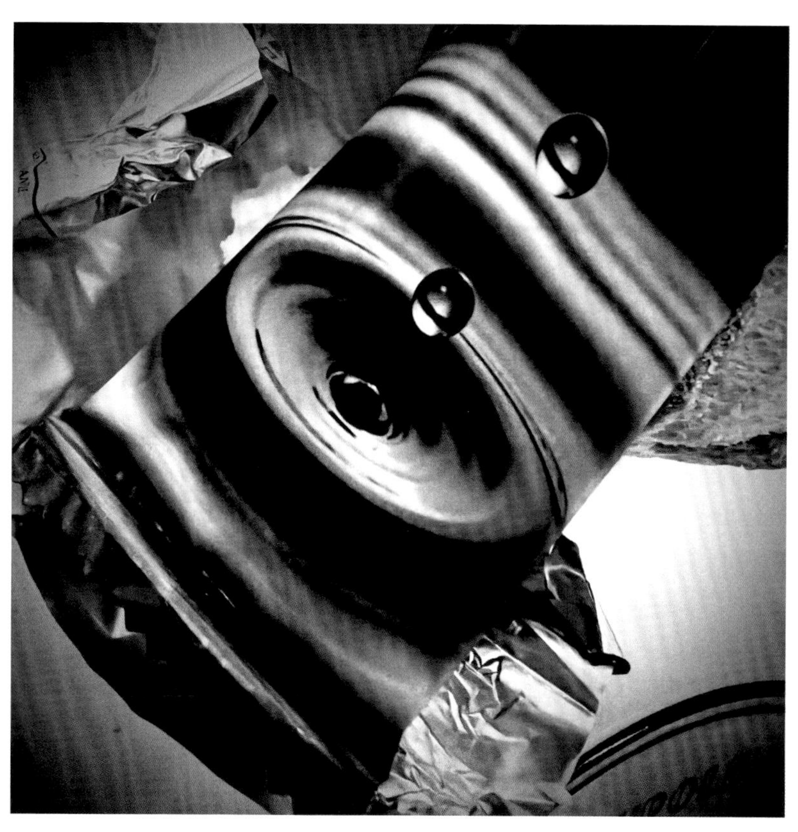

Odyssey

奥德赛

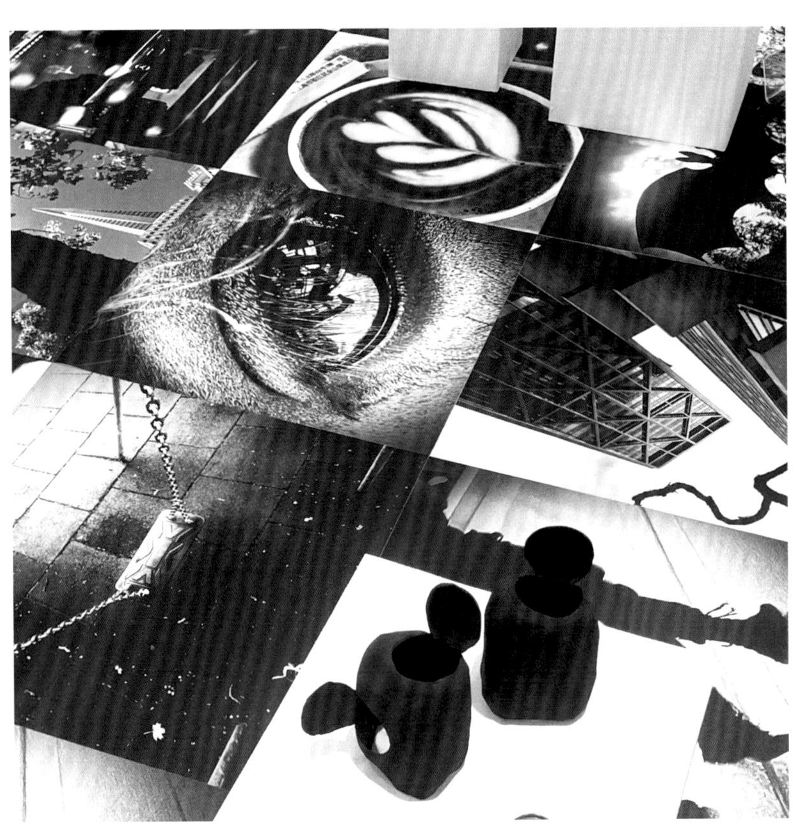

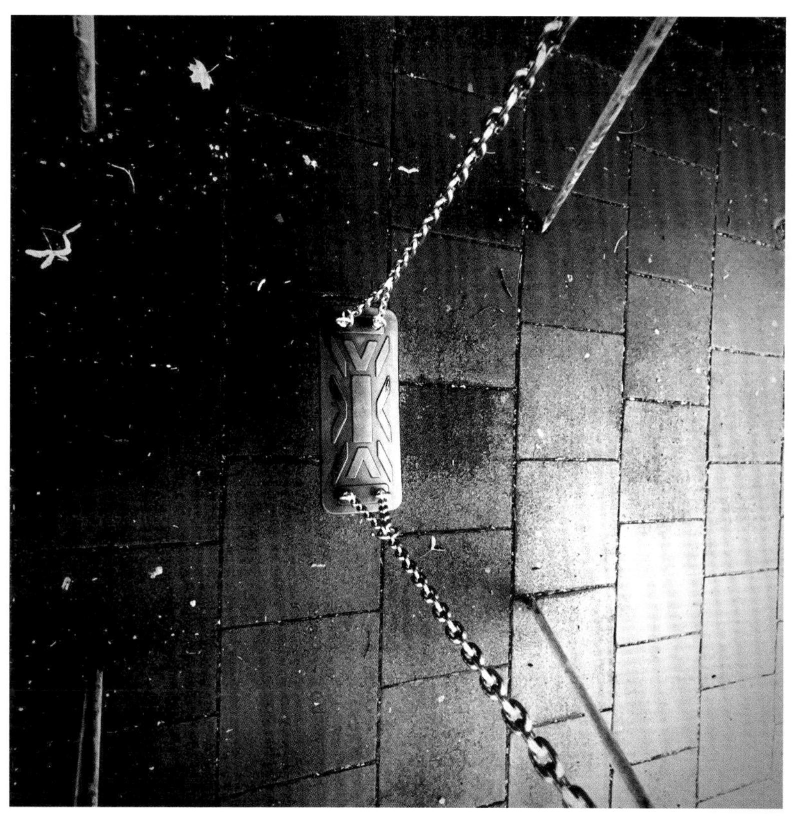

Single Frame

单帧

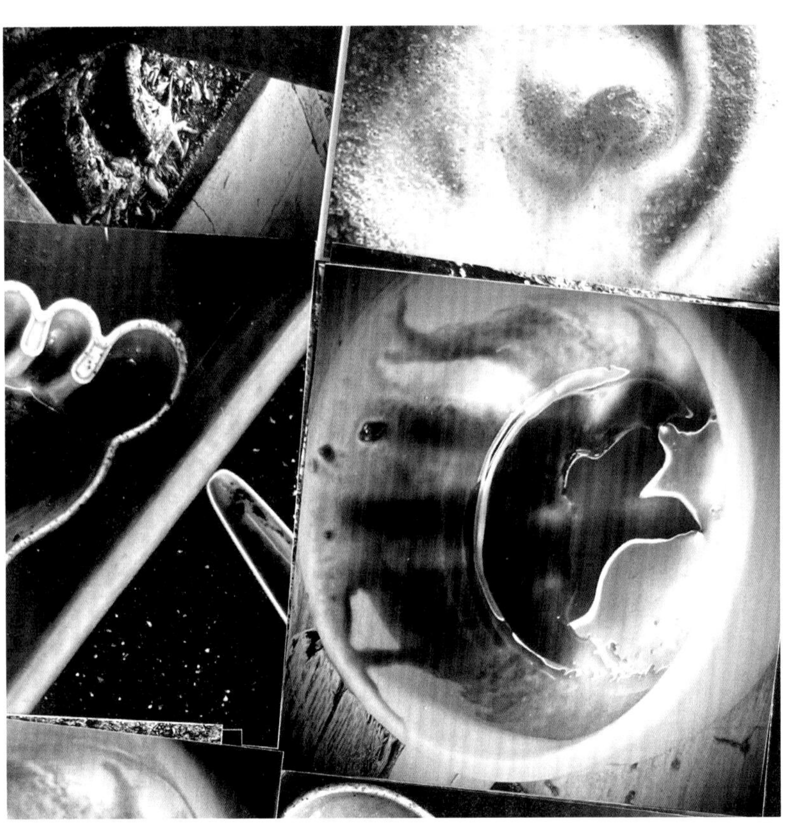

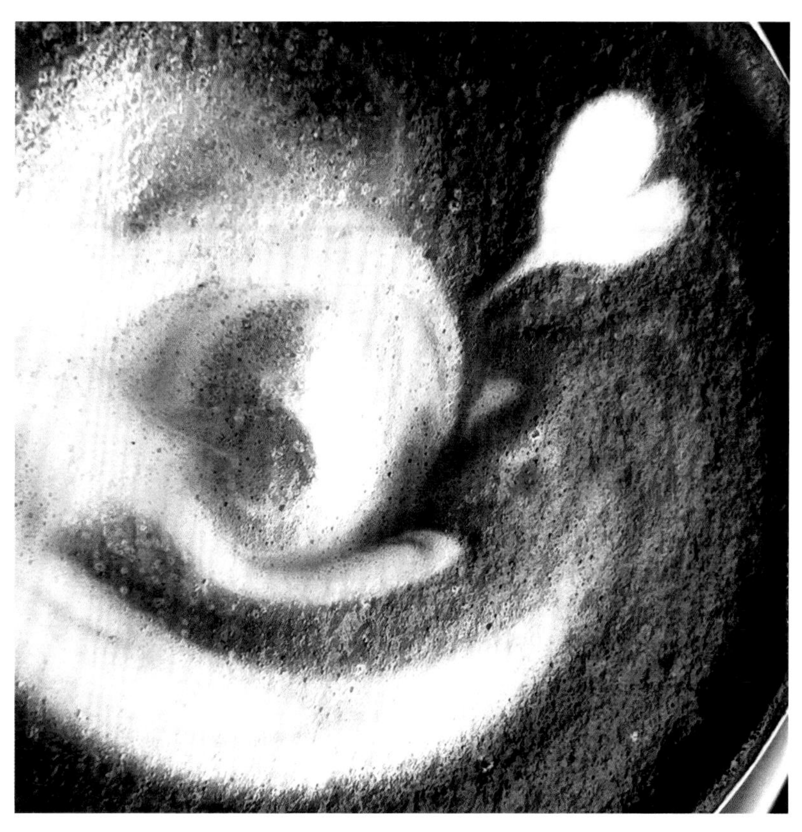

The Apology Impulse

道歉冲动

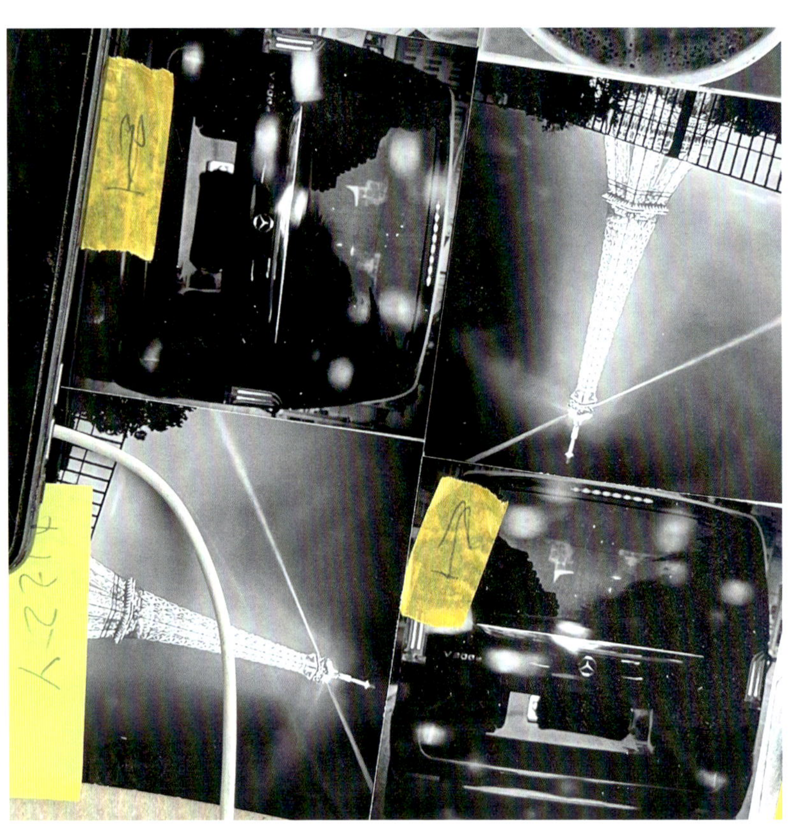

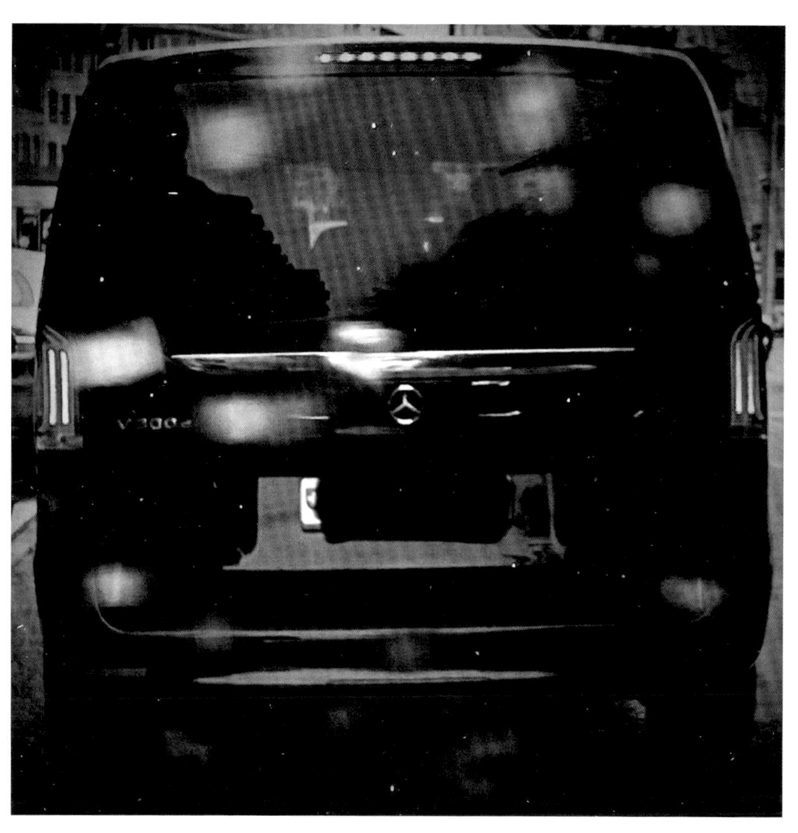

Mapping the Universe

绘制宇宙

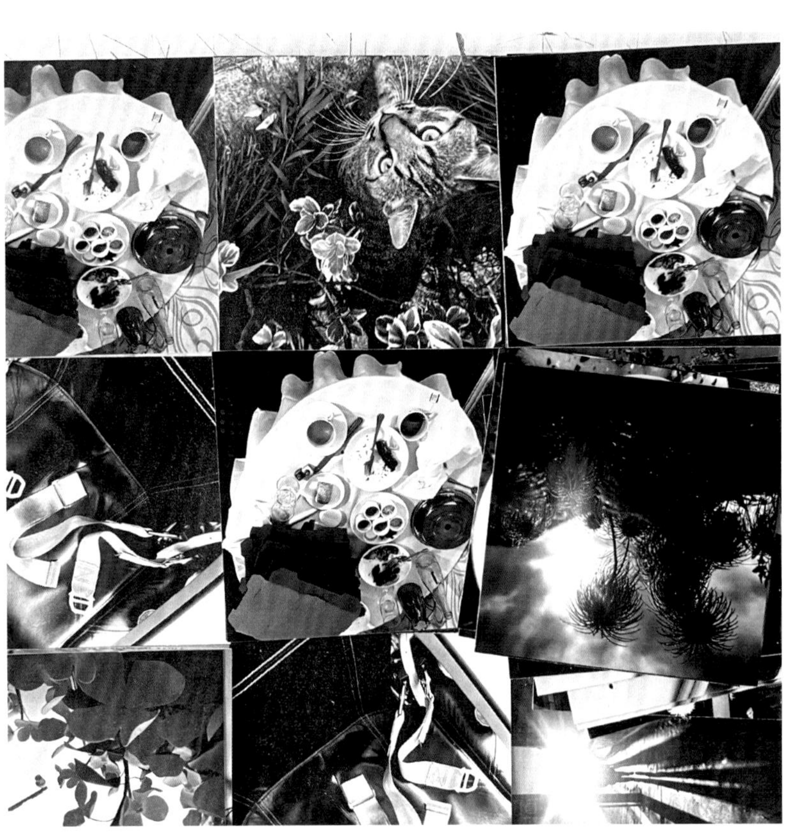

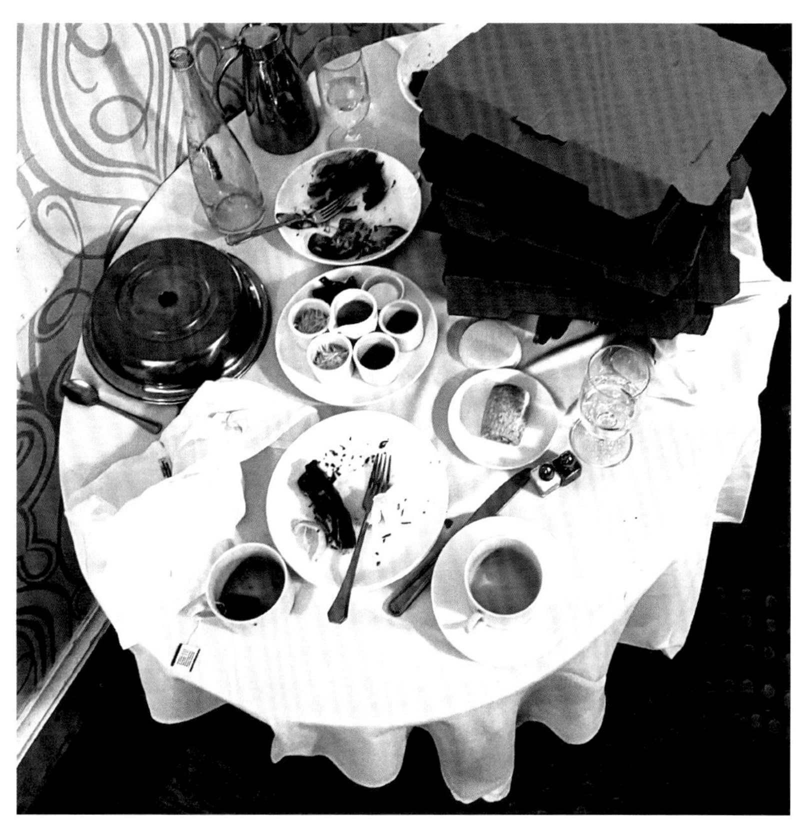

In a Fairytale

在童话中

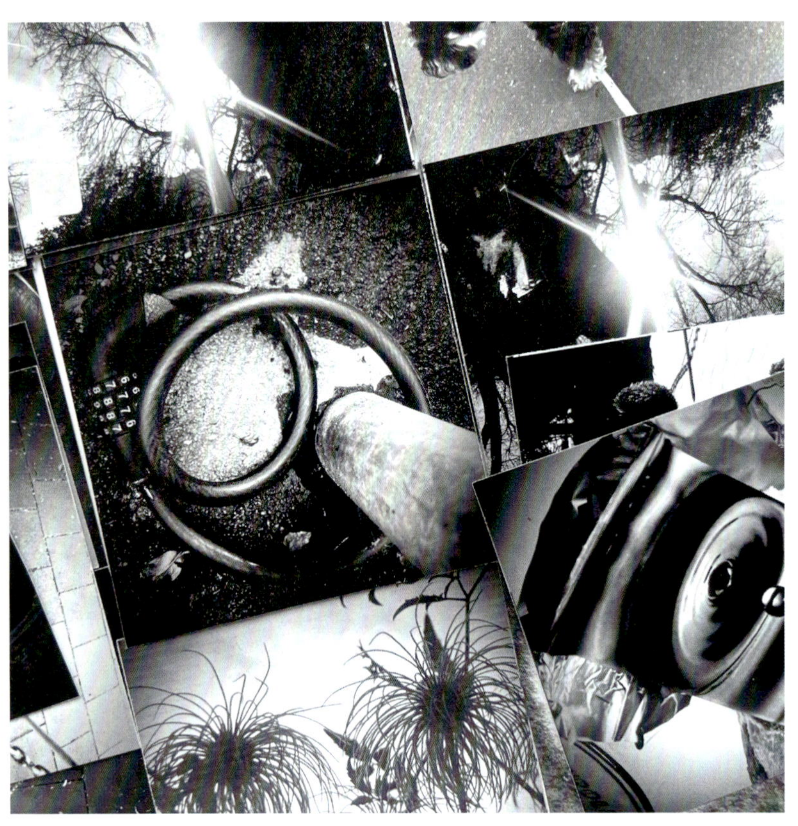

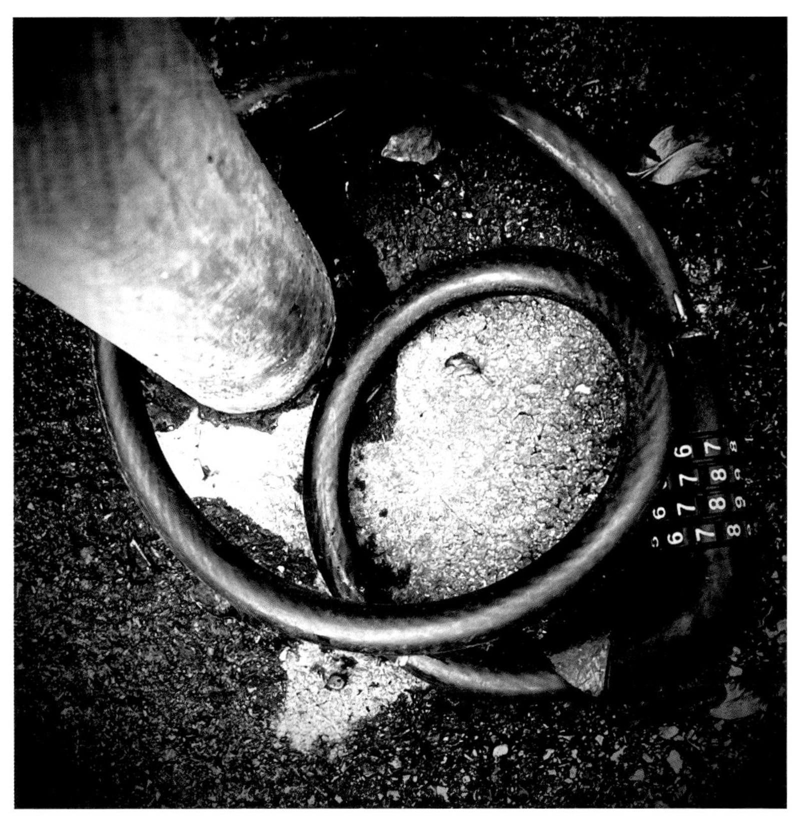

Ignoring

忽略

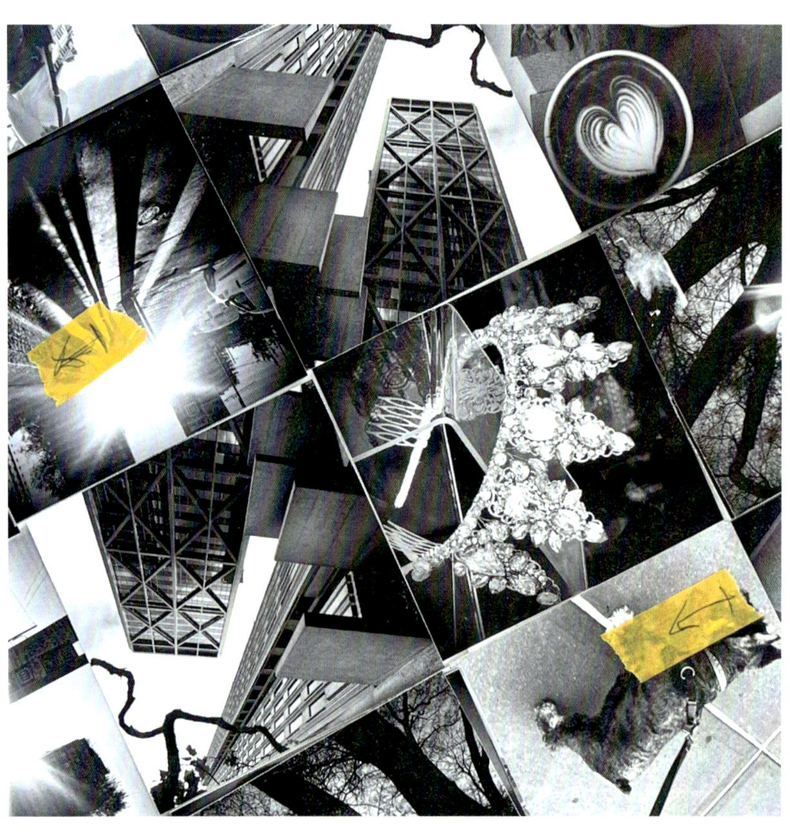

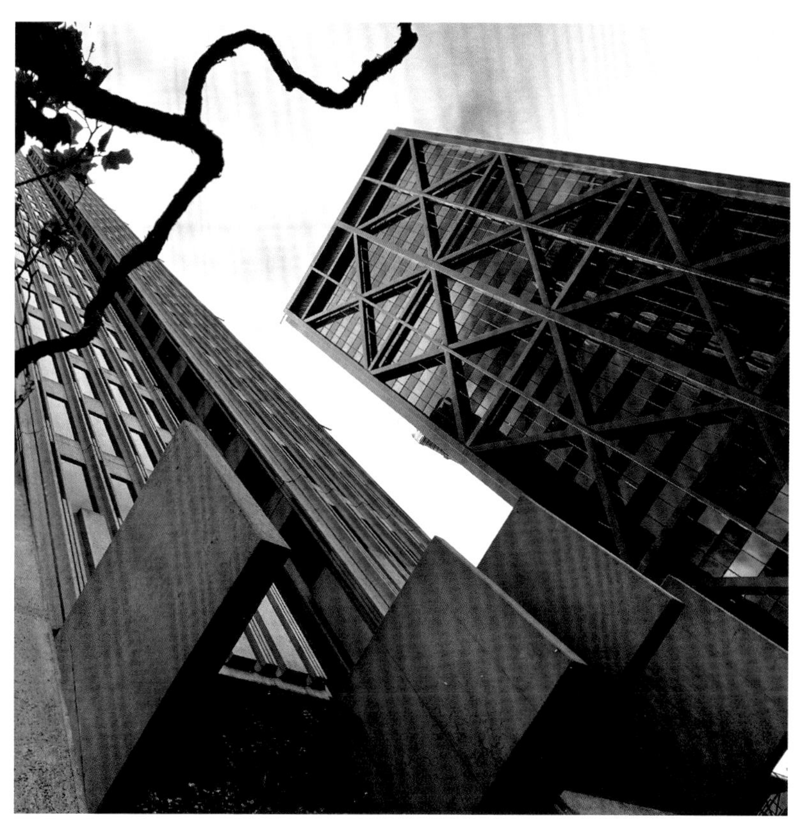

Drama

戏剧

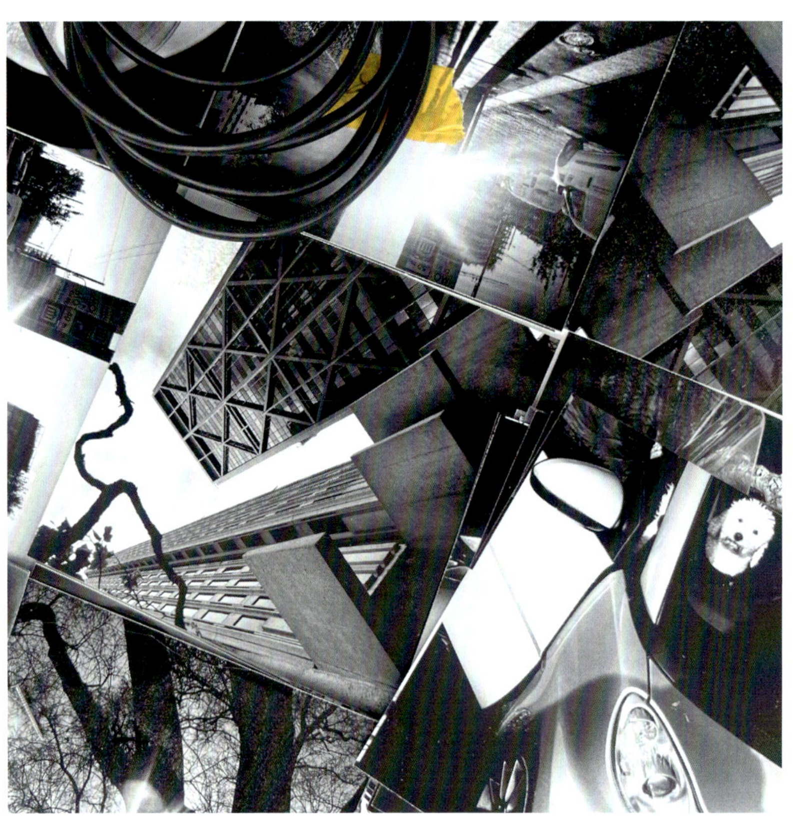

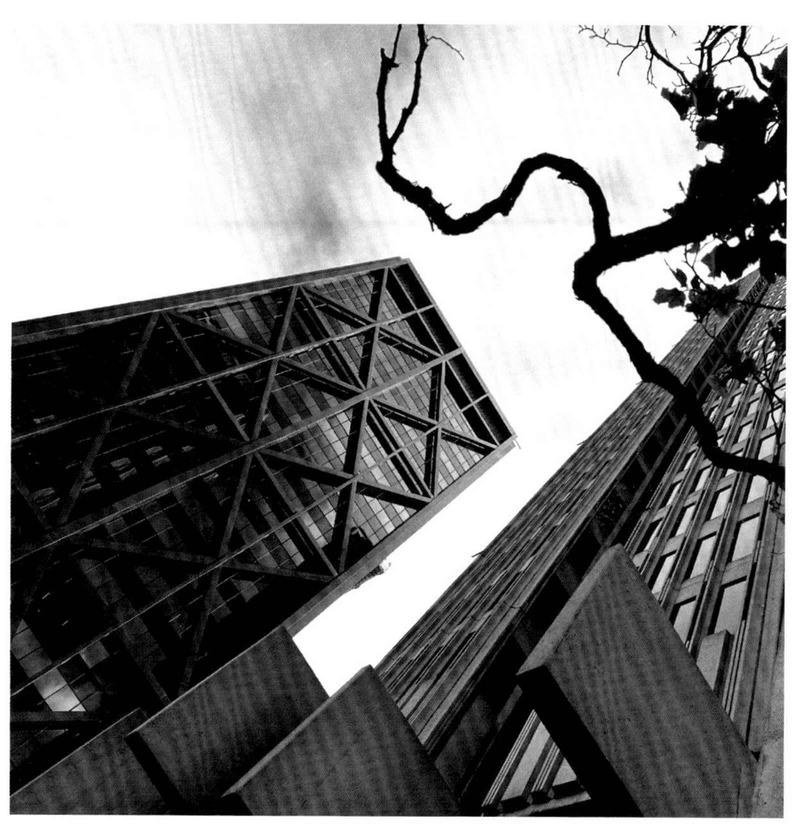

Worldwide

全球范围

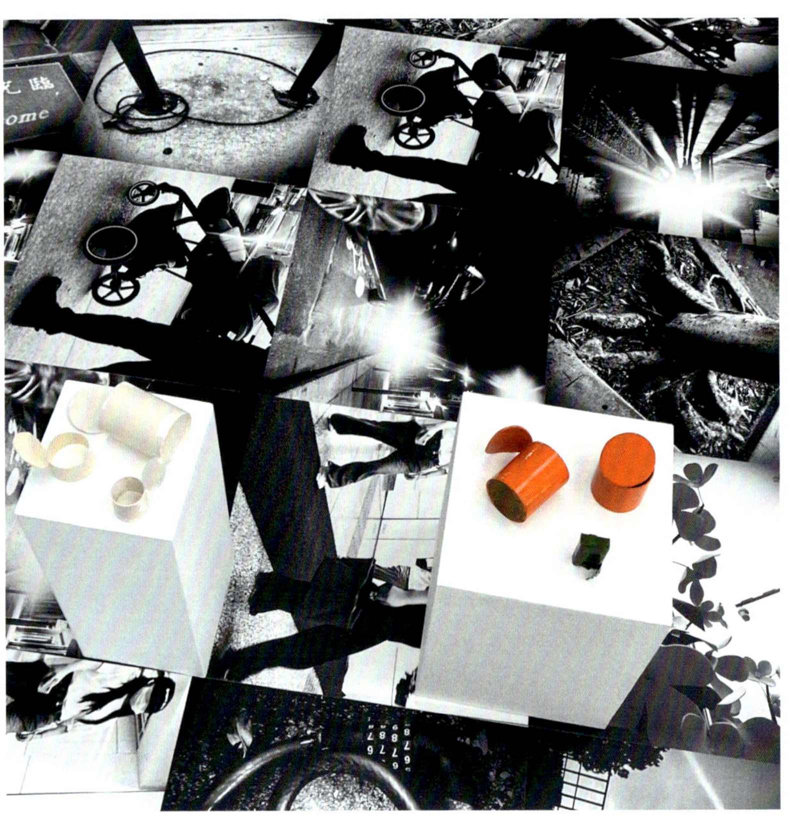

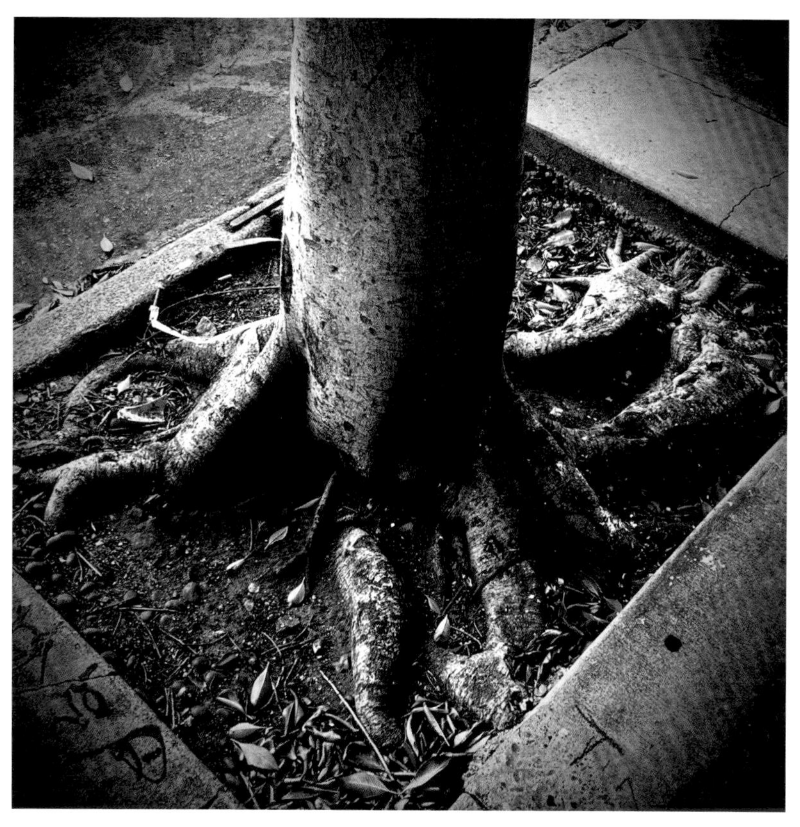

The Effect of Light on Plants

光对植物的影响

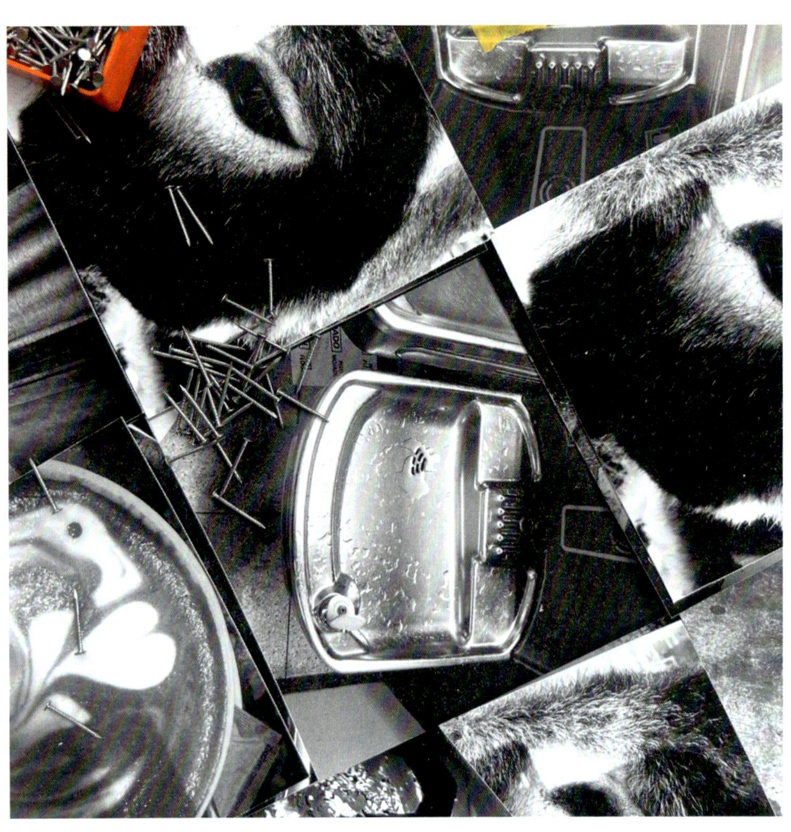

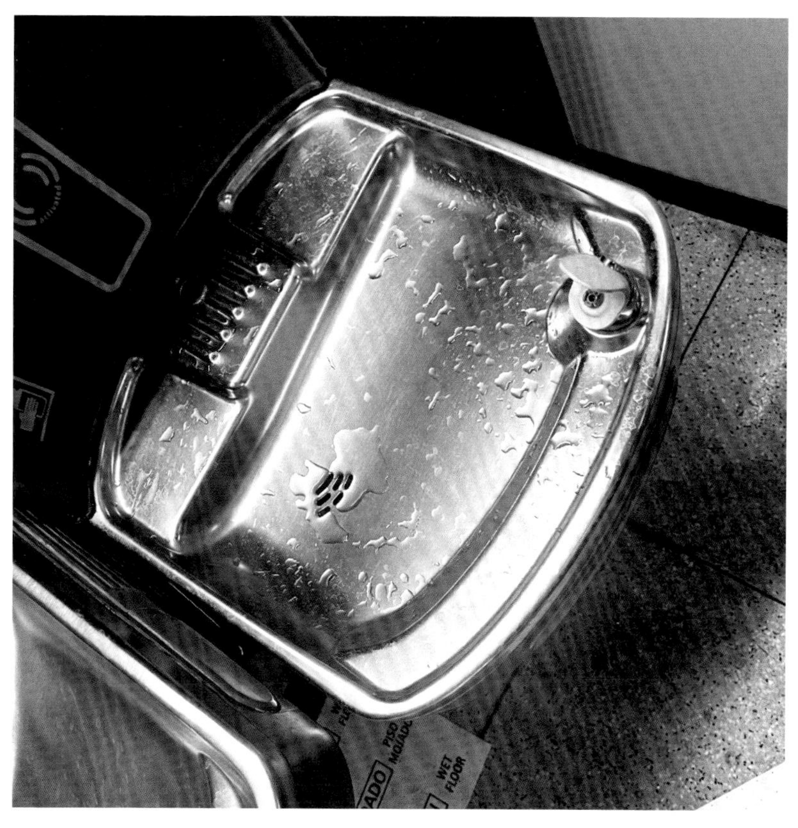

Attractive Surface

迷人的表面

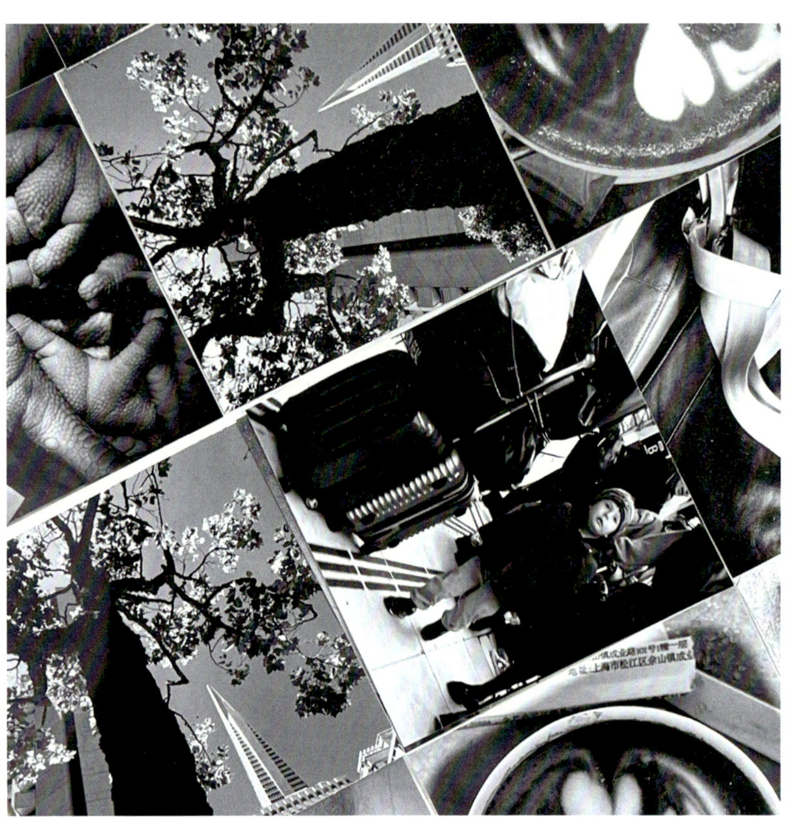
上海市松江区佘山镇

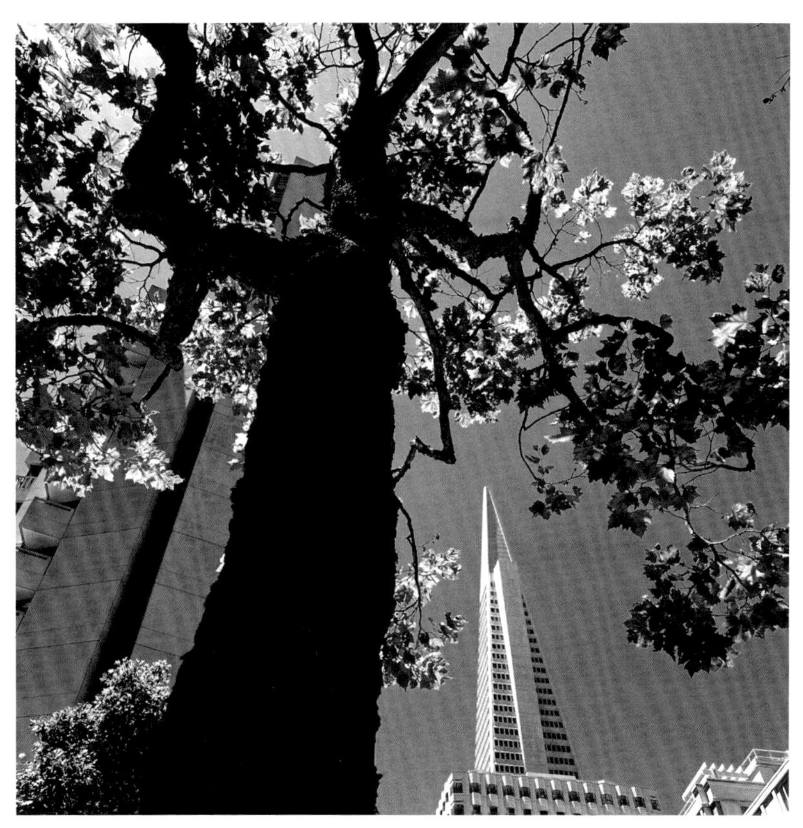

Blueprint

蓝图

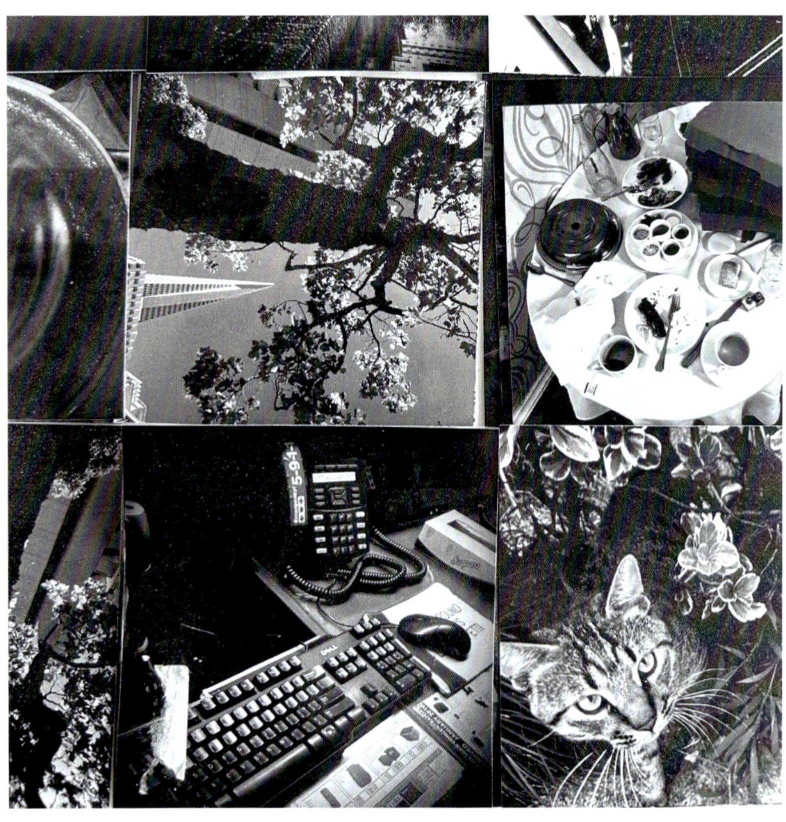

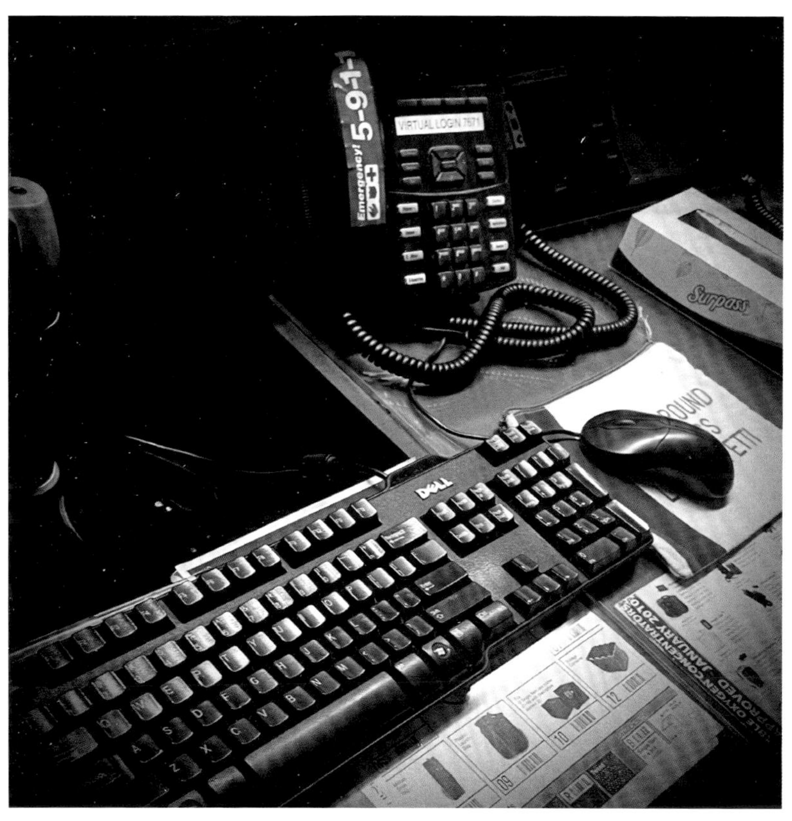

The 21st Century

21世纪

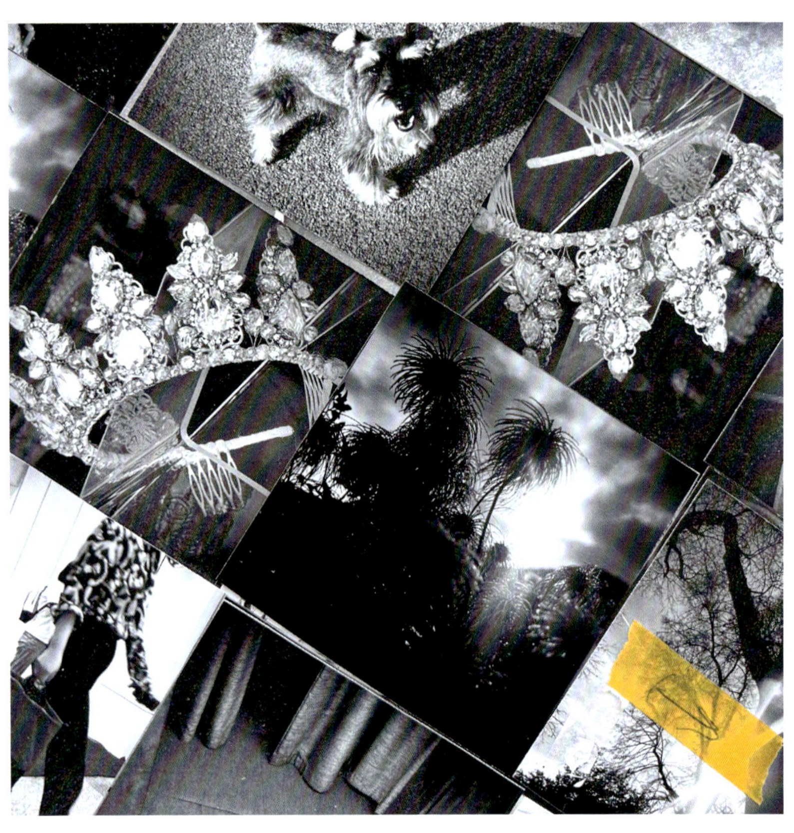

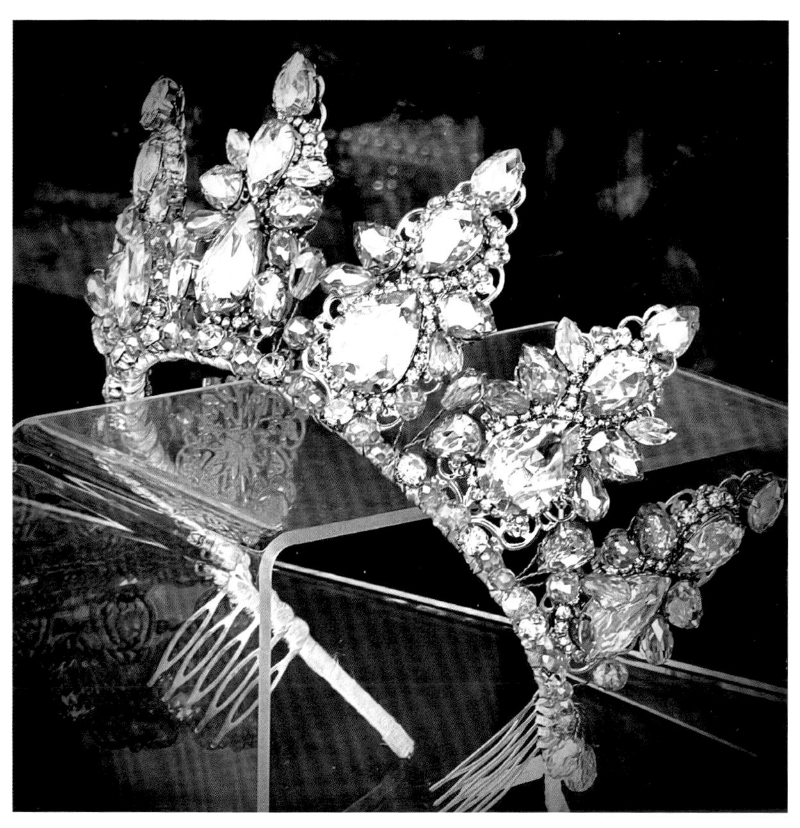

As If

仿佛

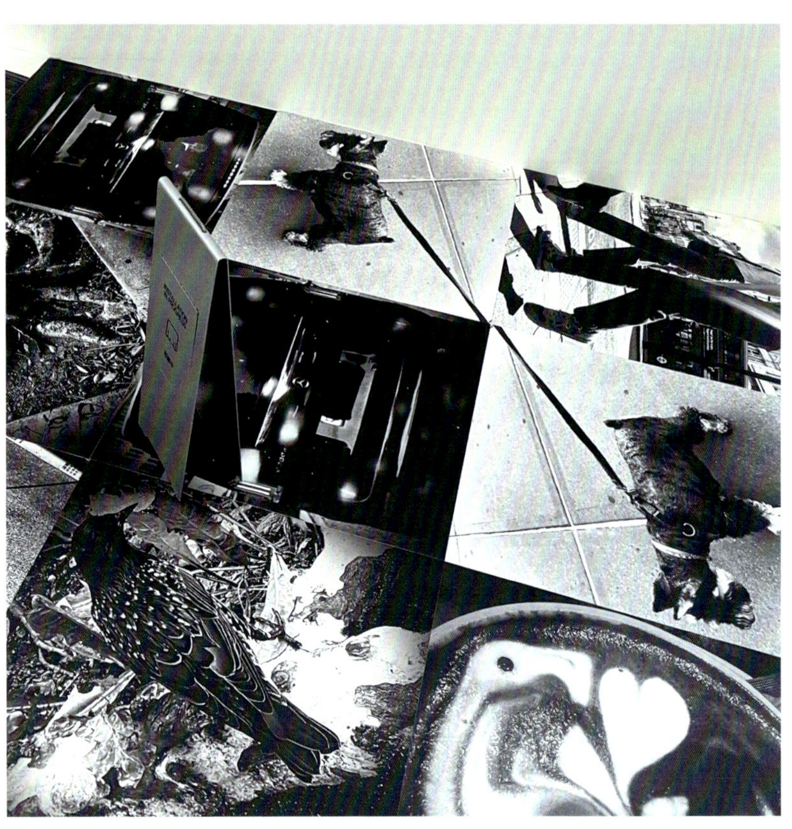

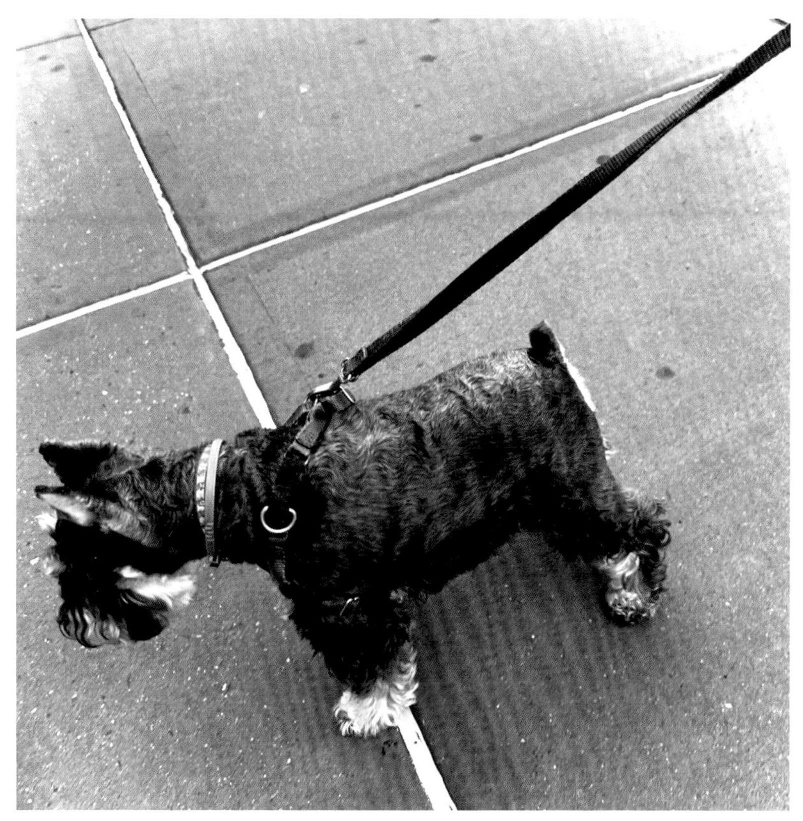

Compass

罗盘

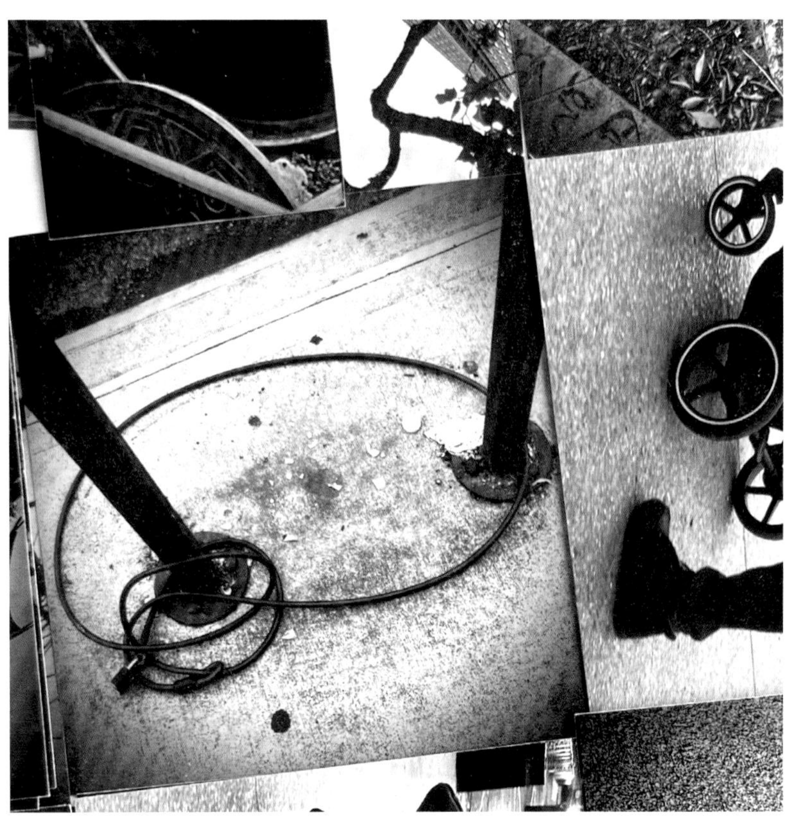

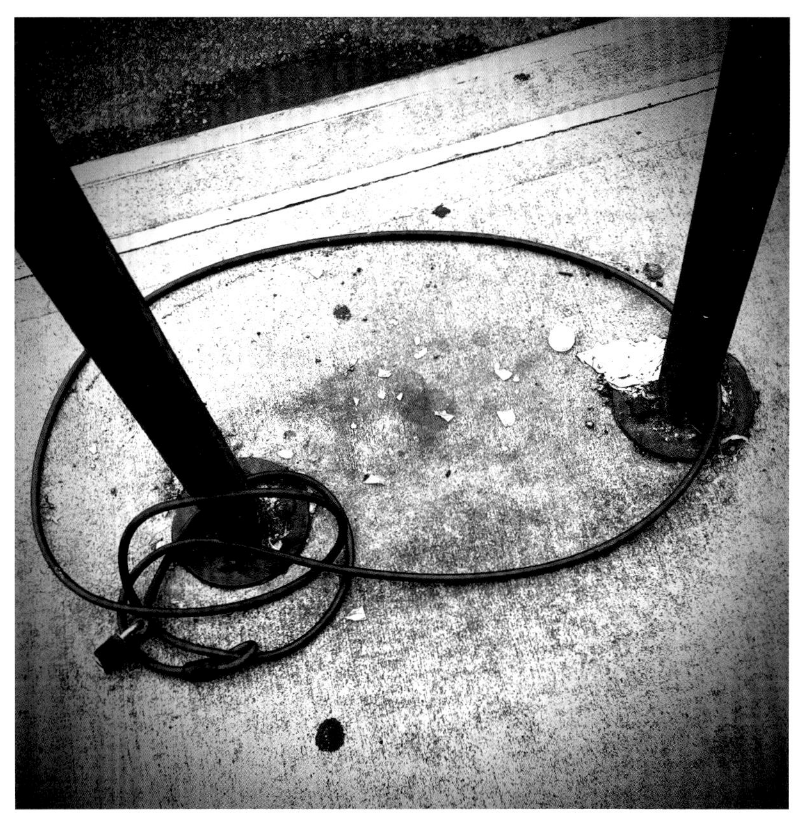

The Production of Subjectivity

主体性的生产

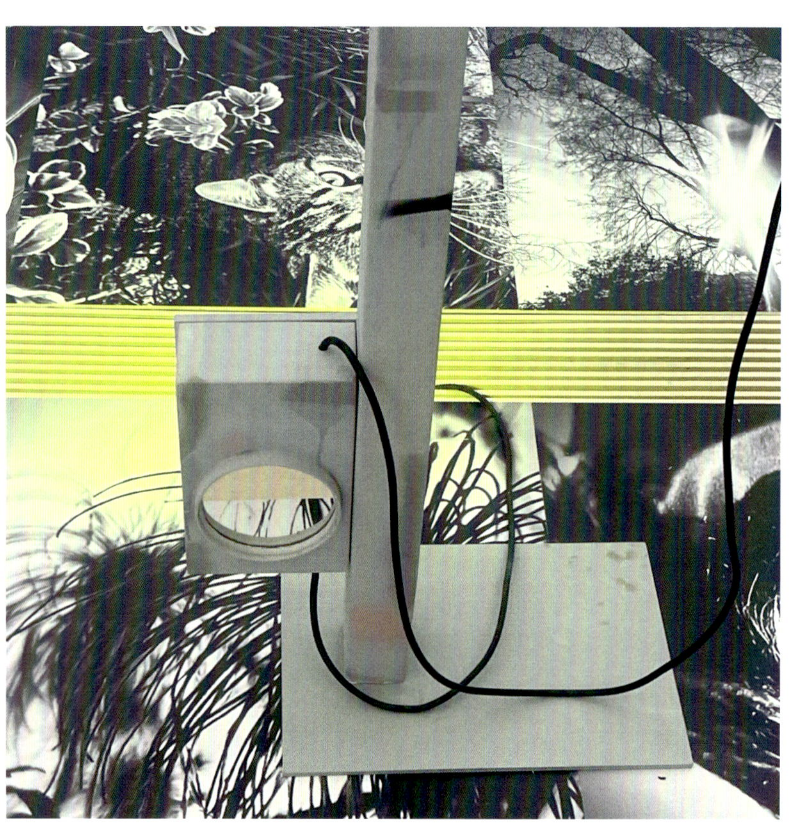

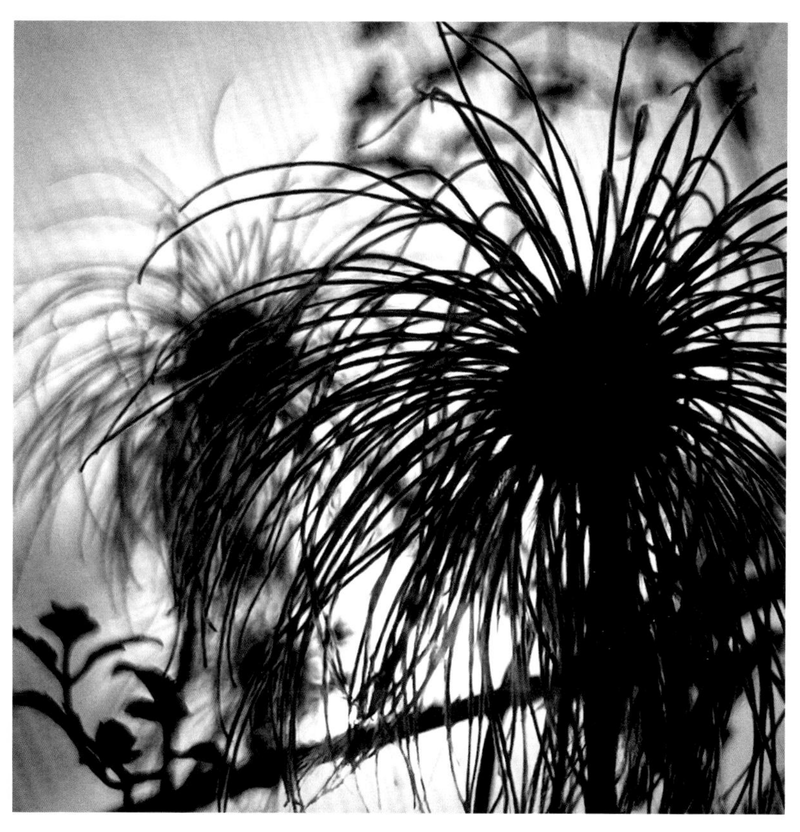

Two Sun Universe

双太阳宇宙

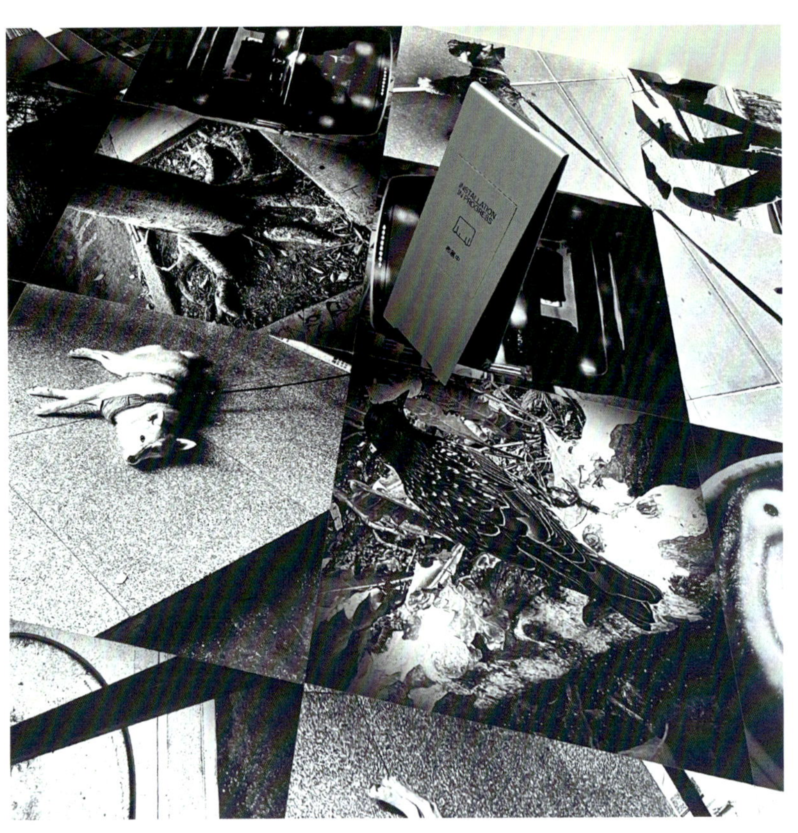
INSTALLATION
IN PROGRESS

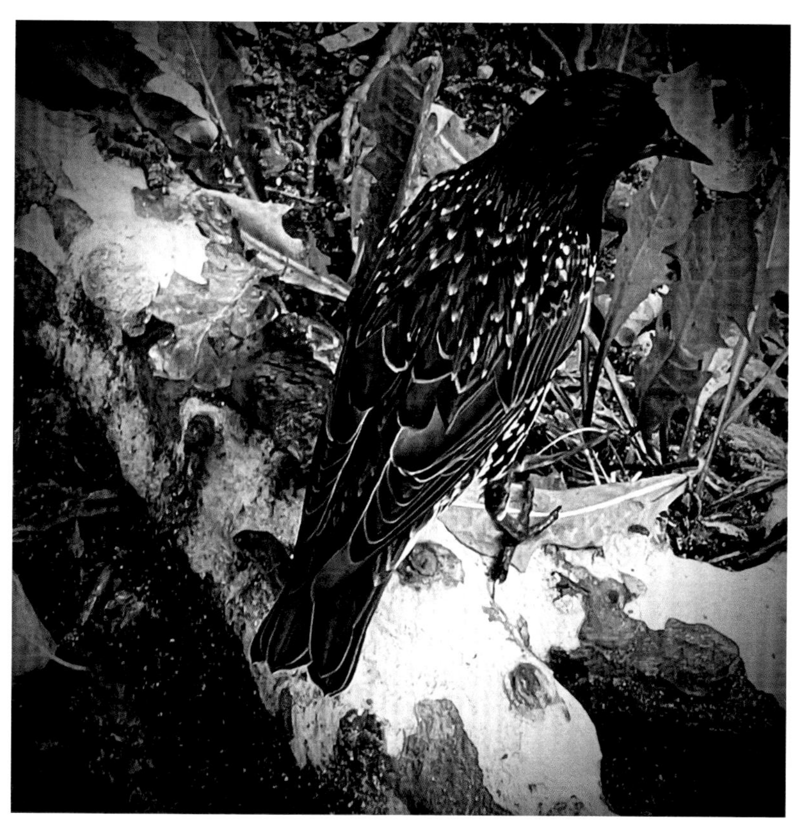

Wait till Midnight

等到午夜

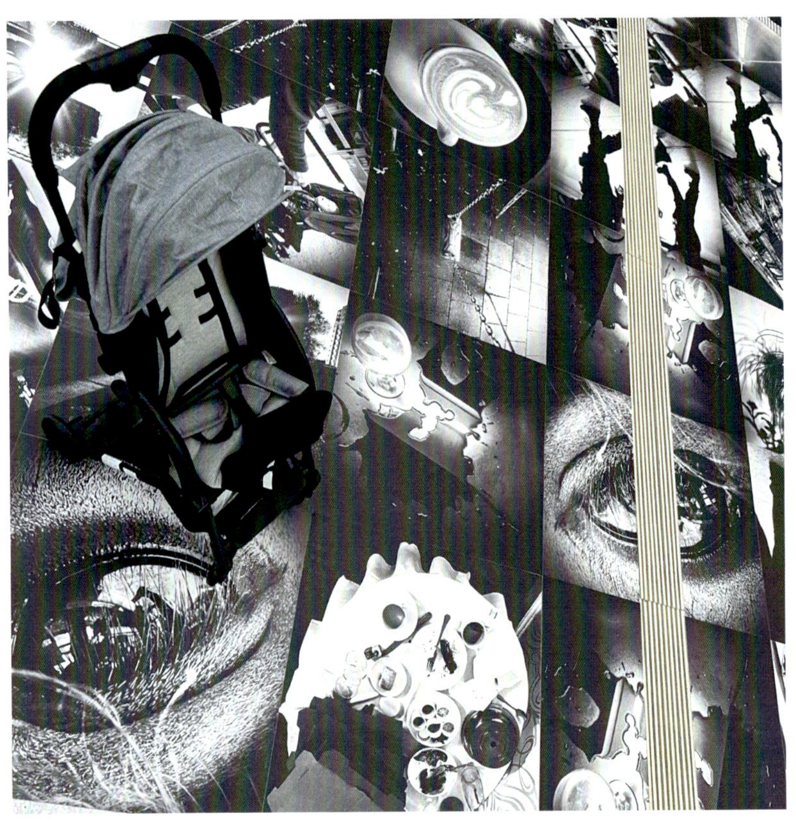

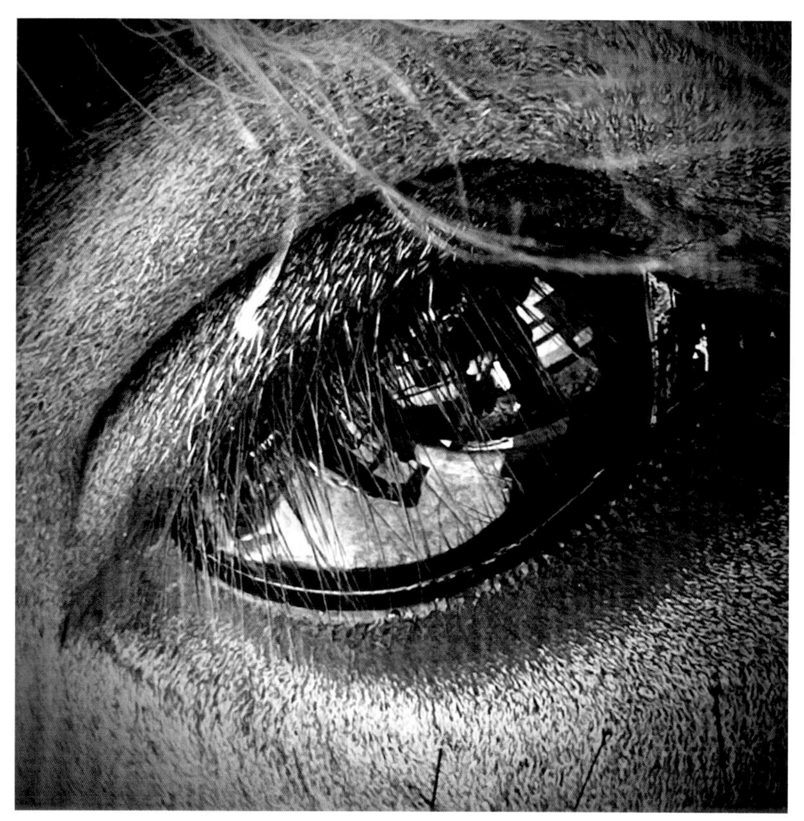

Cosmic

宇宙的

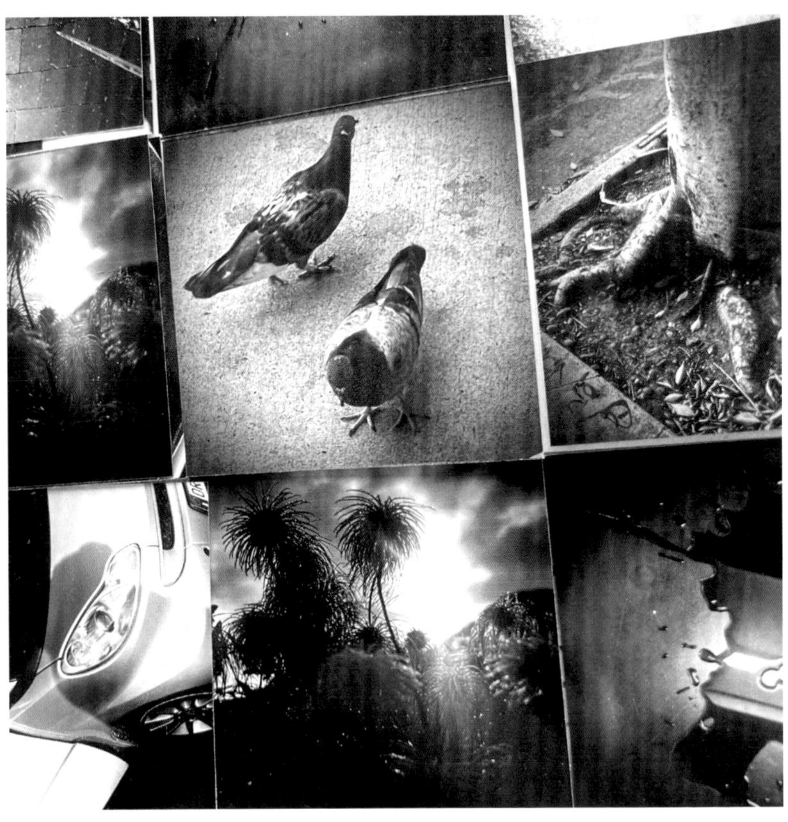

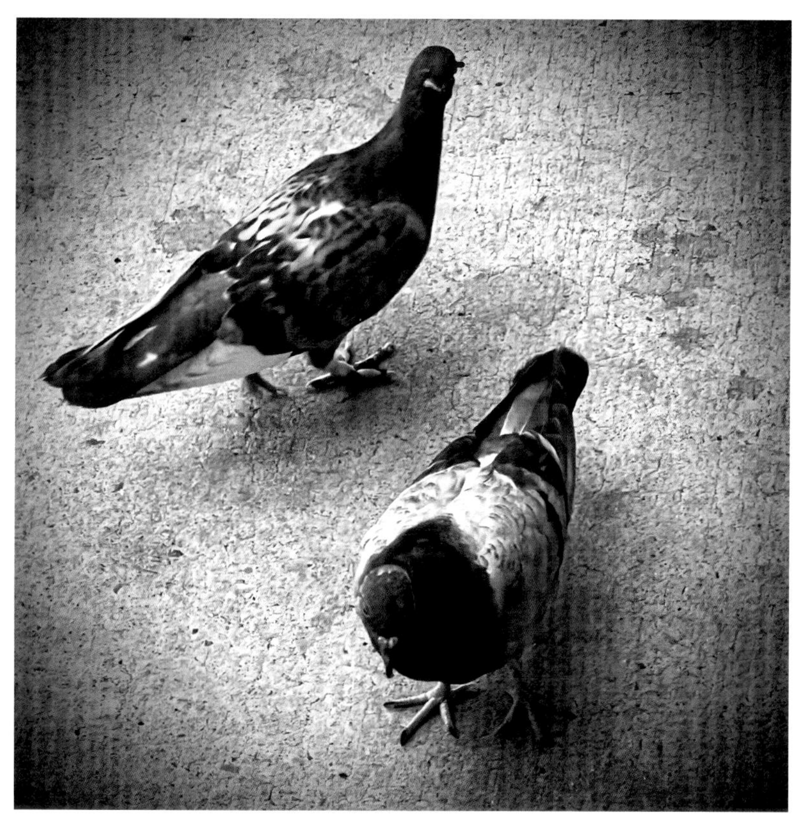

A Calmer Life

更平静的生活

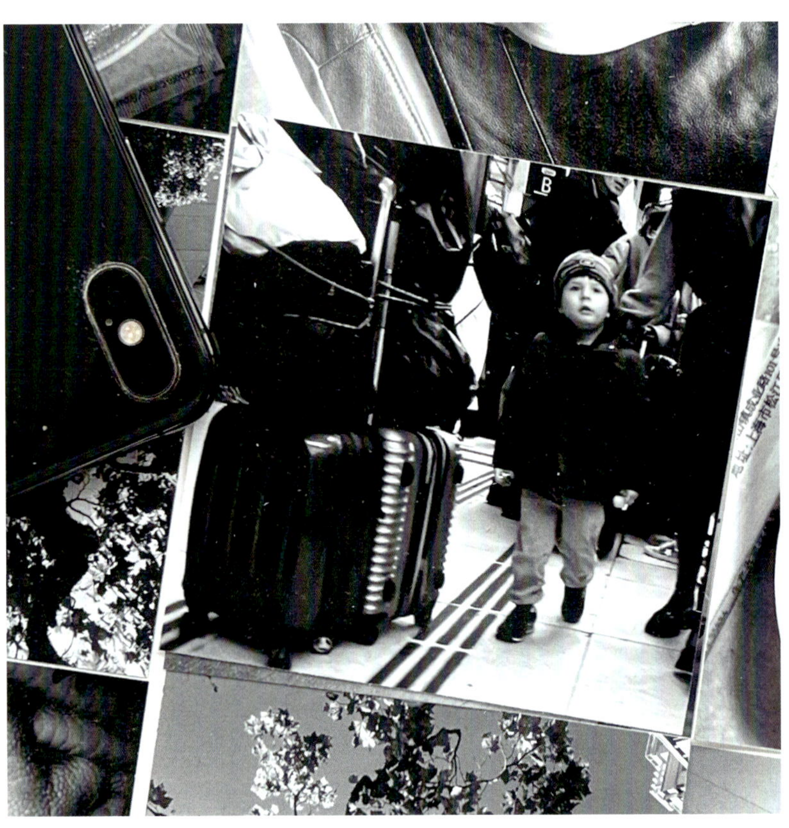

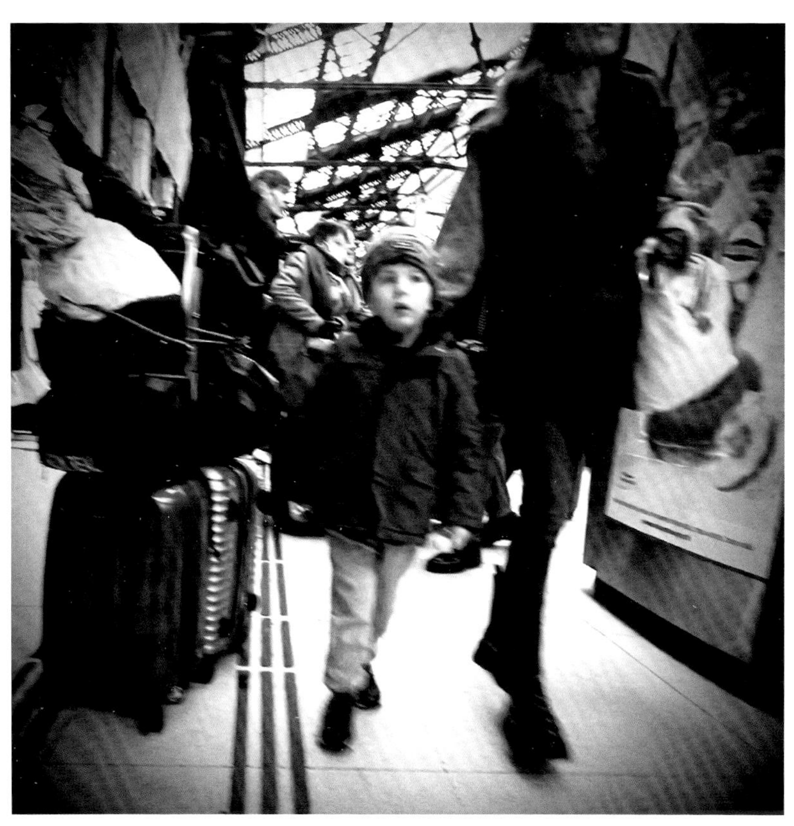

Peter

彼得

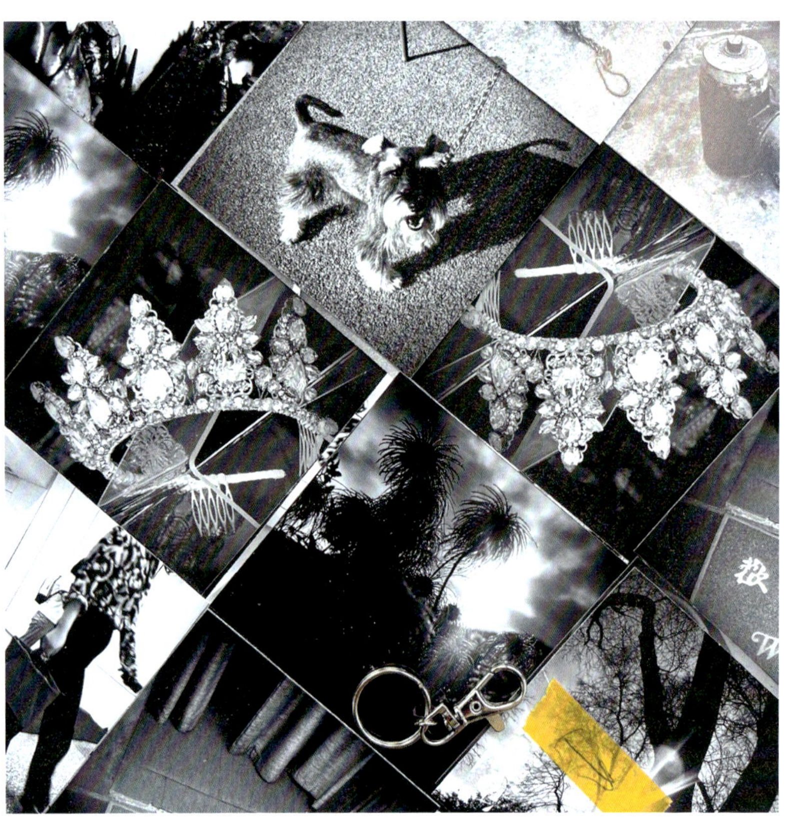

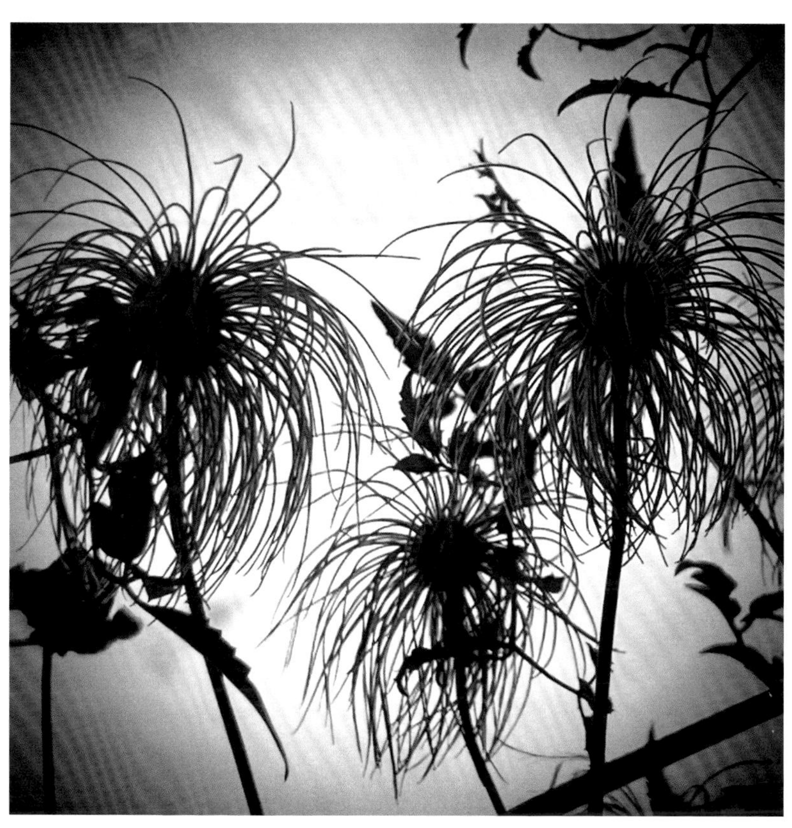

Three Sun Universe

三阳宇宙

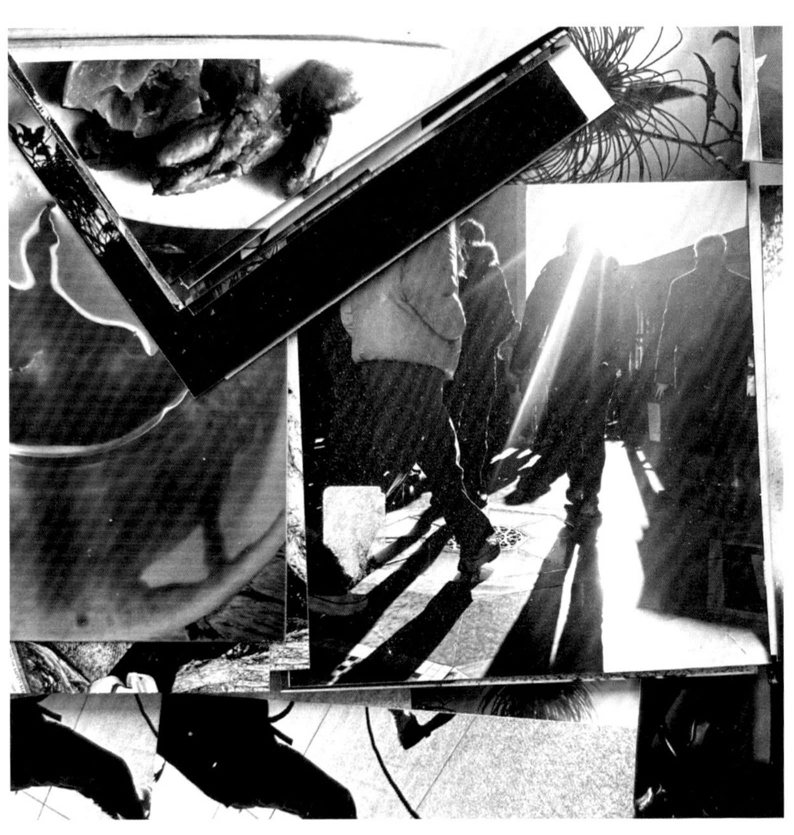

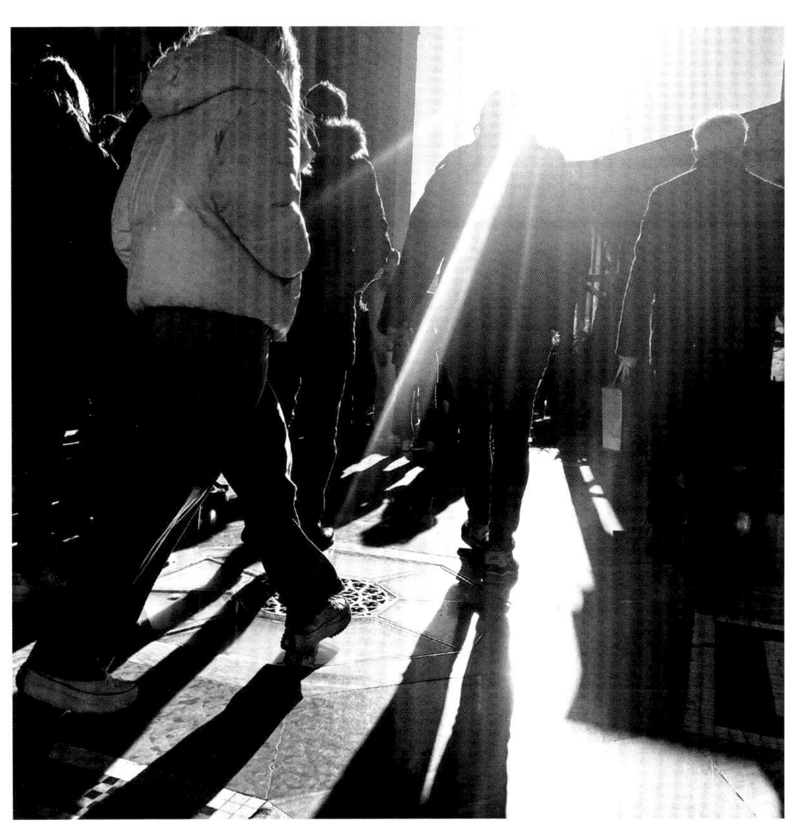

Fallout

辐射尘

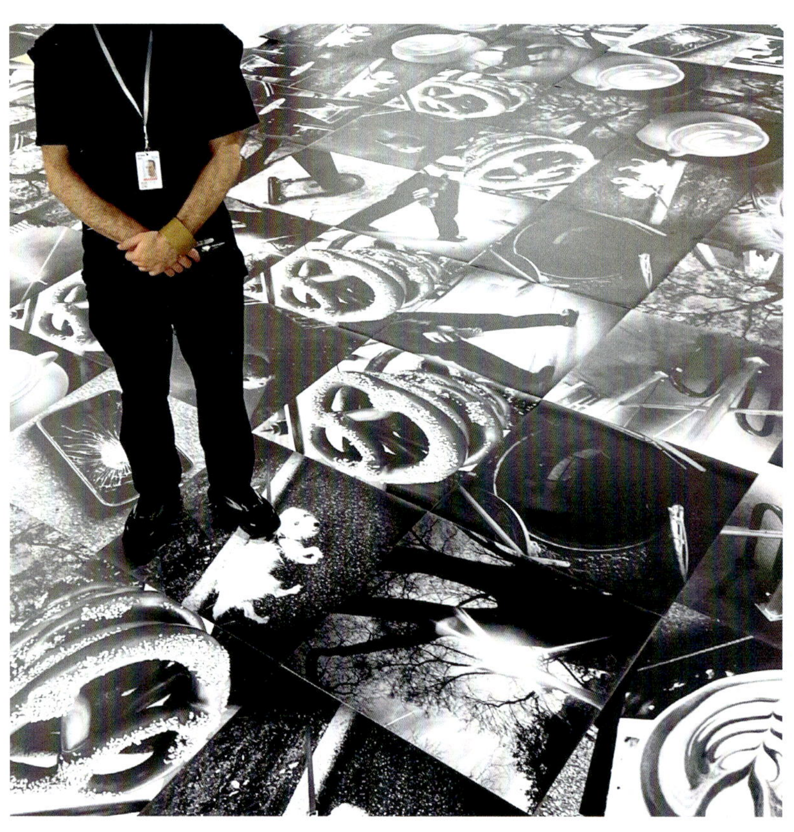

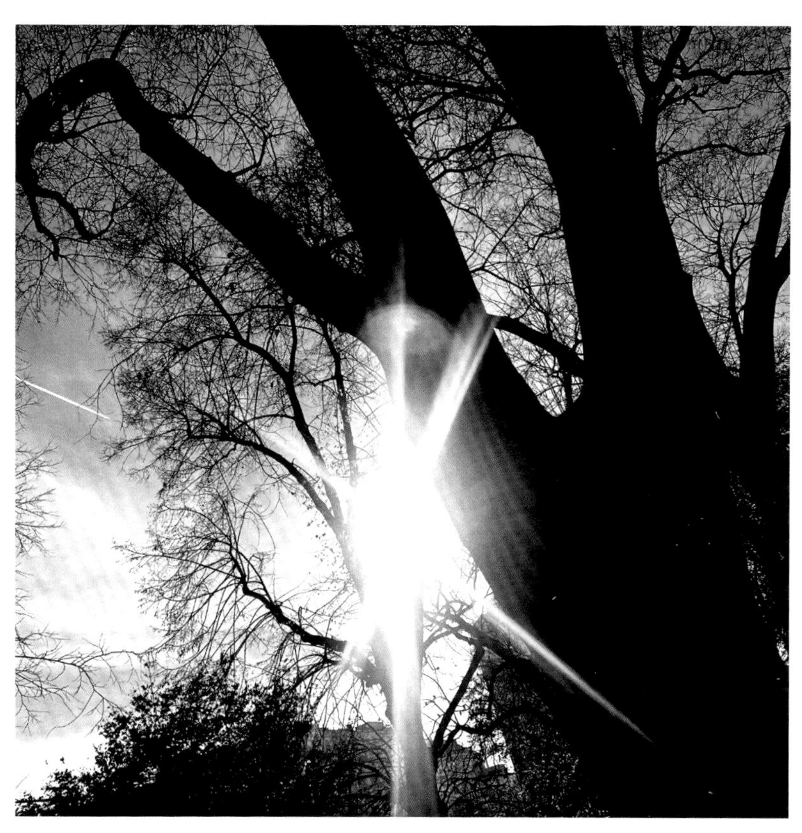

Hinkypunk

鬼火

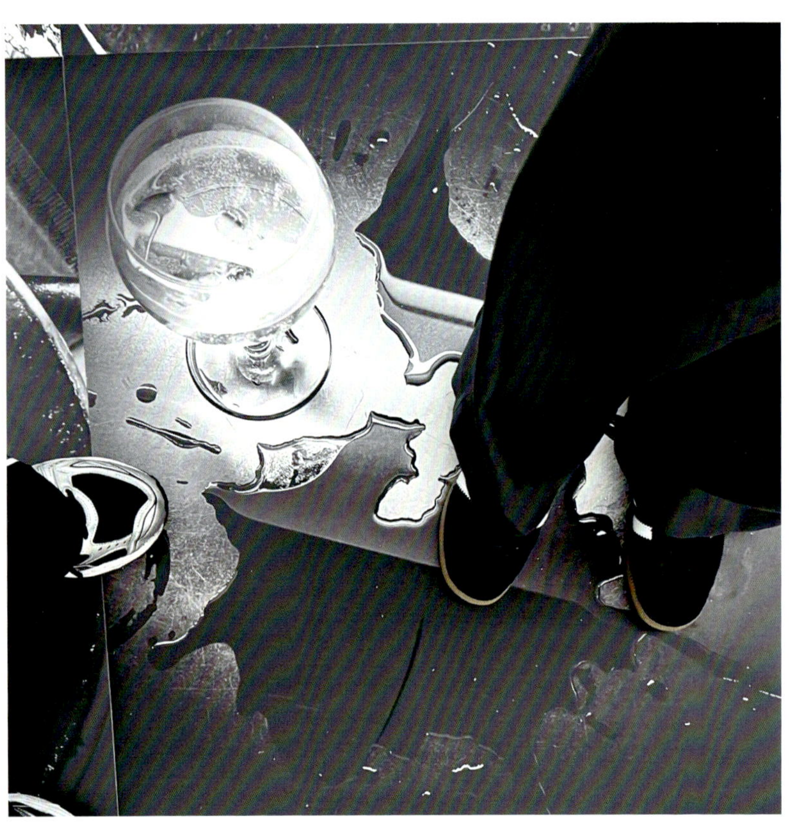

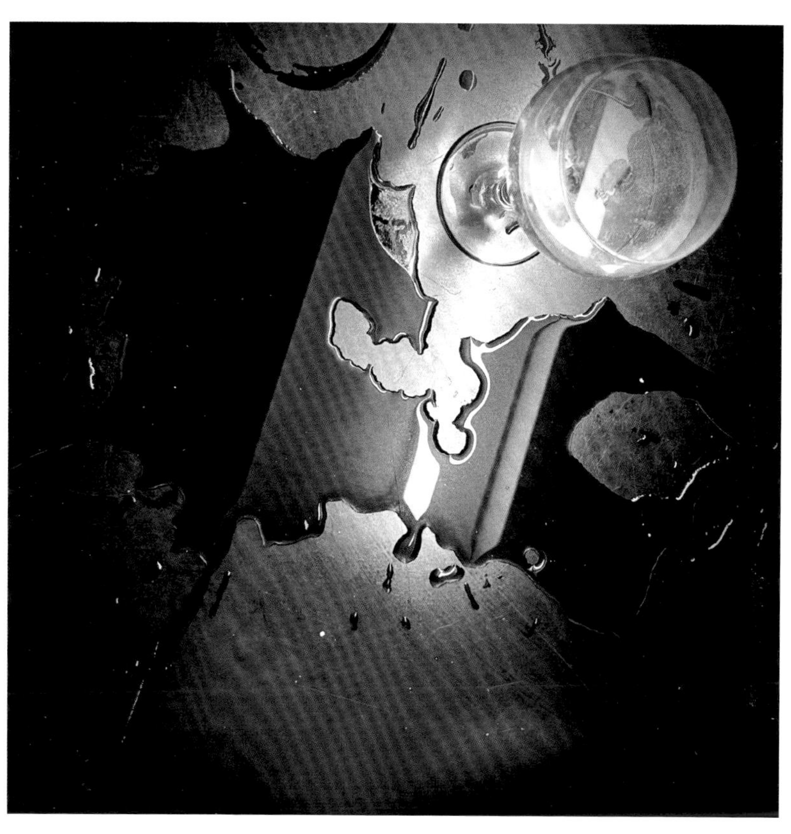

Free Gift

免费礼物

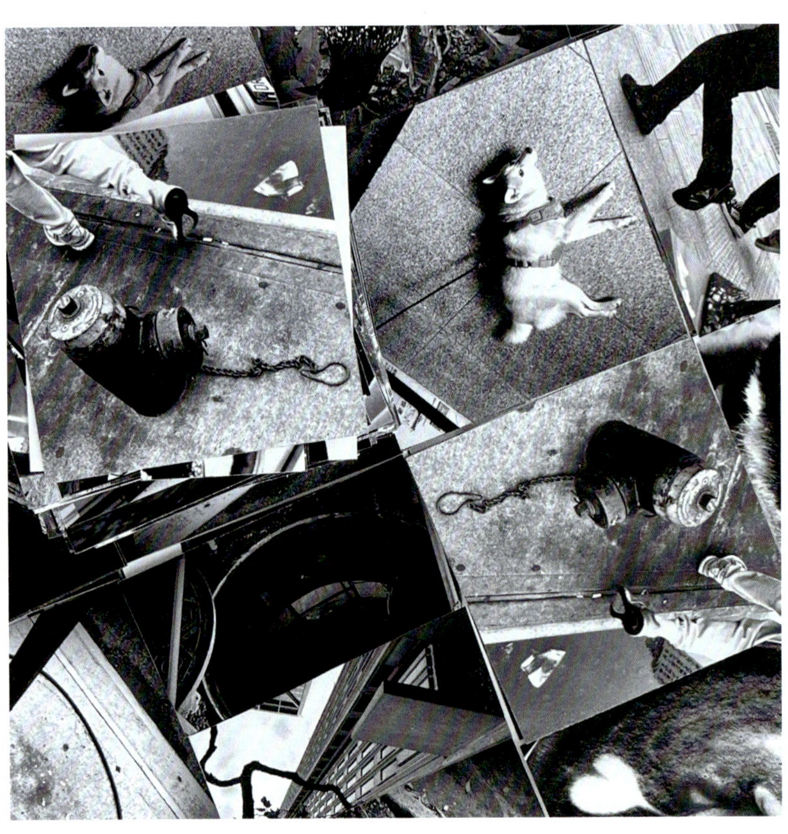

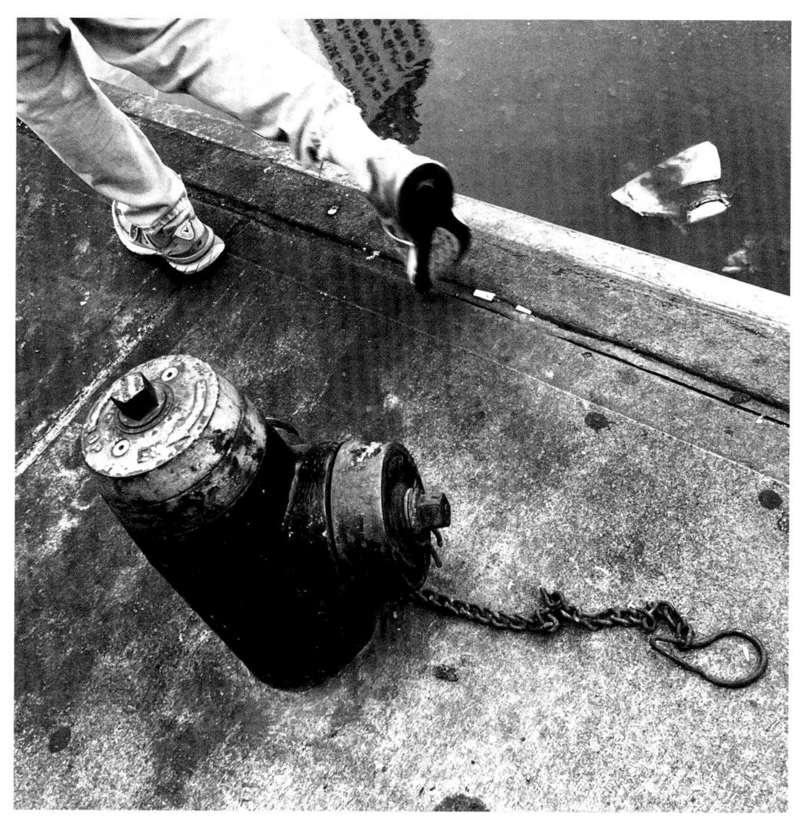

Haunted House

鬼屋

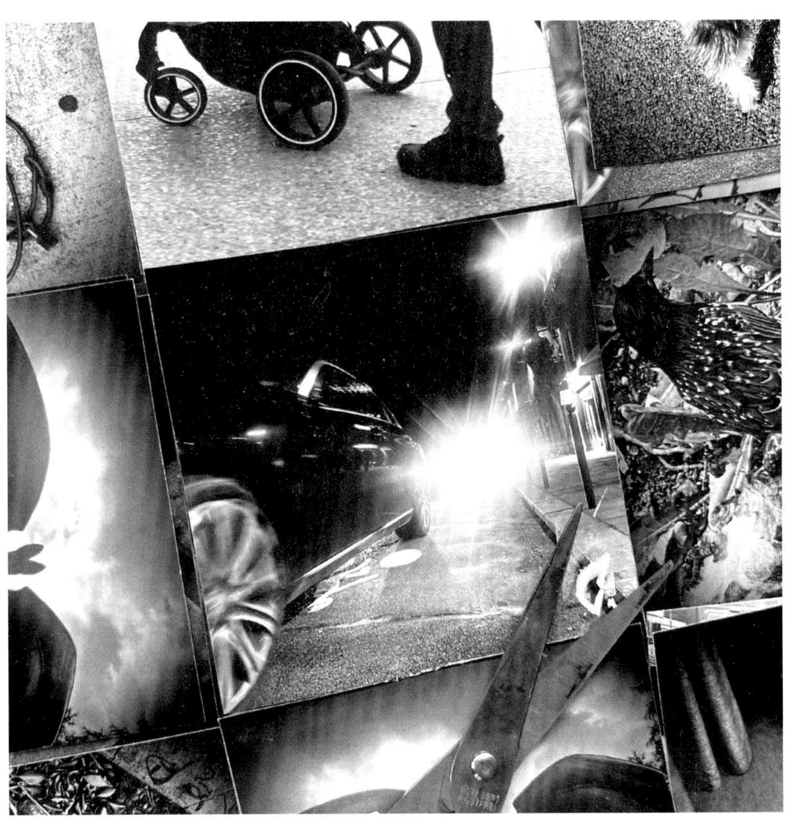

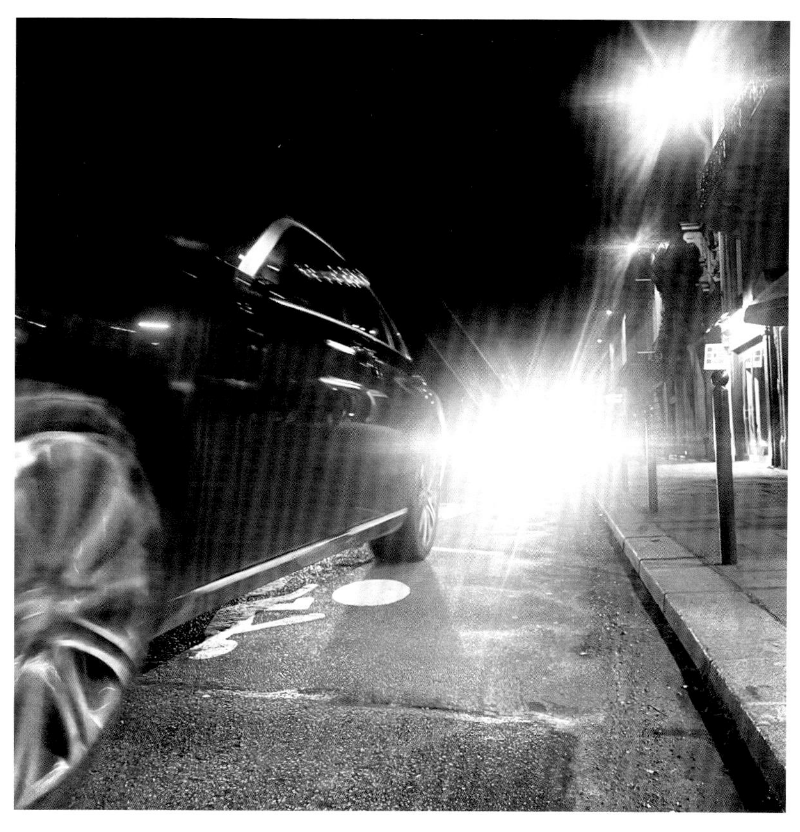

Double Enlightenment

双重启蒙

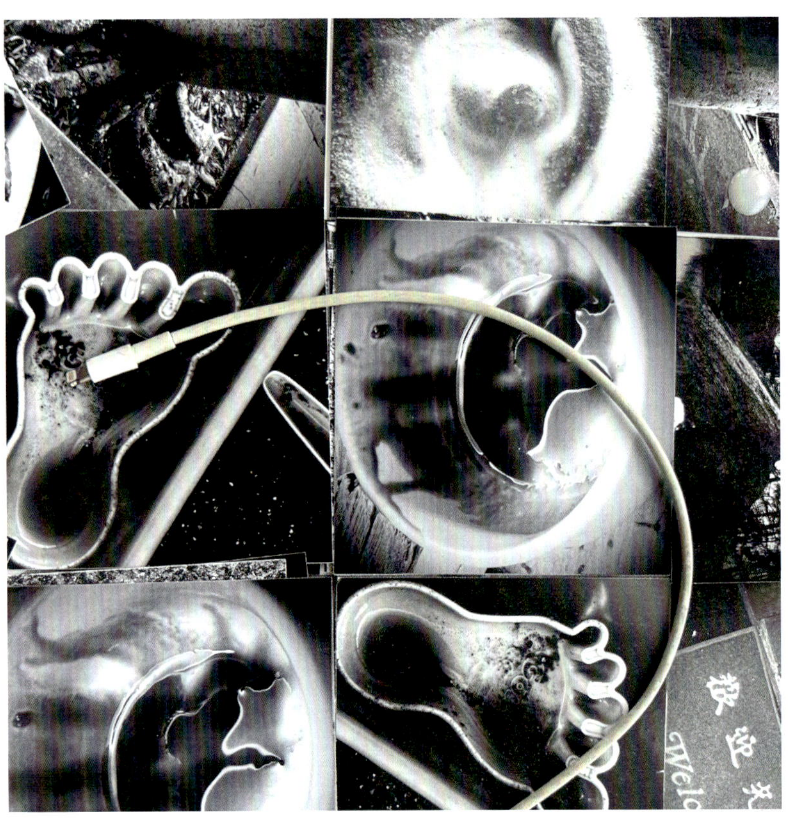

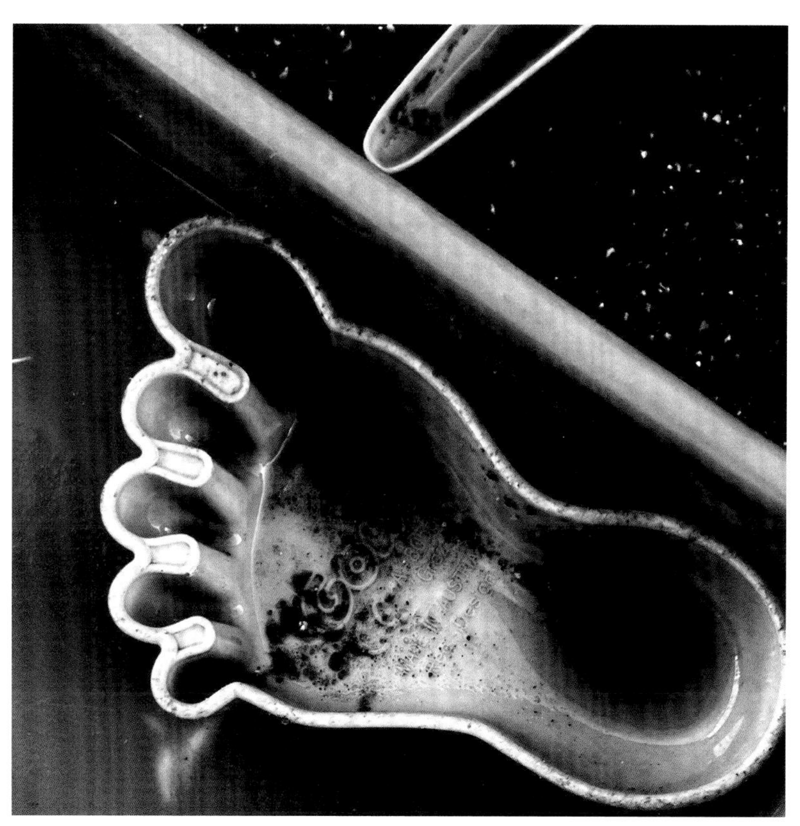

Stupid

愚蠢

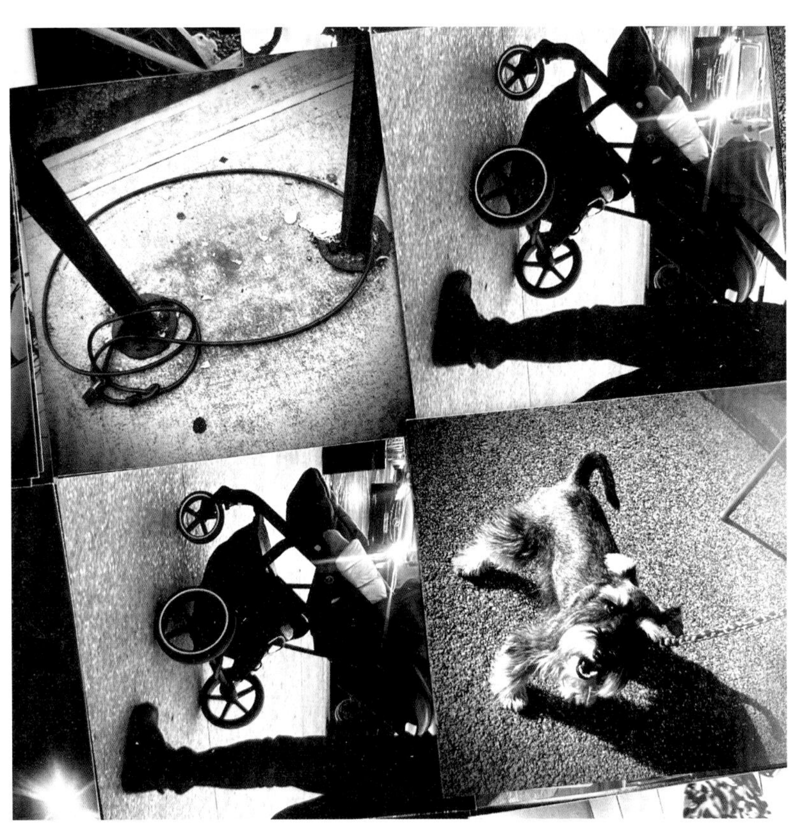

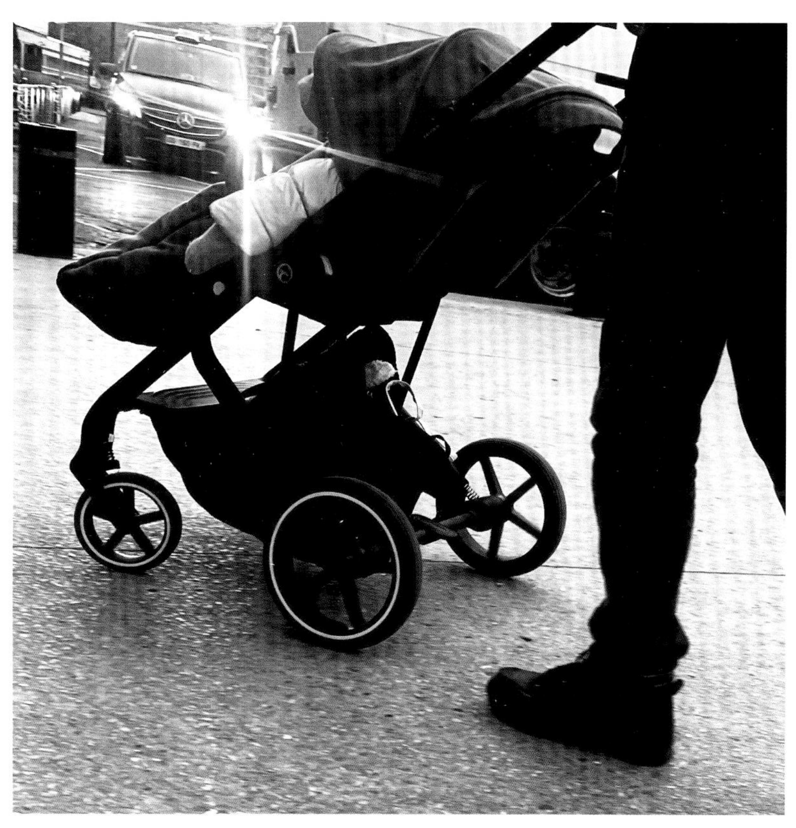

On the Way Home

回家路上

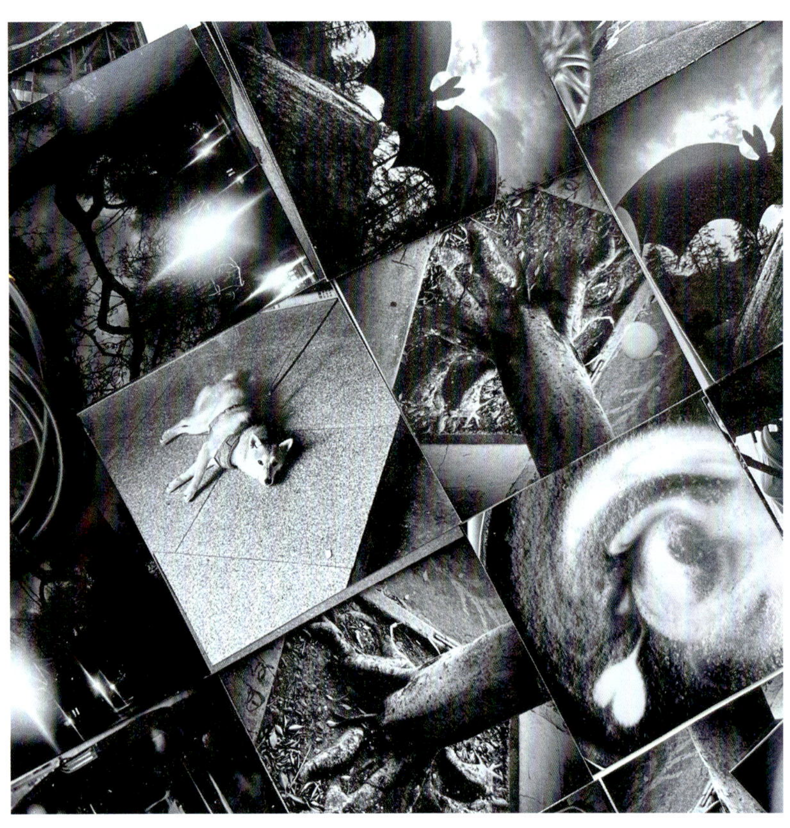

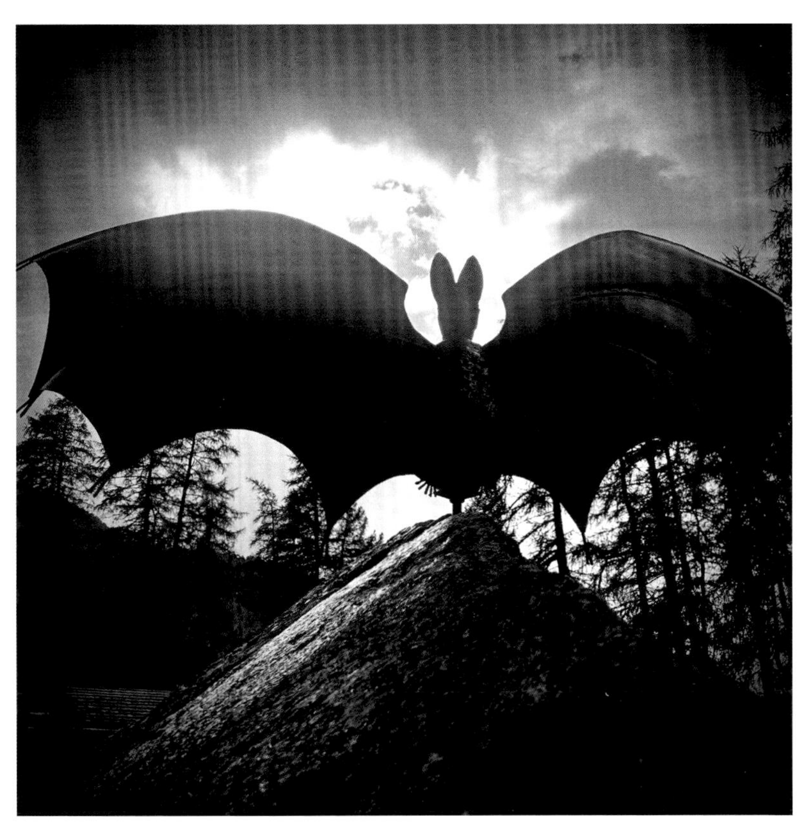

A Scenario

场景

I am at home when the email arrives. *Seven different groups of works will be on display. Four of them inside the museum, two outside.* I read it on my smartphone, standing, shoes on, bag in hand, stopped at the very moment I am about to step out. *Often, I found myself taking the same photos in different cities, like a hole on the sidewalk or fragments of pedestrians. Sometimes, I saw myself as an artist acting like a tourist, and sometimes as a tourist acting like an artist—stumbling through the so-called public spaces, looking down or up, taking photographs of dogs and trees and seeing these images immediately again on the grid of my phone—my phone that felt partly also like public space.* These are notes from private conversations, held on morning drives to Peter Fischli's studio. Peter gives my colleague Beni and me a ride in his black sedan, the car that in our group chat we jokingly call the "job bus." We take the same route every time, skirting the Altstadt, over bridges that ford the Limmat then on to a highway—one fast and wide enough to make Zurich feel, briefly, like a proper city. *Wavering between interpretation and observation, I tried to explain what I would see as everyday banalities, often mirrored in distorted subjective sensations. Often these images are hybrids of stereotypes and archetypes—symbols and signs, full or empty depending on our energy or mood to decode or interpret them. I gave them titles, imitating the process of dream interpretation or naming them to fix their existence for a moment, driven by the fear that they might mean nothing to me—that I could become alienated from what I was surrounded by and observed.* By the time I board the job bus, I have usually been put in my place: the twelve-year-old poodle Jimmy rides shotgun, stretched across the front seat, tongue lolling, as the three of us strike up our discussion of the day's plans. Through the car's windows, a dull mosaic rolls by, its tiles the walls and roofs of the suburbs—the anonymous non-spaces of the city, devoid of distinguishing landmarks. Look closely, and it could be anywhere, only the recurring blue rectangular signs with their street names suggest a sense of place. *I tried to create an interrupted pattern, repeating certain images so they would*

邮件送达时，我正在家里。“展览将呈现不同的七组作品。其中四组在馆内展出，两组在馆外。”那时我已经穿上了鞋，拿起了包，正要踏出门去，但在那一刻停了下来，站在那里，用智能手机读起了邮件。“我时常发现自己在不同的城市拍摄同样的照片，比如人行道上的一个洞或一些行人片段。我感觉自己有时像是以游客身份行动的艺术家，有时又像是以艺术家身份行动的游客——跌跌撞撞在所谓公共空间中穿行，时而抬头仰视，时而低头俯瞰，拍摄狗和树木，然后立即在手机相册的图像网格里再次察看这些照片——我感觉手机在某种程度上也像是一个公共空间。”这些笔记记录的，是在前往彼得·费茨利工作室的车程中发生的私人对话。彼得会开着他那辆在我们的群聊中被戏称为“工作巴士”的黑色轿车，载上我和我们的同事贝尼。每一趟车程走的都是同样的路线，绕过苏黎世老城，驶过横跨利马特河的桥梁，然后开上一条高速路——一条路面足够宽、车速足够快的道路，让行经这条路上的乘客短暂地感觉苏黎世就像是一座真正的城市。“我在阐释和观察之间动摇不定，试图解释那些会被我视为日常凡庸的事物，它们常常反映在扭曲的主观感受中。浮现出来的这些图像往往是各种刻板印象和典型形象——象征与符号——的混合体，会因我们解码或阐释它们时的精力或心情，而变得充实或空洞。我为这些图像起了标题，要么是在模仿解梦的过程，要么是想通过为它们命名以暂时固定住其存在，而这样做，是因为我担心它们可能对我毫无意义——担心我可能会与我周遭的和我所观察到的事物疏离。”在登上工作巴士的那一刻，我通常已然就位：十二岁的贵宾犬吉米坐在副驾驶的位置，伸展着身体横躺在座椅上，舌头耷拉，我和彼得、贝尼三人则开始讨论当天的计划。一幅沉闷单调的马赛克画面缓缓掠过车窗外，马赛克的每一颗瓷砖都代表着郊区的墙壁和屋顶——城市中那些无名的非空间，完全缺乏任何可以辨识的地标。这幅马赛克也许可以代表任何地方，只有当你更仔细地观看时，那些反复出现的蓝色长

briefly appear as ornaments, providing a micro-orientation. Red, green. Stop, start. *Later, I printed them on ordinary vinyl floor pieces and laid them out in a gallery space, so visitors could walk and observe them as they might stumble through a simulacrum of the city—partly resembling a questionable interior decoration—or as if they were walking on the image grid of my phone, filled with the same typology of images as other people's collections: food, dogs, cars, buildings, trees, babies, flowers—all square and black and white.* My phone vibrates; Peter is outside. I press the home button, open the door.[1]

1 Those familiar with Peter Fischli's writing know that he enjoys thinking at the wheel. Speed is essential: he's quick with a quip. He has a taste for quotations, often speaking in lines—sometimes exclusively in book titles, as in the series *Planet People Profit* (2021), where sequences of photographed book covers suggest, if not a narrative, then at least the ghostly trace of one. It's another pun on quickness—how to read cover-to-cover in the shortest time possible. These succinct snippets, one-line breakdowns strung together, create a syntax all his own, mirroring his approach to image-making. The choice of books resonates with the selection of images in Fischli's photo-floors: a range of therapy, business and sightseeing titles whose bland promises of self-betterment are arranged to emphasize the recurrence of certain nouns and phrases—work, money, zen, peace—that, collectively, bear

方形路牌以及路牌上的街道名称才为你显露出一种地方感。“我试图创造一种不连续的排列模式，使某些图像重复出现，从而让它们短暂地作为装饰呈现在画面上，并提供一种微小的方向指引。红灯，绿灯。停车，又起步。然后，我将这些图像印刷在普通的乙烯基地板上，铺展在画廊空间的地面上，这样，观众就可以一边走在上面一边观察，就如同他们也许会跌跌撞撞地穿过某个城市的拟像一样——这种拟像在一定程度上类似于值得质疑的室内装饰；或者，就仿佛他们行走在我手机里的图像网格上一样，网格里充满了任何人都会在相册收藏的同一类型图像：食物、狗、汽车、建筑、树木、婴儿、花朵——全都呈现为黑白方格。”我的手机震动了起来；彼得在门外。我按下home键，打开门。[1]

---

1 熟悉彼得·费茨利写作的人都知道，他喜欢在驾驶时思考。速度至关重要：他能飞快地做出敏锐的观察，更快地想到双关笑话，最快地丢出爆笑梗。他热衷于引用，经常用排比来表达——有时甚至完全使用图书的标题，正如他在《星球·人类·利润》（2021）系列中那样，一连串拍摄下来书籍封面哪怕无法构成一个完整叙事，至少也呈现了一个叙事中那些如鬼魅般难以捉摸的模糊痕迹。这是对速度的另一个双关——如何在最短的时间内“从封面读到封底／从一张封面读到另一张封面”。这些简短断章和单行概述组合在一起，创造出完全独属于他的句法，也呼应着他的图像创作方法。费茨利对于他所拍摄书籍的选择，与他在“照片地板”这个装置中对图像的选择是相呼应的：一系列心理治疗、商业经管和旅行观光类书籍，这些

the irreducible trace of human complexity, just as his snap of an empty airplane seat still contains the imprint of a human body. From the accumulation of meaninglessness, a form of meaning emerges; out of repetition comes something singular.

Fischli's work and its focus on the urban psyche can be well understood through Georg Simmel's essay 'The Metropolis and Mental Life' (1903). Simmel explores how the city's constant external stimuli alter mental life, intensifying emotional experience. The rapid changes in the urban environment—from the streets to social and professional interactions—continually challenge people's perceptions. Simmel was interested in how individuals in cities either connect with or distance themselves from others. He argues that urban dwellers develop distinct identities and personality traits shaped by city life's dynamic and diverse nature, resulting in a detached yet sensitive mentality typical of metropolitan living. He argues that the consequences of rapidly shifting stimuli and the anonymity of the city, too crowded to

书为读者许下的自我提升的乏味承诺被艺术家刻意排列，从而凸显了某些名词和短语——工作、金钱、禅、和平——的反复出现，而这些词语共同承载了人类复杂性的不可磨灭的踪迹，就像他所拍摄的那张空飞机座椅上仍然包含着一具人类躯体的印记一样。从无意义的积累中，某种形式的意义涌现出来；在不断的重复中，某种独特的事物应运而生。

要清晰地理解费茨利的作品及其对都市心灵的关注，我们可以借助格奥尔格·齐美尔的《大都市与精神生活》（1903年）一文。齐美尔探讨了城市所施予的持续外部刺激，是如何改变精神生活，强化情感体验的。从街市道路，到社交和职业互动，这些城市环境的快速变化不断挑战着人们的感知。齐美尔所关注的，是城市中的个体如何与他人建立联系或保持距离。他认为，城市居民会发展出由城市生活的动态和多样性所形塑的独特身份认同与性格特征，最终形成大都市生活典型的那种既疏离又敏感的心态。他指出，快速变化的刺激和城市的匿名性（城市过于拥挤而无法容纳个人化的体验或关系），导致了他所称的城市的“无情客观性”，将定性价值简化为定量值。

allow for the personal, lead to what he calls the city's "merciless objectivity," reducing qualitative values to quantitative ones.

In Simmel's account, the urban dweller, the metropolitan type, reacts with a detached, rational attitude, formally designated as one of reserve. The city demands intellectual qualities, he claims, not emotional ones. In resisting being leveled and swallowed up by the social-technological mechanism: "there is perhaps no psychic phenomenon which is so unconditionally reserved to the city as the blasé outlook." The essence of the blasé attitude, Simmel writes, is indifference toward distinctions between things—not that they are not perceived, but rather that the meaning and value of such distinctions, and therefore of the things themselves, are experienced as meaningless: "They appear to the blasé person in an evenly flat and gray tone; no one object deserves preference over any other. This mood is the faithful subjective reflection of the completely internalized money economy." Work, money, zen, peace.

在齐美尔的描述中，城市居民，也就是所谓的大都市类型，是以一种疏离、理性的态度来应对外在事物的，而这种态度被齐美尔正式地定义为“矜持”。他声称，城市所需要的，是智力品质，而不是情感品质。在人们努力抵抗被社会技术机制均化和吞噬的过程中，“也许没有哪种心理现象像腻烦态度那样，被如此无条件地专门保留给了城市”，齐美尔这样写道，而腻烦态度的本质，是对事物之间差异的漠然——不是说这些差异没有被察觉，而是这些差异的意义和价值，以及它们所进而勾连的事物本身的意义与价值，都让人感觉是毫无意义的。“对于腻烦的人来说，它们都呈现出一种平坦均匀的灰暗色调；没有任何一个客体比其他客体更值得受到青睐。这样的情绪是对已经完全内化于心灵的那种货币经济的忠实的主观反映。”工作、禅、和平。

The term *blasé*—meaning apathetic to excitement due to excessive indulgence; worldly-wise and at the same time world-weary—expresses the affective note struck by Fischli's work. The blasé pose is one of having seen it all before, but Fischli's 'way of seeing' remains attentive and critical; repeated returns to an object—or its likeness—could as easily be a sign of fascination as a cause for boredom. "All things float with equally specific gravity in the constantly moving stream of money. All things lie on the same level and differ from one another only in the size of the area which they cover," writes Simmel, not anticipating that Fischli would one day take this one step further, transforming the blasé attitude into a blasé perspective, in which Cologne Cathedral and a pretzel occupy the same amount of space. Fischli, though, is reflexive in his own indifference, actualizing Simmel's claim that "from each point on the surface of existence—however closely attached to the surface alone—one may drop a sounding into the depth of the psyche." In doing so, "all the most banal externalities of life are finally connected with the ultimate decisions concerning the meaning and style of life." It matters, then, how one walks the floor.

齐美尔选用的这个术语“腻烦”——意指由于过度放纵而对刺激无动于衷；积极入世的同时而又消极厌世——道出了费茨利的作品所传达的那种情感基调。然而，腻烦的姿态是一种“从前全都见过”的态度，费茨利的“观看之道”却仍然保持着对周围世界的高度关注和批判性眼光；复返同一个物体——或其相似物——既有可能是着迷的表现，也同样很可能是导致倦怠的原因。“所有事物都以同等的比重在不断奔涌的金钱之流中漂浮。所有事物都处于同样的层次上，彼此之间只有所占面积的尺寸的不同。”齐美尔这样写道，但他并没有预料到有朝一日费茨利会更进一步地推进这种观念，将腻烦态度转化成一种腻烦视角，而在这种视角中，科隆大教堂和椒盐卷饼占据着同等的空间。然而，费茨利在自己的漠然中保持了一份自反，使得他将齐美尔关于“人们从个体存在的表层上任何一点出发——无论这一点是多么紧密地附着于表层上——都可以探入心灵深层”的论断化为实践。这样一来，“生活中一切最庸常的外部事物，归根结底都与关乎生命意义和生活方式的终极决定联系在了一起。”因此，如何行走于费茨利的地板之上，就变成了一个重要问题。

A month later. I'm on a train, sitting with my back to the direction of travel. My friend Emanuel sits across from me. We're on our way to his show at Kunsthaus Glarus. Wanting to pick his brain, I tell him that I'm writing about the photo-floors but that I haven't yet found an angle, and that perhaps that's what interests me about the work: I haven't developed a liking for it. Still, lots of room for drifting. The only thing that comes to mind is wanting to read some of those flâneur novels I never have, taking a *dérive* through modern urban literature. I tell Emanuel that I had thought of writing the text as a series of lengthy footnotes—a form in which one can stroll.

Emanuel has walked the floor before but asks to see the single images. I pull out my phone and hand it to him. After a moment of scrolling, he stops at a picture and turns it back to me: a sun-shaped crack splintering across an iPhone screen, captioned 'Sunshine'.

A pause. Then he asks me, half-jokingly, if Peter "used to be a Mod."

I raise my eyebrows, unsure how to place the question.

'Mod'... as in subculture, 'mod' as in modernist. He mentions he had just stumbled upon a funny text about the Mods, as seen through the eyes of three Italian leftists who visited London in the early '60s. They were shocked by the ultra-hedonistic, clothing-conscious working class and their conspicuous consumption of Italian aesthetics: Lambretta scooters, espresso (a gateway to other forms of chemical accelerant), slim-cut designer suits that undermined the conventional meaning of 'suiting up'. The text, he says, is interesting in how it describes the Mods embracing modernity for its kitsch, simultaneously experiencing and understanding it through parody.

I knew exactly what Emanuel was getting at: the last thing you see as you leave Peter's studio is a poster of an exhibition on moped culture. The

一个月后。我坐在火车上，背对行进的方向。我的朋友埃马纽埃尔坐在我对面。我们正在去往格拉鲁斯美术馆的路上，他在那里有场展览。我想请教他的见解，便告诉他我正在写一篇有关费茨利照片地板装置的东西，但还没有找到切入点——也许这正是这件作品让我产生兴趣的所在：我对它还没有产生喜爱之情。不过，这留下了许多自由游走的空间。我脑子里唯一浮现的头绪，是想去阅读一些游荡者小说，在现代都市文学中进行一番漂移。我告诉埃马纽埃尔，我曾考虑过把这篇文本写成一系列长篇脚注——这种形式让读者可以在文本中信步游荡。

在今天的讨论之前，埃马纽埃尔就曾踏足在这个照片地板上，但他还是要求看看地板中单独的一张张图像。我拿出手机，递给他。滑动片刻之后，他停在一张图片上，把手机摆回我眼前：一个太阳光芒形状的裂纹在 iPhone 屏幕上蔓延，照片的标题是“阳光”。

沉默片刻。然后他半开玩笑地问我，彼得以前是不是一个摩登族。

我扬起眉毛，不确定要如何理解这个问题。

摩登族……指的是那个亚文化群体呢，还是指现代主义者呢。他提到，他最近才偶然看到一篇讨论摩登族的有趣文章，是从三位在1960年代初访问伦敦的意大利左翼人士的视角写的。他们十分震惊于极度享乐主义、注重着装的工人阶级，以及他们对意大利美学的炫耀性消费：兰美达牌踏板机车、意式浓缩咖啡（通往其他化学兴奋剂的窗口），以及打破了“穿西装”传统含义的修身剪裁的设计师定制套装。他说，这篇文章有趣之处在于，它描述了摩登族如何因其媚俗而拥抱现代性，同时又通过讽刺性的戏仿来体验和理解现代性。

background is composed of a church's granite-block walls, over which the layering of a sticker ('I ♥ Maxi') has been artfully suggested through photo-editing. At the center of the red heart icon, the circle of the white-and-green-checkered PUCH logo. A blonde teenager, dressed in a blue jacket and darker blue jeans, sits below, outside the church, on a rust-colored moped. Below the front wheel, the show's title, *2-Takt* (Two-Stroke), in bold black.

It's about tuning and tuning in—adjusting the pitch to align with what is experienced every day, attuning oneself to the surroundings, and calibrating one's senses to the pitch of lived reality. Yet, there's also a distinctly youthful tweak detectable, the sound of an engine revving above its default settings. Extracting more power out of the factory-made. Peter's work contains the same tinkering impulse, only this time within the machinery of arts and culture. In this sense art is not a passive reflection but an active recalibration of life itself, reshaping and rewiring it into something more dynamic and compelling: "Art is what makes life more interesting than art," as the quote—one of Peter's favorites—from Robert Filliou runs.

I'm hesitant, and tell Emanuel I've always known Peter to be more of a car guy.

Well, by the late '70s, Mods had pretty much died out, Emanuel concedes, then adds, jokingly, that Peter would have been more of a Post-Mod, like The Specials. *Ghost Town*. Two-Tone. Checkered pattern. Checks out.[2]

我完全明白埃马纽埃尔的意思：在你走出彼得的工作室时，最后看到的东西是一张海报，主题是一个小型摩托车文化的展会。海报背景是教堂的花岗岩砌块墙，墙上通过图片处理巧妙地呈现了一张贴纸（“我 ♥ Maxi”）。在红心图案的中心，是PUCH摩托绿白格子的圆形车标。一个金发少年，穿着蓝色夹克和深蓝色牛仔裤，坐在教堂外面一辆铁锈色小型摩托车上。前轮下方，加粗黑字写着展会标题：“2-Takt”（二冲程）。

它的意义在于调整和适应——调整音调使之与每日经验相协，调适自己来顺应周遭的环境，校准自己的感官从而磨合周遭活生生的现实的音调。然而，你也能从中明显地察觉到一种年轻人特有的调整：引擎超高转速的轰鸣声比出厂时的默认设置更加响亮。年轻人们从出厂设定的性能值中榨取出了更多的马力。彼得的作品中包含了与年轻人改装摩托车一样的驱动力，虽然他所改装的对象是艺术和文化的机器。从这个意义上说，艺术并不是被动地反映着生活，而是对生活本身主动的重新校准，将其重塑和重组成更具生命力、更打动人的东西：正如罗伯特·菲利乌的名言——这是彼得最喜欢的一句话之一——“所谓艺术，就是让生活变得比艺术更有趣的东西”。

我犹豫了片刻，然后告诉埃马纽埃尔，我一直觉得彼得更像是玩汽车的。

好吧，到1970年代末时，摩登族差不多消亡殆尽了，埃马纽埃尔承认道，然后开玩笑地补充道，彼得可能更像后摩登族，就像The Specials乐队那样。名曲《鬼城》。Two-Tone风格。黑白棋盘格图案。都对上了。[2]

2 *Vertigo Vinyl Floor Patterns I, II, III,* consists of black-and-white photographs: a myriad of square images of cityscapes and everything spotted within, each printed multiple times on vinyl, turned into nearly three-foot-long individual tiles, rotated, and laid into intricate patterns, forming three distinct grid-pattern photographic mosaic floors. The photo-floors are walk-in collections of pictures taken over the past two years in various cities across continents— a topography of the universal metropolitan experience in a kaleidoscopic array. Covering a broad range of subject matter, whether grand or modest, the city lies at your feet, with a martini just a hop away from the Eiffel Tower, a skip from a pair of chopsticks, or a jump to a well-groomed poodle, depending on the direction you take.

2 《眩晕乙烯基地板图案I、II、III》由一系列黑白照片组成：许多不同的城市景观以及其中被捕捉下来的一切事物，它们各自呈现为一张张方形图像，每张图像都被多次印刷在乙烯基上，制成80厘米见方的地砖，这些地砖被旋转并排列成复杂的图案，形成三组不同的网格图案照片的马赛克地板。这些让观众行走的照片地板上，集合了过去两年间艺术家跨越数个大洲在多个城市中拍摄的照片，它们以复杂多端的排列呈现，展示了一种普世性都市体验的地景。照片的主题包罗万象，无论宏大壮阔或渺小平凡，一切城市景观尽在脚下，要从一杯马提尼到达埃菲尔铁塔只需轻轻一跃，如果再跳一下还可以跳到一双筷子，或一只修剪整齐的贵宾犬上，取决于你选择的跳跃方向。

Fischli's photos, transformed into an installation, are enigmatic in both purpose and perspective. As he 'stumbles' upon his subjects while wandering the streets, the intention behind each shot remains unclear, as does the rationale behind the selection and arrangement of the images—or, more broadly, the choice to print and display these spontaneous encounters as a disorienting surface, liminal space patterned for further stumbling.

The work is whimsical; at first glance, it's difficult to discern what the floor represents. Was it once part of a fairground stall or a stage set? It hardly matters once you're on it—it's fun to wander across the surface of someone else's photo album. You might even press your heel down a bit harder when you step on a cappuccino heart. This playful act of trampling captures the curious sensation of profanation—an aggrandizing defilement of what lies beneath—as if you can truly step on anything within this already steamrollered reality. Here, the foot naturally follows the eye's path, each step a gesture which, through exaggeration, lays bare the cheap romance we call reality.

这些被转化为装置的照片，在拍摄目的和视角选择上都如同谜团一般神秘莫测。费茨利的拍摄对象都是他在街头漫步时“跌跌撞撞”偶然遇见的，每张照片背后的拍摄意图都不甚明了，观众也很难看清楚选择和排列这些图像的理由——或更宽泛地说，也很难看清费茨利为何要选择这些不期而遇的场景来印刷和展示，让它们呈现为一个令观众失去方向感的表面，一个排列成使得他们也在这些场景上跌跌撞撞的阈限空间。

这件作品奇异迷离；初看之下，你很难分辨清楚，这地板究竟寓意着什么。它曾经是游乐场摊位或舞台布景的一部分吗？然而你一旦踏足其上，这些都无关紧要了——踩在别人的手机相册上漫步的感觉实在太有趣了。当你踏上一杯顶着心形拉花的卡布奇诺图像，你的脚尖甚至可能会稍微多用点力。这种玩闹式的践踏捕捉了某种异乎寻常的亵渎之感——一种对脚下之物的过度玷污——就好像你真的能够在这个已经被碾压成平面的现实中踏上什么东西一样。走上作品时，你的脚会自然跟随眼睛的路径迈出一步又一步，经由每一步踏出的夸张姿态，不加掩饰地将被我们称作现实的廉价浪漫揭露出来。

Slowly, though, the head grows heavy and starts to droop, weighed down by imagery. There aren't many bright spots among these recurring motifs; reencountering them becomes almost painful—a forced *déjà vu*, or, in Proust's term, a *mémoire involontaire*—distorted terrain upon which public symbols have hollowed into discarded shells. Again and again, one is confronted with the most jaded of them all: the top-down views of perfectly foamed *cappuccini*: artisanal, adorned with rosettes and tulips, quaffable trinkets in paper cups, black-and-white filtered—no image expresses the gentrified mind better than a fake retro. No need to have read *Ornament and Crime* to detect this degeneracy: cultural criticism is rendered way too easy here. The work leads to questions not of orientation but of purpose: to what do all these photos add up? What is the point of navigating this ghost town of JPEGs, this photo dump? A hint of unease sneaks up on you—is it a malaise of modernity or a symptom of preexisting digital communication fatigue? Both. It's not clear on what level one should approach this work: is this street-photography-turned-Op-Art-floor-piece our era's inverted answer to the Sistine Chapel ceiling? There's a subtle sting in the absurdity, a quiet hurt masked by deadpan humor: of course, *everything is like this now.*

然而，你的头会开始慢慢变得沉重，被图像的重负压得低垂下来。你在这些反复出现的拍摄主题中找不到多少亮点；与这些意象的每一次重新遭遇甚至几乎变成了一种痛苦的体验：一种强加于你的既视感，或一种普鲁斯特所形容的“不由自主的回忆”——一块畸变的文化地形，而这片领域上曾经有意义的公共符号已然全都被掏空成废弃的空壳。人们一次又一次地面对已经反复观看到令人腻烦的场景：一杯又一杯俯视视角中覆盖完美奶泡的卡布奇诺：每一杯可以一饮而尽的咖啡都是手工制作，顶着叶子和郁金香形状的拉花，盛装在纸杯里，整个场景沉浸在黑白滤镜之中——没有哪种图像比这种虚假复古更能表达士绅化的心态。你并不需要读过《装饰与罪恶》就能觉察这种堕落：对它进行文化批评简直变得太过容易。这件作品引导观众去发想的问题并不关乎方向，而是关涉目的：所有这些照片组合在一起到底意味着什么？浏览这座JPEG“鬼城”、这块照片堆填场又有什么意义？你会感到一丝不安悄无声息地攫住了你——这是现代性的痼疾，还是你对数字通讯久已积累的倦怠所再度显现的症候？两者都是。我们不清楚究竟应当以哪个层面作为理解这件作品的进路：这件由街头摄影转化而成的欧普艺术地板作品，是否是我们当下时代以完全颠倒反转的形式对西斯廷教堂的天顶壁画作出的回应？在这种荒谬中，你能感到一种微妙的刺痛，一种被面容冷峻的幽默所掩盖的静默伤痛：当然，现在一切都是如此。

There's no detached way to behold this work; it is hard to focus on how to piece the images together, let alone draw meaning from them. The floor resists an objective external perspective, making a critically distanced view—the bourgeois ideal of an aloof examination—difficult. You can't see it all at once. Rather than outside-in, one must reckon with it from the inside-out, standing in its midst and engaging with the piece from within its depths. Look down and a quasi-cubist multiperspectivity opens up, flattening everything—earth and sky, skyscraper and manhole. High and low culture, digital and analog, past and present, private and public, ordinary and extraordinary, the sincere and the insincere—all merge into a checkered field of contrasts. Self and world, expression and document, technological advance and cultural stasis, place and non-place all coexist, blurring the boundary between 'photo'–'floor'.

不存在一种超脱物外的方式来观看这件作品；你很难找到一个观察的焦点来将这些图像拼接在一起，更不用说找到一个可以映射意义的点了。这块由照片组成的地板拒绝客观的外部视角，使得疏离远观的批判性视角——在中产阶级那里被推崇为理想姿态的冷眼审视——难以实现。你一眼看不到整个作品的全貌。你无法从外向内地进入它，而是必须从内向外地来思考它，站在其中，从作品的深处介入它。你低头向脚下看去，一种类立体主义的多重视角展开，展平了一切事物——大地与天空、摩天大楼与窨井盖。高雅文化与通俗文化、数字与模拟、过去与现在、私人与公共、平凡与非凡、真诚与虚伪——所有一切都融合成了一块呈现对比的棋盘格。自我与世界、表达与记录、技术进步与文化停滞、地点与非地点全都共存于此，模糊了“照片”与“地板”的界限。

The quality—or lack thereof—in Fischli's photos is also hard to pin down. An analysis of the individual images divided into subject, composition, and style, would certainly miss the point. Suffice to say, there are no selfies in the series. The photos are too stock to be personal—neither true snapshots nor posed pictures. If the pictures make an impact, it is in a peculiarly worn-out way, the 'vintage' effect of secondhand sentimentality. They are pseudo-existentialist, it's all about 'being-in-the-world', being thrown into its 'aroundness', but with one small twist: the subject of this experience is conspicuously absent. Gentrified is the term that best expresses not only the subjects of the pictures—drawn from the bland cityscape—but also their displacing qualities. The photographs have lost their indexical certainty, making it difficult to trace them back to any definitive 'real'. They could just as easily be products of artificial intelligence—computer-generated images, language-based and prompted by a text-to-image generator. The absence of clearly recognizable human faces in the series could even be attributed to the algorithm's heightened sensitivity to data protection.

费茨利所选这些照片的质量——或者说缺乏质量——也是难以把握的。对单个图像按主题、构图和风格等分解开来的层面进行分析，肯定会偏离作品的要旨所在。可以说，这一系列照片中并没有自拍照。同时，这些照片也太过普通，体现不出任何个人的特质——它们既不是真正的随手快拍，也不是摆拍。如果这些照片使观看者产生了某种触动的话，那么这种影响也是以一种殊为陈旧的方式实现的，就像体验了二手情感所具有的“复古”效果一样。这些照片也是伪存在主义的——它们都关乎“在世之在”，都被抛入了它们的“周围性”之中，但只有一个微小的不同：这种经验的主体明显缺位。“士绅化”这个词最贴切地表达了这些照片的主题——它们都取材于索然无味的城市景观——同时也最恰如其分地反映了它们在表面上所展现的魅力，以及它们让观众感到错位的属性。这些照片失去了它们指示现实的确定性，而这使得它们难以被追溯到任何明确的“真实”。它们可以很容易地被当成人工智能的产物——由计算机生成的图像，产生于以语言为基础的模型，由图像生成器根据提示词创建而成。这一系列作品中明显缺乏可辨识的人脸，甚至都可以归因于算法对数据保护的高度敏感。

Walking across the floor, where endlessly scrolling, virtualized visuals are scaled, retranslated, or re-analogized into a kind of pseudo-flânerie, reveals more than just a flick book of retro-kitsch. The images are sincerely insincere. They draw attention to photography's authenticity problem, along with that of the metropolises it depicts, and so provoke questions about authenticity itself. The visual world of the philistine (square) consumer is both a reflection of Fischli's surroundings as lived experience and a manifestation of his alienation from it. But Fischli doesn't stoop to the snark or cynicism common to many artists who engage with the rhetoric of consumer culture only to produce works of commodified dissent. Instead, he maintains a delicate *équilibre* where critique and complicity intertwine. His work is elusive precisely because it resists immediate interpretation as commentary. It adheres to Marcel Broodthaers' notion that making art is something insincere. To appreciate both the art and the artifice, modernism and kitsch, Fischli adopts a faux-naïve perspective. Through this amateur lens, the focus extends beyond the exploration of photography and transgresses into faux-tography, into the realm of the *faux pas*, the misstep. This is what Fischli describes as "the questionable." The floor has a specific interest in redrawing and rezoning the boundaries of what counts as art. It gerrymanders good taste, prompting the reader of this catalog to question whether what they are holding in their hand might just be a coffee table book. And if so, so what?

费茨利的这件地板装置，无穷无尽地滚动呈现着虚拟化的视觉内容，它们被缩放、重新转译或重新模拟成某种伪都市游荡，当观众走过时，它所揭示的绝不仅仅只是一本怀旧媚俗的翻页动画书而已。这些图像真诚地展现出了一种不真诚。它们引起观看者注意到摄影的本真性问题，以及摄影所描绘的大都市的本真性问题，从而促使观众拷问本真性本身。庸俗（古板）消费者的视觉世界对费茨利来说，既反映了他通过个人生活经验所感受到的周遭环境，也体现了他与这种环境之间的疏离。但是，费茨利并不自甘于像许多艺术家所惯常采用的那样，对消费文化发表一番讥讽或愤世嫉俗，这些艺术家们挞伐着消费文化的修辞，然而最终创作出的作品，仍然只是一种商品化的异议而已。与他们不同的是，费茨利保持着一种微妙的平衡，批判和共谋在他的作品中相互交织在一起。他的作品之所以难以把握，恰恰是因为它们拒绝被直接当作对某种事物的评论来解读。它们遵循着马塞尔·布达埃尔所谓的艺术创作是“一种不真诚之事”的观念。为了同时看到并欣赏艺术和人为造作、现代主义和媚俗，费茨利采用了一种伪天真的视角。经由这种业余的视角，费茨利的关注点延伸开来，超越了对摄影的探索，闯入了“伪摄影”的领域，闯入了“不当行为”的领域。这就是费茨利所描述的“值得质疑”之处。这件地板装置尤其注重对“什么可以被算作艺术”进行重新界定和重新规划。它操纵着好品味与坏品味的界限，促使本书的读者诘问自己拿在手中的这本展览画册，是否只是一本摆在咖啡桌边供人随意翻阅的装饰书。而且如果是的话，那又怎样呢？

Yet another month later, I find myself not in a car or on a train but stationed in Santiago Calatrava's Zurich Law Library. It's a multi-story construction with elliptical floors suspended inwards, often likened to a ship's hull. And things are drifting off course. The library initially seemed like the ideal setting to write this essay; Calatrava's architecture features twice in Fischli's latest video: the sweeping, dynamic curves of the whale-rib skeleton designed for the World Trade Center Transportation Hub and its predecessor, the Stadelhofen station—a version with fewer ribs. These are places of circulation, where trains arrive as empty vessels and slither into the city full of commuters. An architectural experience for the administered world. Fischli's playground.

Calatrava's architecture embodies an immersive experience of placelessness. Existing anywhere and everywhere, his buildings travel the world faster than its visitors, beating tourists in a race they cannot win. This structure captures the essence of urban development's march toward global sameness, where every city begins to mirror the next. The same theme lies at the heart of Fischli's photo-floor. As Peter explained in the car, it's about observing the generic urban landscapes shaped by dominant power structures, often disguised as collective efforts, or worse, as individual creations. It's about a nameless ideology that works quietly beneath the surface, infiltrating every aspect of daily life, embedding itself in the most routine rituals, and shaping even the smallest social interactions. It's a process of internalizing the external step by step, as this mundane exterior world is absorbed and takes root within. This ongoing exchange between the production of space and the shaping of subjectivity or, as he puts it, using the title of a book by Austrian writer Peter Handke, it's about: "The Innerworld of the Outerworld of the Innerworld."

又过了一个月，这次我不是在轿车里，也不是在火车上，而是驻足于由圣地亚哥 · 卡拉特拉瓦所设计的苏黎世法律图书馆中。这是一座多层建筑，椭圆形的楼层在内中庭挑空，常常被人们比作船体。而事情正在漂移偏航。图书馆最初似乎是写作这篇文章的理想场所；卡拉特拉瓦的建筑在费茨利的最新录像作品中出现了两次：拥有鲸鱼肋骨骨架般恢宏动感曲线的世界贸易中心交通枢纽，以及它的前序版本——肋骨更少的施塔德尔霍芬车站。在这些流通往来的地点，列车作为空荡荡的容器抵达，然后满载通勤者蜿蜒驶向城市。这些建筑体验是为被管治的世界所构造的。它们是费茨利的游乐场。

卡拉特拉瓦的建筑体现了一种沉浸式的“无地点感”——这些由他所营造的建筑可以存在于任何地方，它们传布到世界各地的速度比游客周游世界更快，在这场游客无法获胜的比赛中将他们全都击败。这种结构捕捉到了城市发展朝向全球同质化迈进的本质特征，每个城市都开始变得与其他城市相似。同样的主题也是费茨利照片地板的核心关注所在。正如彼得在车里解释的那样，这关乎观察由支配性的权力结构所形塑的通属城市景观，而这些权力结构常常伪装成集体努力，或者更糟糕的是，伪装成个体创造。这关乎一种无名的意识形态，它在表面之下悄然运作，渗透了日常生活的每个层面，内嵌于最常规的仪式之中，塑造着哪怕最细微的社交互动。这是一个逐步将外部世界内化的过程，人们将平凡的外部世界逐渐吸收，最终让其在内心之中扎根。这是空间的生产与主体性的形塑之间的持续交流互动，或者就像他借用奥地利作家彼得 · 汉德克某部小说的标题来说的那样，这是关乎“内部世界的外部世界的内部世界”。

I had set out to read the great city novels, but I wandered off course, never getting around to it. I hold one now—Breton's *Nadja*—but every page reads disappointingly… touristy. The book is somehow complicit in the disappointment you experience drawing into the Gare de Lyon by train only to realize, once again, that you've arrived 100 years too late—Paris has become a tourist in search of its own past. Yet, *Nadja*'s beginning jumps out at me; "*Qui suis-je?*" Who am I? Who do I follow? As a comment on today's social media reality, the grid from which Peter's visual world also stems, it feels too perfect, an insincerely sincere way to conclude. I look at pages filled with my handwritten notes, lost. Who am I to follow?[3]

3 In his nested role-play as a camera-wielding tourist, Fischli adopts a layered persona—an artist playing a tourist with artistic ambitions. This faux-naïve stance becomes a critical inquiry into stereotypical identities, vanguard techniques of deskilling and defamiliarization are refracted through the lens of popular culture and mass appeal. Armed with a cellphone camera and ready for captioning the captured, Fischli's interest lies in the fact that now that almost everyone has just such a device to hand, almost everyone has become an amateur semiotician, each contributing to a dynamic yet ambiguous proliferation, or perhaps pollution, of the digital megacity.

我原本打算读一读那些伟大的城市小说，但我偏移了航向，始终没有真正付诸行动。此刻我正手持着其中一本——布勒东的《娜嘉》——但每一页读起来都令人失望……就好像它是在迎合游客。这本书就像一颗埃菲尔铁塔雪花球，某种程度上助长了你乘火车抵达里昂车站时所经历的那股失望感：你再一次意识到，自己来晚了100年——巴黎已经成为一个追寻自己往昔的游客。然而，《娜嘉》的开头引起了我的注意；"Qui suis-je?"我是谁？我跟随谁？作为对当今社交媒体现实（彼得的视觉世界也是源于社交媒体上的网格视图）的评论，用布勒东的这个问句作结好像太完美了，简直是一种不真诚的真诚方式。我看着满是手写笔记的书页，心绪迷失。我该跟随谁呢？[3]

---

3 在费茨利嵌套式地演绎手举相机的游客这一角色的过程中，他采纳了一个多重层次人格——一位化身为怀有艺术抱负的游客的艺术家。这种伪天真的姿态构成了对刻板身份认同所进行的批判性探究，前卫的"去技术化"和"去熟悉化"手法经由大众文化与群众吸引力的视角加以折射。对于随身携带手机相机、随时准备为捕捉到的画面配文的费茨利来说，他的兴趣在于，如今几乎每一个人手边都有这样一部设备，从而使得几乎每一个人都转化成了业余的符号学家，每个人都在为数字大都市不断涌动而又晦暗不明的增殖——或污染——做出贡献。

Fischli's photos, distorted through today's cellphone image files, still echo the vernacular of modernism and its intensive seeing, highlighting the experience of city streets in a manner akin to constructivist photography. The jagged angles, skewed perspectives, long leading lines, geometric patterns, and dramatic interplay of light and its absence are reminiscent of Alexander Rodchenko and László Moholy-Nagy (with whom Fischli also shares an architectural motif, evident in the Hungarian's 1925 *Eiffel Tower* series). Compositionally, Fischli's images, taken from a worm's-eye view, are reminiscent of Berenice Abbott's work. Starting in early 1929, Abbott used a handheld camera, tilting the lens upwards to capture the endlessly tall skyscrapers, documenting the urban canyons of New York. By the end of the year, she completed the New York Album, an index of the rapidly rising metropolis, featuring 266 small black-and-white prints spread over thirty-two pages. These cityscape shots were just the beginning; countless more followed as she continually looked forward and upward: "to the bold foreshadowing the future," exemplifying the principles of modernity's *Vertikal-Tendenz.*

尽管费茨利的照片经过了当下手机图像文件的变形处理，它们仍然在呼应着现代主义及其“密集观察”的日常语言，以一种类似构成主义摄影的方式凸显了人们关于城市街道的经验。锯齿状的角度、倾斜的视角、延伸的引导线、几何图案，以及亮部与暗部的戏剧性强烈交织，这些风格元素都使人想到亚历山大·罗德琴科和拉斯洛·莫霍伊-纳吉（费茨利与莫霍伊-纳吉共同关注某种建筑元素的母题，这一点在这位匈牙利艺术家1925年的《埃菲尔铁塔》系列作品中体现得十分明显）。从构图上看，费茨利的照片采用仰视的虫瞰视角拍摄，让人想起贝伦妮丝·阿博特的作品。从1929年初开始，阿博特举着一台手持式相机，将镜头对准倾斜向上的角度，捕捉高耸得仿佛没有尽头的摩天大楼，记录下了纽约的城市峡谷。该年底，她完成了《纽约相簿》一书，书中展示了分布于32页上的266张小尺寸黑白照片，为一座飞速崛起的大都市留存了一份索引。这些城市景观照只是她创作的开始；在接下来的岁月中，她不断向前看，向上看，“朝着大胆预示未来的方向”，继续拍摄无数照片，为现代性的“垂直倾向性”原则给出了一个绝佳的例证。

But photography, as Susan Sontag once argued in her essay on the subject, isn't what it used to be. Originally a radical means of seeing beauty in the banal, its early Surrealist aesthetics have become stereotypes. Its radical techniques have been absorbed into mainstream visual culture, rendering what was once subversive into clichés of a photographic way of seeing, reducing the avant-garde to mere visual style. Sontag: "In principle, photography executes the Surrealist mandate to adopt an uncompromisingly egalitarian attitude toward subject matter." This collapse of boundaries between high and low culture is key to understanding how photography has become a vehicle for both modernist taste and commercial exploitation. Photography, once subversive, now commodifies reality, turning the world into a department store where everything is up for grabs. This commodification highlights photography's contradictory nature: it reconciles avant-garde ambitions with commercial demands. It is this tension between populism and artistic sophistication that defines modernism. Concordantly, a core of modernist art is precisely this: to question what counts as art. Sontag argues that photography embodies the modernist impulse because it subverts traditional artistic aims by elevating the mundane and the unpretentious into high art, consumed almost in spite of itself.

但是摄影，正如苏珊·桑塔格在她关于这个主题的文章中曾经论述过的那样，已经不复过去的模样。最初，摄影是一种在平凡中发现美的激进的艺术创作方式，可是，其早期的超现实主义美学已经成为当下的主流俗套，其激进手法已经被主流视觉文化收编，使得曾经具有颠覆性意义的东西，变成了一种摄影观看之道的俗套，前卫的艺术态度和表现方式被降格为仅仅只是视觉风格。桑塔格说："原则上，摄影需要执行超现实主义所托付的使命，即对拍摄主题采取一种毫不妥协的平等主义态度。"高雅文化和通俗文化之间界限的崩塌，对于理解摄影如何同时成为现代主义品味和商业开发这两种倾向的载体来说，至为关键。摄影曾经是颠覆性的，而今却将现实商品化，把世界变成了一个百货商店，一切都"可以被抓取"。这种商品化突显了摄影的矛盾本质：它需要调和前卫的艺术抱负与商业的需求。平民主义与艺术的复杂深奥之间的张力定义了现代主义。现代主义艺术的一个核心关注恰恰在于：拷问什么才算作艺术。桑塔格认为，摄影体现了现代主义冲动，因为它通过将平凡和"不矫饰"的东西提升为高雅艺术，让它几乎"不由自主"地被观众所欣赏和接受，从而颠覆了传统的艺术目标。

All of this speaks directly to Fischli's work, making Emanuel's question of whether he is a 'Mod' seem all the more justified. Fischli's gaze is modern, not only in its vertical tendency but also in its downward dodge. This hidden perspective is evident in his many images of passers-by walking, their back feet already raised. Photographing them from the waist down, these photos are what Fischli calls "Fragments of Pedestrians." This lowered gaze is what Simmel, in his essay 'Sociology of the Senses', refers to as the ostrich tactic, a manoeuvre integral to the anonymity of modern urban life, one which is essential for "self-preservation in the face of the large city."

In 1929, the same year that Berenice Abbott published *New York Album*, Franz Hessel, a writer and translator, published *Walking in Berlin: A Flaneur in the Capital*. He turned the art of walking into one of turning pages, conveying the experience of being in the big city as akin to reading: "Strolling is a kind of reading of the street, in which people's faces, shop windows, café terraces, trains, cars, and trees become a series of equal letters that together form the words, sentences, and pages of an ever-changing book." Modernist literature is, of course, known for its strolling protagonists, such as Virginia Woolf's Clarissa Dalloway and James Joyce's Leopold Bloom. Both *Ulysses* and *Mrs Dalloway* are prime examples of the

所有这些讨论都直接指向费茨利的作品，使埃马纽埃尔所问的那个关于他是否是“摩登族”的问题显得更加合理。费茨利的目光是现代的，这一点不仅体现于他的“垂直倾向”上，还体现在他向下的闪避上。这种隐藏的视角得见于他拍摄的许多行人行走的图像，这些照片中的行人后脚已经抬起，画面只拍到腰部以下，费茨利将它们称为“行人片段”。这种低垂的目光正是齐美尔在其《感官社会学》一文中所称的“鸵鸟策略”，现代城市生活匿名性的一个组成部分，对于“面对大城市的自我保护”至关重要。

1929年，就在贝伦妮丝·阿博特出版《纽约相簿》的同一年，作家兼翻译家弗朗茨·黑塞尔出版了《柏林漫步：首都中的游荡者》。他将漫步街头的艺术转化为翻阅书页的艺术，将身处大城市中的体验比作阅读：“漫步是一种阅读街道的方式，人们的面孔、商店橱窗、咖啡馆露台、火车、汽车和树木化身为一系列彼此等同的字母，共同组成了一本不断变化的书中无数个词语、句子和页面。”当然，现代主义文学以其钟情于漫步的主人公而闻名，比如弗吉尼亚·伍尔夫笔下的克拉丽莎·达洛维夫人，还有詹姆斯·乔伊斯书写的利奥波德·布鲁姆。《尤利西斯》和《达洛维夫人》都是意识流技巧的典范，描绘了在街

stream-of-consciousness technique, depicting the rush of thoughts, memories, unfiltered impressions and associations that arise when walking through the streets. This aspect of the connection between walking and processes of consciousness and perception also emerges in the work of surrealists such as André Breton, for whom aimless wandering became a means of activating the unconscious, akin to *écriture automatique*. A walk through the city can spark what Breton described as the "productive unconscious of sight," akin to his notion of automatic writing as "a true photography of thought."

"*Qui suis-je?*" Breton understood that this question could never be satisfactorily answered by ontology and so, eschewing traditional notions of identity and authenticity, he posed it as a problem for fiction. Approaching it as literary critics, we can unmask a double entendre. The *suis* conjugation carries dual meanings: it is the first-person singular form of both *être* (to be) and *suivre* (to follow). Thus, 'who am I?' also asks 'who do I follow?' or, as he puts it in the opening line, 'who I haunt'. Breton's alter-ego narrator, André, shadows Nadja through the streets to find himself. All the collected texts, thoughts, and documents that compose the book are souvenirs of this journey. Each piece, a fragment of memory, forms a mosaic of his exploration of identity, haunting, and the perpetual interplay between being and

头漫步时涌现的思绪、记忆、未经过滤的印象和联想。行走和意识与感知过程之间联系的这一层面，也体现在诸如安德烈·布勒东等超现实主义者的作品中，对他们来说，漫无目的地在城市中漫游成为激活潜意识的一种方式，类似于所谓的自动书写。都市漫步可以激发布勒东所谓的“视觉的生产性无意识”，类似于他将自动书写视为“对思想进行真实摄影”的观念。

“我是谁？”布勒东知道，这个问题永远无法通过本体论得到完满解答，因此，他摒弃了传统意义上的身份认同和本真性概念，将这一问题作为一个虚构的问题来提出。以文本批评的进路切入，我们可以揭示其中的双关。法语词“suis”的变位带有这样的双重意义：它既是“être”（是）这个词的第一人称单数形式，也是“suivre”（跟随）这个词的第一人称单数形式。因此，在问“我是谁？”的时候，这个问题也是在问“我跟随谁？”或者，如布勒东在开篇所问的，“我与谁相纠缠”。布勒东的另我叙述者安德烈，在街头如影随形般跟在娜嘉后面，从而寻找自我。所有收集的文本、思绪和档案都是这段旅程的纪念品。每一个记忆的碎片，形成了一块块马赛克，拼凑成了他对于身份、纠缠，以及存在与跟随之间永恒互动的探索。“纪念品移置了本真

following. "The souvenir displaces the point of authenticity as it itself becomes the point of origin for narrative." The narrative of self is performed through Nadja, who becomes the perfect *sou-venir*—what comes from the ground and within: the insight of the street / the interiorization of the exterior—while Breton's protagonist occupies the perspective of the *sur-venir*—what comes from above and beyond, the epiphany.

"Lost steps? But there's no such thing!" Nadja exclaims upon seeing Breton's *Les Pas Perdus, Manifeste du Surréalisme* in the novel that bears her name. She flips eagerly through the pages, and André becomes entranced by her. Their chance encounter on a bustling street sparks his obsession, for she possesses a rare gift: to spot the extra within the ordinary. *Nadja*—a novel that never quite takes shape—begins with seemingly aimless wanderings, capturing trivial details often dismissed by grand literature. What's more, the marginalia of life find their way into the story through pictures. The first-person narrative is enriched by forty-four images, woven into the text, each captioned—a vivid stand-in for what might otherwise be laboriously described. Breton's anti-literary stance is expressed through his use of raw material, including cityscapes, facades, portraits and sketches—often of Nadja's making. Other miscellanies, like a photo of a

性所在，因为纪念品本身成为了叙事的起点。”自我的叙事经由娜嘉而被操演着，她成为一个完美的纪念品（sou-venir，法语“下方”与“来自”这两个单词的拼合）——某种来自地面和内心的东西：街头的洞察力 / 外部世界的内在化；而布勒东的主角，则占据了某种来自上方、超越性的视角（sur-venir，法语“上方”和“来自”这两个单词的组合），某种灵悟

“迷失的脚步？可是迷失的脚步不存在啊！”《娜嘉》小说中的同名女主角在读到布勒东的《迷失的脚步》和《超现实主义宣言》时惊呼道。她急切地翻阅着书页，安德烈在一旁看得入了迷。他们在嘈杂街道上的偶然相遇，激起了他对娜嘉的痴迷，因为这姑娘拥有一种罕见的天赋：能在平凡中发现不凡。《娜佳》——一部从未真正成形的小说——始于一场场看似漫无目的的漫游，而这些漫游捕捉了那些常被宏大文学所忽视的琐碎细节。然而，生活的边角之物通过图片找到了进入故事的方式。第一人称叙事的文本因四十四张图片的插入而变得更为充实，这些图片无缝地与文字紧密结合，每一张都配有说明文字——它们生动地替代了原本可能需要冗长繁杂的文字来描述的内容。布勒东的反文学立场体现于他对某些未经文学加工的

discarded glove are eerily reminiscent of Fischli's *Empire*. The novel's approach aligns with Breton's theoretical writings; his 'Disdainful Confession'—the opening essay in *Lost Steps*—illustrates a commitment to the street. These surprising detours shape lives under capitalist modernity. No one embodies the avant-garde spirit better than Nadja, who "enjoyed being nowhere but in the streets, the only region of valid experience for her." She and the street—electrifying and unforgiving—intertwine and clash. Reality hits, Nadja's extraordinary perceptions are dismissed as vertigo and hallucinations, her fear of falling through the cracks finally realized when she is committed to a mental hospital. Taken to the brink of madness, Nadja keeps going, while the narrator stops short. Staying just within the boundaries of reason, he distances himself abruptly until Nadja becomes a ghost to him.

Breton's photo-text left a mark on Walter Benjamin. The philosopher was staggered by the novel and how "photography intervenes in a very strange way." He gives a critical assessment of *Nadja*, in his essay 'Surrealism: 'The Last Snapshot of the European Intelligentsia' (1929). In the essay he emphasizes how the text exemplifies this "profane illumination," which dissolves the boundaries between the public and private, allowing the mundane and the marvelous

原始素材的使用，包括城市景观、建筑立面、肖像和速写——其中许多由娜嘉所作。还有其他一些难以归类的元素，比如一张丢弃的手套的照片，令人联想到费茨利拍摄的照片《帝国》，二者之间的相似几乎显得有几分诡异。布勒东这部小说的创作手法与他的理论著作是相呼应的；《迷失的脚步》中的开篇文章——“轻蔑的告白”——就描绘了他对街道的关注。这些“惊奇的曲径”形塑了资本主义现代性下的生活。没有谁是比娜嘉更好的前卫精神的具身体现了，她“只喜欢徜徉街头，这是她唯一能获得切身实感的疆域”。她与街道——令人心醉神迷，却又无情冷峻的街道——纠缠相融而又激烈碰撞。现实向娜嘉袭来，她非凡的感知却被当作仅仅是眩晕和幻觉，她对堕入罅隙之中的恐惧最终在她被送入精神病院时化为现实。被推到疯狂边缘的娜嘉继续前行，而叙述者却止步不前。他停留在理性的边界之内，与她倏然拉开距离，直到她在他的生命中成为一个越来越不真实的鬼魅。

布勒东这部图文作品产生了不可磨灭的影响：例如，瓦尔特·本雅明就曾被这部小说击中，“摄影以一种非常奇怪的方式介入其中”尤其让他感到震撼。本雅明在《超现实主义：欧洲知识界

to collide. He describes *Nadja* as: "a book with a banging door," and uses the metaphor of a glass house to highlight the openness and vulnerability that characterize revolutionary consciousness—an "intoxication, a moral exhibitionism, that we badly need." For Benjamin, Paris plays a central role in *Nadja*, symbolizing both the dreamscape of surrealism and the potential for revolutionary change. He asserts that: "at the centre of this world of things stands the most dreamed-of object, the city of Paris itself." The city becomes a space where surrealist imagination and political revolt converge, noting that "only revolt completely exposes its Surrealist face." The novel, along with Franz Hessel's *Walking in Berlin* and the photographs of Eugène Atget—whom Abbott called "the Balzac of the camera," himself a great flâneur of Paris—significantly influenced the creation of *Berlin Childhood Around 1900*. In his memoir, Benjamin presents a rapid succession of vivid images—brief scenes etched into memory—resembling the way photography captures portable picture-puzzles, sometimes miniaturizing, sometimes magnifying. Benjamin aspired to achieve a similar effect in his writing, crafting intense little vignettes that transform the depiction of reality into a kind of verbal picture-puzzle.

的最后一张快照》（1929年）一文中对《娜嘉》进行批判性的审视时，强调了这份文本如何体现了某种“世俗的启迪”，它消解了公共和私人之间的界限，让平凡与超凡相互碰撞。本雅明在描述《娜嘉》时，称“这本书具有一扇不断开合的门”，而他同时还使用“玻璃屋”这一比喻来强调革命意识所特有的开放性和脆弱性——这是“我们急需的一种沉醉，一种道德上的公开暴露”。在本雅明看来，巴黎在《娜嘉》中扮演着核心角色，这座城市象征着一个超现实主义的梦境，也象征着革命变革的潜力。他断言，“在这个物质世界的中心，站立着世人最梦寐以求的对象——巴黎这座城市本身”。这座城市成为超现实主义想象和政治反抗交汇的空间，而本雅明指出，“只有反抗才能完全展露它的超现实主义面貌”。这部小说，连同弗朗茨·黑塞尔的《柏林漫步》和欧仁·阿特热的摄影作品——阿博特称阿特热为“摄影界的巴尔扎克”，而阿特热本人也是一位伟大的巴黎游荡者——对本雅明《柏林童年》的创作产生了重大影响。本雅明在这份回忆录中，呈现了一连串快速闪现的生动画面——镌刻在他记忆中的简短场景——类似于通过摄影来捕捉随身携带图像谜题的方式，时而聚焦于宏观场景，时而又突显微观细节。本雅明渴望在他的写作中实现类似的效果，他用文字打磨出一系列效果强烈的小小片段，将对现实的描绘，转化成了一种文本的图像谜题。

There is a passage in Benjamin's *History of Photography* that particularly resonates with Fischli, namely its connection to psychoanalysis and dream interpretation: "through photography … with its time lapses and enlargements … one first learns of this optical unconscious, just as one learns of the drives of the unconscious through psychoanalysis… Photography opens up in this material the physiognomic aspects of the world of images, which reside in the smallest details, clear and yet hidden enough to have found shelter in daydreams." One can see this idea playing out in Fischli's work, as he subjects himself to an image association test in which he replaces the inkblot with his own city photos. It functions as an unconventional Rorschach test. The association or interpretation becomes the image's caption, the title of the tile. By both finding and lending language to the image—a mini-mimicry of the psychoanalytic process of interpretation—a signified is determined, allowing these photographs to reappear from the depths of digital data storage as souvenirs. Attributing meaning, finding this title, is thus the process of authorization. Fischli's captions signal the intrusion of the unconscious and a breakout from the constraints of the immediate architectural surroundings.

本雅明的《摄影小史》中有一段尤其呼应着费茨利的内容，也就是本雅明讨论摄影与精神分析和梦的解析之间的联系："经由摄影……借助其延时与放大技术……人们首次认识到了这种无意识的视像，就如同精神分析使我们了解到了无意识的驱力一样。……摄影在这种材料中同时还揭示了图像世界的相貌学特征，这些特征存在于最微小的细节中，相当清晰而又足够隐秘，足以在白日梦中找到庇护之所。"这一观点与费茨利的共鸣在于，他使自己接受了一场图像联想测试，而在这场非传统的罗夏测试中，他用自己所拍摄的城市照片取代了一般的罗夏测试会使用的墨迹图。他对这些城市照片的联想或诠释派生为他为每一幅图像所书写的配文，为每一块乙烯基地砖所赋予的标题。通过为图像找寻并添加语言——这个过程就是在小规模地模仿着精神分析的解释过程——一个所指被确定下来，使得这些照片能够在数字数据存储的深渊之中作为纪念品而重新出现。因此，赋予意义，找寻标题，就是一个赋权的过程。费茨利为照片添加的这些说明文字，标志着无意识的突然侵入，标志着他打破直接的建筑环境所施加的限制，而从中成功实现的一次突围。

Fischli's kaleidoscopic installations are a simulacrum of Instagram's simulacra, today's glass house in which the private is publicly displayed, filtered through the visual jargon of authenticity represented by Instagram's black-and-white retro filters, then curated into grid patterns. These works are symptomatic of a hauntological condition in which the search for authenticity becomes trapped in a repetitive loop. This vertigo is a result of the rapid movement of cultural stasis; its disorienting effects heightened by a fixation on art's past.

The way forward, then, lies in *unfollowing*, allowing oneself to drift into uncharted territory. Watch your step.

费茨利这件如万花筒般斑斓驳杂的装置是对 Instagram 拟像的一个拟像，是今日世界的“玻璃屋”——私密的内容透过这幢“玻璃屋”，经由 Instagram 黑白复古滤镜所代表的本真性视觉语言进行处理，再被组织成网格视图，公开地展示在观众脚下。这件作品是某种“魂在论”的症候——其中，对本真性的追求困足于重复循环之中无法逃脱。费茨利的作品就体现了这样一种在两种倾向之间摆荡不定的现代主义幻痛：一方面渴望着逃离数字漂移，另一方面又耽溺于过去的本真性，而这种本真性本身就是一个幻象。这种迷失感，是文化的停滞状况快速发展的结果，无论在数字领域还是文化领域都感受得到。它并非源于本真性的丧失，而是源于在过去的迷宫中迷失，找不到通往未来道路的眩晕感。

因此，前进的道路在于“取消跟随”——任由自己漂荡到未知领域。艺术的未来就像乌托邦（一个未曾踏足的人反而对它了解最深的地方）一样，仍然未曾绘出。当心脚下。

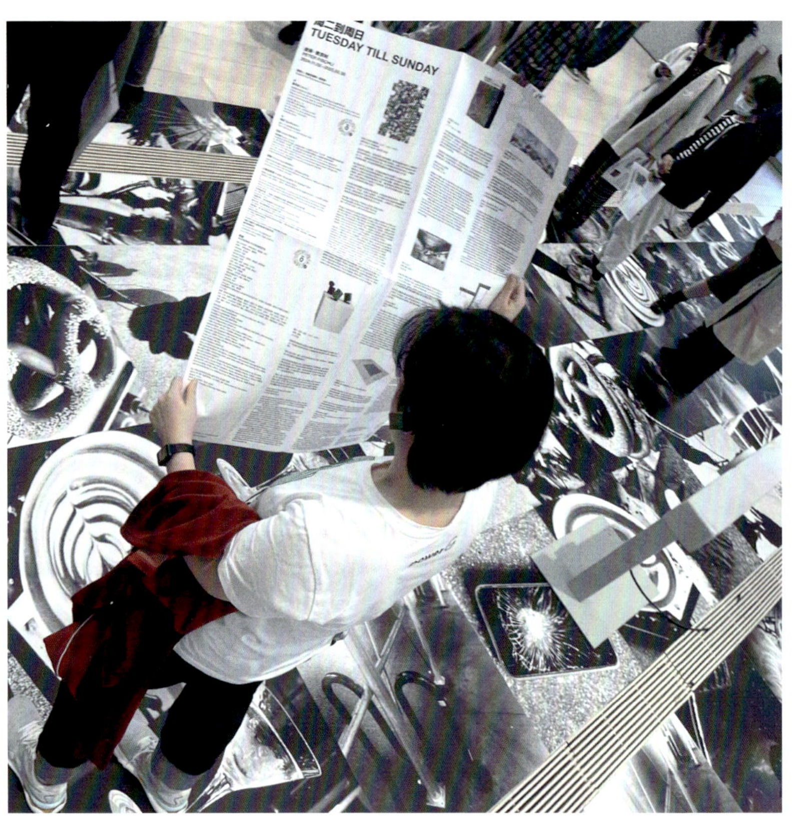
TUESDAY TILL SUNDAY

Published on the occasion of the exhibition Peter Fischli, *Tuesday till Sunday*, held at BY ART MATTERS天目里美术馆 (November 2, 2024 – March 30, 2025).

This catalog is organized by BY ART MATTERS天目里美术馆.

Director and Deputy Director: Francesco Bonami, WU Tian
Curator: Francesco Bonami
Project Coordination: TANG Yunyan
Exhibition Research: SUN Man
Exhibition Design and Execution: GUO Jiahuan, CAI Saihu
Artwork Registration: ZHOU Jia
Public Education: SU Qian, TAO Liwei, KONG Lokyi
General Affairs: JIN Xin, CHENG Wenyuan, WU Haonan, JIANG Yixin
Artwork and Equipment Maintenance: LIU Lei
Operation and Business: LOU Yuhang
Publicity: CHEN Zixuan, ZHANG Wenjie, TONG Luyao
Poster and Brochure Design: Teo Schifferli
Visual Design: MA Rui
Public Relations: ZHAO Ye
Shop and Merchandise: Dolly YU, HUANG Luan, HUANG Yousai

With special thanks to all interns, volunteers, the property management team, the information technology team, and other staff who worked hard for the exhibition and provided support.

Peter Fischli would like to thank: Bernhard Hegglin, Pascal Schneuwly, Andreas Selg, Katja Bruhin, Jessie Fischer, Teo Schifferli, Valentin Altorfer, Fabian Lüscher, Juri Mischler, John Kelsey, HAO Jingfang, Dunes Workshop (LI Yalun, CHEN Feiyue), Reena Spaulings, Filippo Weck, Christopher Müller, Daniel Buchholz, Laila Schnurrenberger, Cara Manes, LI Lin, Francesco Bonami, TANG Yunyan

Published in 2025 by
Verlag der Buchhandlung Walther und Franz König, Ehrenstrasse 4, D-50672 Köln

Distribution:
Buchhandlung Walther König
Ehrenstr. 4, D-50672 Köln
Fon +49 (0) 221 / 20 59 6 53
verlag@buchhandlung-walther-koenig.de

ISBN 978-3-7533-0729-9

Design: Teo Schifferli
Authors: WU Tian, John Kelsey, Hao Jingfang, Dunes Workshop (LI Yalun, CHEN Feiyue), Andreas Selg
Translation: YE Han, CHEN Silin
Proofreading: Tim Crowley, Georgia Petersen, Luker Studio

出版于展览“周二到周日”在BY ART MATTERS天目里美术馆举办之际（2024年11月2日至2025年3月30日）。
本书由BY ART MATTERS天目里美术馆策划。

展览工作团队

馆长及副馆长：弗朗切斯科·博纳米、吴天
策展人：弗朗切斯科·博纳米
项目统筹：汤云艳
展览研究：孙熳
展览设计及执行：郭家欢、蔡赛虎
作品登记：周佳
公共教育：苏芊、陶莉薇、江乐宜
馆务：金昕、程雯媛、武昊楠、姜逸心
展厅及设备管理：刘磊
运营及商务：楼雨航
宣传推广：张文婕、陈紫璇、童璐瑶
海报及画册设计：特奥·席费尔利
视觉设计：马睿
公共关系：赵烨
美术馆商店及衍生品：虞玲杰、黄銮、黄友赛

特别感谢所有为展览付出心血和给予支持的实习生、志愿者、物业团队、信息技术团队及其他工作人员们。

彼得·费茨利特别感谢：伯恩哈德·赫格林、帕斯卡尔·施诺利、安德烈亚斯·塞尔格、卡特娅·布鲁欣、杰西·费舍尔、特奥·席费尔利、瓦伦丁·阿尔托弗、法比安·吕谢尔、尤里·米舍尔、约翰·卡尔赛、郝景芳、沙丘研究所（李雅伦、陈飞樾）、Reena Spaulings画廊、菲利波·韦克、克里斯托弗·穆勒、丹尼尔·布赫霍尔兹、莱拉·施努伦伯格、卡拉·马内斯、李琳、弗朗切斯科·博纳米、汤云艳

由Verlag der Buchhandlung Walther und Franz König, Köln 出版

设计：特奥·席费尔利
文章作者：吴天、约翰·卡尔赛、郝景芳、沙丘研究所（李雅伦、陈飞樾）、安德烈亚斯·塞尔格
翻译：叶晗、陈思霖
校对：柯好埋、乔治娅·彼得森

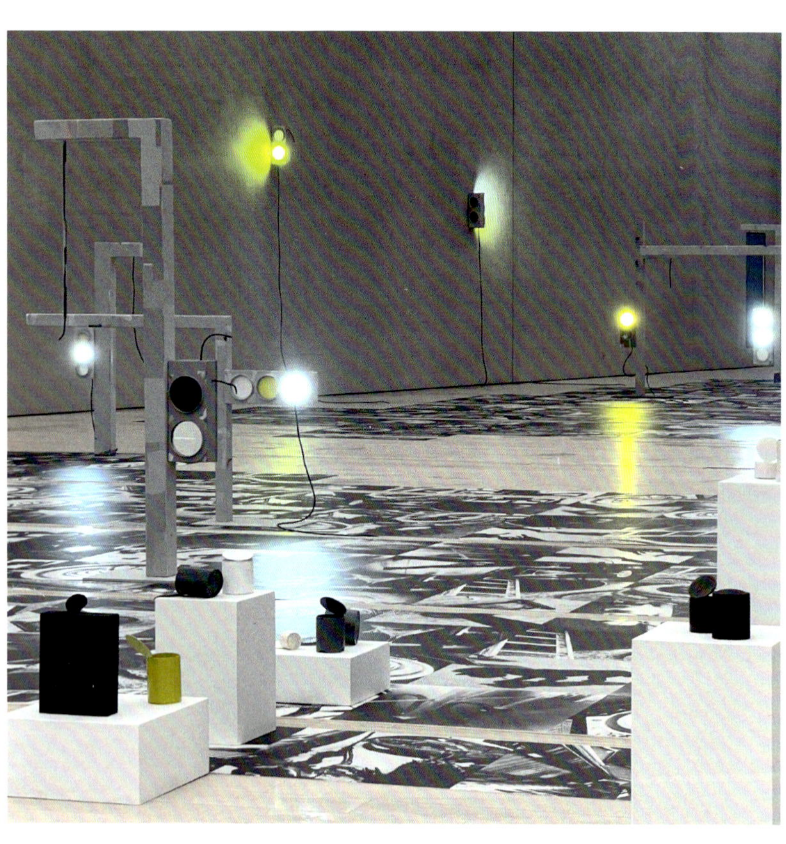